CONSUMING IDENTITY

CONSUMING IDENTITY

The Role of Food in Redefining the South

ASHLI QUESINBERRY STOKES AND WENDY ATKINS-SAYRE

University Press of Mississippi
Jackson

www.upress.state.ms.us

Designed by Peter D. Halverson

The University Press of Mississippi is a member of the Association of
American University Presses.

First printing 2016

∞

Library of Congress Cataloging-in-Publication Data

Names: Stokes, Ashli Quesinberry, author. | Atkins-Sayre, Wendy, 1972– author.
Title: Consuming identity : the role of food in redefining the South / Ashli
Quesinberry Stokes and Wendy Atkins-Sayre.
Other titles: Role of food in redefining the South
Description: Jackson: University Press of Mississippi, [2016] | Includes
bibliographical references and index.
Identifiers: LCCN 2016008683 | ISBN 9781496809186 (cloth : alk. paper)
Subjects: LCSH: Food habits—Southern States. | Cooking, American—Southern
style. | Food—Social aspects—Southern States. | Identity
(Psychology)—Social aspects—Southern States. | Southern States—Social
life and customs.
Classification: LCC GT2860 .S76 2016 | DDC 394.1/20975—dc23 LC record
available at http://lccn.loc.gov/2016008683

British Library Cataloging-in-Publication Data available

CONTENTS

Preface   vii

Introduction
The Stories, Subjectivities, and Spaces of Southern Food   3

PART ONE: THE RHETORICAL POTENTIAL OF SOUTHERN FOOD

CHAPTER ONE
Consuming Rhetoric
How Southern Food Speaks   21

CHAPTER TWO
A Troubled Region and Its Possible Culinary Fix   50

PART TWO: EXPLORING THE SOUTHERN TABLE

CHAPTER THREE
Sipping on Southern Hospitality
Drink as Rhetorical Invitation   79

CHAPTER FOUR
Turf Tussle
Uniting through North Carolina Barbecue   103

CHAPTER FIVE
Authenticating Southernism
Creating a Sense of Place through Food   134

CHAPTER SIX

Nostalgia, Ritual, and the Rhetorical Possibility of Southern Baking   159

PART THREE: AFTER-DINNER CONVERSATION

CHAPTER SEVEN

Redefining the South through Food   189

References   203

Index   222

PREFACE

Everyone has a story about a food experience. Whether it is a childhood memory of first encountering a particular food, learning to make a prized family recipe, or going on a pilgrimage to eat at a certain restaurant, it is clear that food plays an important role in our lives. It is cliché to say that "you are what you eat," yet there is certainly some truth to that saying in that food crafts part of our identities. That is, we recognize that although food serves the mundane role of providing nutrition, it does much more than that. We build family, community, and cultural memories around food. We let foods become symbolic of holidays, special events, and places. For these reasons, we argue that identity is partially cultivated through foods and experiencing certain food cultures—in this case, Southern ones.

One of Ashli's earliest memories is attending a summertime family re-union in the mountains of southwest Virginia. She remembers getting out of the car and seeing tables piled with food. After what seemed like an eternity of exchanging greetings, it was finally time to eat. The simple folding tables were arranged loosely by course. First there were breads: still warm yeast rolls, biscuits, and cornbread. Salads were next, the table loaded down with macaroni salad, potato salad, egg salad, various types of coleslaw, and even the South's bizarre Watergate salad, made with pistachio pudding, canned fruit, and marshmallows. Main dishes followed, with platters of fried chicken, glazed ham, egg salad and pimento cheese sandwiches, and various types of casseroles. Baked beans, green beans, platters of tomatoes and cucumbers, corn on the cob, and even potato chips sat next to these stars of the show. Finally, heaven to a sweet-toothed kid, the desserts: chocolate pie piled high with meringue; pound cake with whipped cream and strawberries; "chocolate delight"; and platters of homegrown watermelon sprinkled with salt. That endless supply of dishes came to signify what communal eating in the South meant to her as a child. Whether it was a funeral, fellowship in a Presbyterian church hall, the Fourth of July, or just a typical weekend in the summertime, that same collection of dishes would be there, steadfastly anchoring the gathering at hand. Sharing these foods taught Ashli about friendship, family, and who she was as a young girl growing up in Virginia in the late seventies.

One of Wendy's most significant family memories was when her mother and grandmother taught her how to make the family cornbread recipe. Step by step her grandmother walked her through the "proper" way to make the Southern manna, explaining how the German influence in their family probably accounted for the slight amount of sugar (not too much—no sweet cornbread in our family!). The ingredients were never measured precisely— phrases such as "heaping spoonful," "just about this much," and "enough to make it wet" had to suffice for the family recipe. And, of course, cornbread was to be made in a well-worn cast-iron skillet handed down through the generations and seasoned to perfection. It was a small task, but at that moment, it was clear to Wendy that she was part of a family tradition. Even a cooking injury—the hot oil dripping onto her hand as she prepared the skillet—couldn't taint this memory. Cornbread might be made from simple ingredients, but those ingredients brought her family together at that moment and made it apparent that she was a vested member. And with the handing over of the family recipe, she became a part of the family story that she would add to and pass down to future generations. This was no mere cornbread—these were some of the ingredients of the family tradition of breaking bread together.

Not surprisingly, the idea for this project grew out of some delicious shared Southern meals. Having gone to graduate school together at the University of Georgia to study our true academic love—rhetoric—we happened upon a shared interest. Ashli had been studying food through the Slow Food movement and, in a roundabout way, Wendy had been studying food through animal rights rhetoric. It struck us that combining our love of rhetoric, social movements, and Southern food might make for some very interesting insight into those areas. What began with one short essay grew into two, and before we knew it, we had so many ideas for projects centered on Southern food that we decided to take the plunge with this book. Selling the idea for this project to others was difficult at times ("Yes, grant committee, I AM requesting money to travel through the South and eat!"), yet in many ways it was an easy sell. After all, as we mention above, everyone has a food story. As we presented our early works to audiences, we found people eager to add to our collection of stories, jumping at the chance to continue the discussion about food and finding a particular interest in the topic of

Southern food. Many papers, presentations, trips, meals, and conversations later, we embarked on this food journey. Our intent was not only to add to our understanding of how food is rhetorical, but also to add to our understanding of how Southern culture is so clearly shaped by its foodways. And, thus, with these goals in mind, we began our effort to prove this connection.

There are several people we would like to thank for their help in this journey. Our departments—the Department of Communication Studies at the University of North Carolina at Charlotte, and the Department of Communication Studies at the University of Southern Mississippi—and colleges have been supportive both with money and with time. Deborah Gurt and our graduate research assistants, Angela McGowan and Beth Booker, helped track down sources and helped with revisions. Ellen Weinauer, Joyce Inman, Tasha Dubriwny, and Dan Grano read early essays and provided invaluable feedback. Our colleagues, friends, neighbors, and fellow community members were willing to share their food stories (and oftentimes their food), recipes, and opinions. There were numerous offers to accompany us on our food trips, and some even went along for the ride. Those who did so put up with our note taking, videos, and nonstop discussion about food. Our families supported our cross-regional excursions and last minute requests for more time to write. Ward Sayre and Jeff Stokes (as well as Gillian, Owen, Kate, and Charlie) had infinite patience and offered unwavering support, and we thank you, especially. Finally, to our mothers and grandmothers, who began our lifelong love of Southern food, your influence has shaped us more than you can ever know. Wendy wouldn't be the same without Granny's chicken and dumplin's, Nonnie's Watergate salad, and Mom's cobblers and cornbread, while Ashli was shaped by (her) Granny's skillet-fried chicken, her mother's biscuits and pound cakes, and Mammy's subversive inclination to take a sip of Jack, sit back, and let the rest of the family cook. To all of our supporters—and especially those who fed us physically and spiritually—thank you.

CONSUMING IDENTITY

THE STORIES, SUBJECTIVITIES, AND SPACES OF SOUTHERN FOOD

The signs that we had hit upon an important cultural and rhetorical subject were all apparent to us as we began our research into Southern food. We found that audiences—whether at a roadside stand or a convention hotel ballroom—would open up, smile, and freely share their memories, opinions, and ideas. After all, most people who are from the South or who identify with the region, despite being "of" another region, have opinions on what makes good Southern food. The topic crosses lines of race, class, gender, region, and so forth, providing an opportunity for a common discussion point.

This book explores the types of identities, allegiances, and bonds that are made possible and are strengthened through Southern foods and foodways, or "the study of why we eat, what we eat, and what it means" (Engelhardt, 2013, p. 1). Approaching our study from a rhetorical perspective, we focus on the role that food plays in building identities. Identity scholarship argues for the importance of accounting for how individuals are shaped by the ways they see themselves and others, how we identify with some roles and not others, and how those identities influence our thoughts and actions (Burke, 1950/1969; Butler, 1990; Charland, 1987, for example). Symbols of any type contribute to how we view ourselves, and it makes sense that, given the importance of food to our lives, our scholarship should account for the messages that food can send about who we are, how we see ourselves, and how we see others.

Significantly, we seek to add to the types of texts that communication studies scholarship accounts for in understanding the development and maintenance of identities. Although the study of food as communication has gained traction in recent years (see, for example, Cramer, Greene, & Walters, 2011; Frye & Bruner, 2012; Greene, 2015), there is still a great deal of work to be done to understand the communicative power of food. The chapters in Cramer and colleagues' (2011) volume, for example, look at such topics as popular constructions of food, the way it shapes our communication about health issues, and the way it becomes a part of our cultural experience. The chapters in Frye and Bruner's (2012) edited volume delve into the rhetorical aspects of food, discussing how language can shape our perceptions of it and even the politics surrounding it. Greene (2015) explores the rhetoric of excess that is often attached to discussions about food. All three projects contribute in important ways by beginning the conversation about the role of food in communication. We add to this conversation by providing a sustained argument about the rhetorical nature of food and the part that it has played in shaping a culture. Southern food, in particular, provides a rich example of this kind of rhetorical work.

At the same time, we hope to contribute to current food studies scholarship by explaining how food acts rhetorically. The notion that it reflects and helps sustain a culture is well explored, but accounting for the role that communication plays in that process—that is, *how* we communicate through food—strengthens our understanding of why food is such a vital part of culture. More specifically, while this book is only one of a growing list of volumes that examine Southern cuisine, the focus on the rhetorical nature of Southern food and the communicative effect that the food can have on Southern culture makes what we hope will be a significant contribution to that important conversation.

Consequently, we primarily focus on the story of Southern food and the narratives that surround it. Food experiences are inherently tied to stories, which, as with any narrative, can be rhetorical. Food stories have a peculiar strength, inviting us in and allowing us to reflect on our own narratives. This book develops by telling the stories of Southern food that speak to the identity of the region, explaining how food helps to build individual identities, and then exploring the possibilities of how it can open up dialogue. Three primary arguments follow. The first argument is that food acts rhetorically. The kinds of food that we choose to eat and serve send messages. Food tells stories, intentional or not, about our upbringing, about how we view ourselves and others, about how we read a situation (formal or informal, for example), and about the cultural ties that help shape who we are. We, thus, join the discussion that has recently emerged in communication studies and food studies that argues for the ability of food to send messages and help build relationships. Food serves as a narrative, telling our stories of past and present. The chapters in this book specifically explore the kinds of stories that Southern food tells about the region.

The second argument that we put forth is that food serves an identity-building function. If it tells our stories, it is also reasonable to assume that those stories help to develop our identity in some ways. Using the ideas of Kenneth Burke (1966) about the importance of symbols in the creation of our lived experience, we put forth the argument that food is symbolic, and the narratives that develop around it invite individuals into a particular identity. That is, food serves a constitutive function to, as Charland (1987) argues, "hail forth" an identity by offering up a positive image of Southerners as imagined through their food. Chapter one will more explicitly develop these theoretical concepts. The fact that food factors so heavily into our memories (or personal narratives), especially in the South, means that we must account for that rhetoric in explaining the development of identities.

Finally, we argue that because food and the stories surrounding it are so important to Southern culture, they provide a significant and meaningful way to open up dialogue in the region. By sharing and celebrating the stories of Southern foodways, but more importantly sharing the actual food, Southerners are able to focus on similar histories and traditions, despite the division that has plagued and continues to plague the region. The ritual of cooking and eating in the South is a small, but significant, way to reaffirm the strength of the region and to continue to build connections across racial and class lines. As Rebecca Watts (2008) points out in her discussion about new Southern identity, a subject that will be taken up more fully in chapter two, "One possible resolution to the continuing debate over Southern identity is to continue the gradual shift from the old order of division to a new order of identification. Such a shift would entail Southerners of differing perspectives and backgrounds emphasizing their common concerns as Southerners while continuing to recognize the value of each other's differences" (p. 16). Food may be one way to do just this. After all, Southern food is not monolithic; we find numerous differences among Southern foodways. At the same time, the topos transcends these differences in many ways. As a result, the possibility of using Southern food to emphasize similarities and open up opportunities for celebrating a shared culture is a noteworthy rhetorical moment. Taken together, these three arguments make it clear why we believe that Southern food provides a significant starting point for understanding the rhetorical potential of food.

SOUTHERN FOOD'S ASCENSION

Called the nation's most clearly defined, vital, and vibrant cuisine, Southern food has been dubbed the region's greatest contribution to American culture (Edge, 2012; Knoblauch, 2002). John Egerton (1993), author of what many consider to be the bible of Southern fare, *Southern Food: At Home, on the Road, in History*, explains the significance of the food to the region:

> Within the South itself, no other form of cultural expression, not even music, is as distinctively characteristic of the region as the spreading of a feast of native food and drink before a gathering of kin and friends. For as long as there has been a South, and people who think of themselves as Southerners, food has been central to the region's image, its personality, and its character. (p. 2)

Food is, thus, central to the Southern experience and understanding the area. Other regional cuisines might be able to make similar claims, yet it is clear that Southern fare provides a strong case study for the significance of food in defining a cultural identity. This centrality can partially be explained by the diversity of Southern foodways.

The cornerstones that make up Southern cuisine reflect the complex race and class history of the region, combining African, European, and Native American cooking roots that today loosely form four categories: soul, Creole, Cajun, and Lowcountry (Gold, 2010). The African emphasis is perhaps the cuisine's most defining characteristic (Edge, 2013a), but hyperregionality is also a key hallmark. Preferences for barbecue sauce change, for example, whether you are in eastern or western North Carolina. Hospitality (as troubled as the concept may be) is also essential to an understanding of the regional cuisine, with an emphasis on feeding the multitudes in times of struggle or celebration (Dupree, 2004). Additionally, Southern food cannot be separated from its agrarian heritage and is one of necessity and resourcefulness; as Severson (2012) explains, "a good Southern dish depends on equal measures of country tradition, economy, and authenticity" (para. 17). Although certain foods such as barbecue, fried chicken, and pimento cheese are iconic Southern dishes, a comprehensive definition of the cuisine is difficult. Southern food, as Kinsman (2010) argues, "isn't just one thing or one way—fried chicken, side of black-eyed peas and cornbread, wham, bam, culture defined—it's a plurality and it's constantly in flux" (para. 8). It is, thus, both distinctive, in that it has many of the characteristics listed above, and malleable enough to allow for a variety of interpretations. That malleability allows for an acceptance of various foodways that all fall under the umbrella of Southern food, emphasizing a shared sense of identification with the region.

There may be hundreds of interpretations of Southern cooking, but as it jumps geographical and cultural boundaries it has become one of the most popular cuisines in the United States (Cobb, 2008; Maynard, 2012; Severson, 2012). It has found a renaissance, with cookbooks and memoirs weighing down the shelves at the bookstores (Acheson, 2011; Brock, 2014; Deen & Clark, 2011; Dupree & Graubart, 2012; Roahen, Edge, & Southern Foodways Alliance, 2010; Willis, Dujardin, & Willan, 2011). Other books explore what it means to be "Southern" in today's global world (Cobb, 2011; Thompson, 2013a) and offer varying accounts of Southern cooking and reflections (Cooley, 2015; Ferris, 2010, 2014; Egerton, 1993; Engelhardt, 2011; Hahne, 2008; Tucker, 2009). The cuisine is also featured on television, in film, and in the media. Magazines such as *Bon Appétit* and *Gourmet* produce issues focused entirely on Southern cuisine. Readers also consume Southern food visually, with *Southern Living* continuing to be the largest regionally focused magazine in the country and helping to popularize Southern foodways (Ferris, 2009). Online sources such as Christy Jordan's website (southernplate.com) and Bitter Southerner (bittersoutherner.com) have also added to the popularity of Southern food. Since its 2008 launch, Jordan's website has had more than 43 million visitors looking for recipes that their grandmothers used to make but never put to paper; meanwhile, Bitter Southerner offers a wry and progressive take on Southern dishes of the past. Films such as *The Help* connect viewers emotionally to Southern food with its much-discussed food-focused subplot. Meanwhile, some feel a connection to Southern food so strongly that they organize in support of it. One group of young Southern chefs, for example, formed the "lardcore movement" to reinvent Southern food for the twenty-first century, while the Southern Foodways Alliance holds events throughout the South to celebrate and promote traditional and contemporary Southern foodways (Ferris, 2009; Ozersky, 2010).

Scholars from a variety of disciplines question why these expressions of Southern food culture endure and expand. Arguments can certainly be made for the significance of other foodways in the creation of cultural identity. The Southern example seems to be strong, however, when it comes to culture and food being bound together. Some argue that the heightened level of attention to Southern cuisine is due to the ability of its comfort classics to transcend time and place (Cobb, 2008), while others contend that it is intriguing because it remains firmly rooted in the past, "entangled in forces that have shaped Southern history and culture for more than four centuries" (Ferris, 2009, p. 4). The nostalgic appeal of the past is echoed by others who argue that Southern food may be appetizing because of its nods to the familiar, to the value of slowing down or looking back (*The Economist*, 1997). As Edge (2013b) argues, "In the midst of an ongoing American nostalgia movement, the South promises the past, preserved in amber, ready to be consumed in the present" (p. 4).

Still others note that the cultural embrace of Southern food may be due in part to the country's larger food movement that seeks a more sustainable approach to eating. Cultivating and cooking with long-forgotten Southern grains and overlooked vegetables has a common interest with the loosely defined sustainable food movement, which has helped develop, for example, a greater mainstream interest in farmers' markets, the support of sustainable food sourcing in restaurant chains and superstores, and an increasing interest in gardening and cooking (Innes, 2007; Martin, 2009). Because Southern foodways are traditionally and strongly aligned with these larger food movement goals, Southern cuisine becomes a unique example of how Americans should be eating. Thus, whether it is the sense of comfort, the fact that it is so rooted in the past, that it acts as an exemplar for the larger sustainable food movement, or the characteristics discussed earlier (diverse, hyperregional, hospitable, and agrarian based), not only is Southern food distinct, but it also serves as one of the strongest examples of foodways defining a region. As Cooley (2015) argues, "the distinctions of the culinary South continue to exist because southerners continue to want them" (p. 154). Those preferences are both a marker of food preferences and a sign of Southerners defining themselves through their foodways.

Of course, Southern food also brings with it some historical and cultural baggage. Former Food Network star Paula Deen's use of racist terms and nostalgic musings about slavery in the South, for example, invited criticism of the regional cuisine (Moskin, 2013). Food is connected to race (as will be discussed throughout this book), and that relationship necessarily means that it can sometimes be caught in the middle of controversy. Although the diversity of Southern food is a key characteristic, it is also important to note that issues of cultural "ownership" are occasionally a part of the discussion: who can lay claim to certain Southern foods and who has been most influential in developing the regional cuisine (Egerton, 1993). Segregation also plays a part in Southern food history. Although restaurants were not the only segregated areas, they were some of the most apparent spaces featured in sit-ins (Conley, 2015), and segregated dining cars, roadside diners, and community cafes often made travel difficult for African Americans (Opie, 2008). Finally, it would be a mistake to ignore the complicated health history that Southerners have with food. Yearly pronouncements note the ongoing problem of obesity in the region. Although not all Southern food is unhealthy, and in fact many modern takes on Southern dishes reject the unhealthy versions (Miller, 2013), the argument still remains that the region's food can play a role in rising obesity rates, increases in diabetes, and other food-related illnesses. Part of the civil rights movement, for example, made an argument for creating healthier versions of soul food dishes in order to make a positive impact on the black community (Opie, 2008). We fully recognize that Southern food is not a panacea for solving the social ills of the region. There is, however, ample evidence that this cuisine is an important part of defining Southerners, and that role in defining a culture means that there is a need to account for its strength, despite its mixed past.

METHODOLOGY

This book is not designed to be a historical or cultural accounting of Southern foodways. Instead, we take a rhetorical approach to our study of the regional cuisine. That is, we focus specifically on how food and foodways can act persuasively to invite individuals to identify with others and to embrace particular identities. Some of this rhetoric is overt, in that Southern food movement organizations, farmers' markets, or restaurants, for example, may make statements about their beliefs, inviting others to join them in their beliefs and actions. Much of the rhetorical work is implicit, however, sending messages about what Southern food should be, how Southerners should cook and eat, and how Southerners should act if they identify with this way of thinking. Because of the diversity in the way that Southern food "speaks," we have chosen to use different methods to collect artifacts and to analyze them.

As we began this exploration of Southern food and the role that it plays in developing Southern identity, it became apparent that the standard research practices of rhetorical criticism would not be sufficient for this project. Although much of the book will include rhetorical criticism (or analysis of symbols in order to understand their persuasive potential) of standard written artifacts such as mission statements, cookbooks, web sites and blogs, and menus, we also read alternative texts. As Ferris (2013) points out:

The "stuff" of southern food—its cast-iron skillets, celery holders, Dutch ovens, iced tea pitchers, beaten biscuit machines, pottery bowls, canning jars, stove ware crocks, choppers, sugar molds, oyster culling hammers, bread bowls, backyard sheds for peanut boil and fish fries—all bear meaning. (p. 300)

Consequently, we also take the objects of Southern culture as important symbols of the region. In the end, we approach this research by opening up the definition of rhetorical texts as much as possible.

We also build our argument based on rhetorical fieldwork, recognizing that only so much of the "texts" that we analyze can be found by seeking it out while driving to and visiting regional gems. Elizabeth Engelhardt (2013), discussing food studies methodology, argues, "We can and should choose the methods most suited to any given food study. We mix and match, reading pieces against each other and in changing combinations" (p. 6). Consequently, our research turns to food experiences to bolster our understanding of Southern culture. As Middleton, Senda-Cook, and Endres (2011) argue, "Participant observation allows critics to experience rhetorical action as it unfolds and offers opportunities to gather insights on how rhetoric is experienced by rhetors, audiences, and critics" (p. 390). This type of rhetorical field research has gained traction in the discipline, being used to explore political upheaval, (McHendry, Middleton, Endres, Senda-Cook, & O'Bryne, 2014), motherhood (Gilbert & Wallmenich, 2014), environmental issues (Pezzullo, 2007), social movement coalition-building efforts (Chavez, 2011), health advocacy groups (Hess, 2011), issues of authenticity (Senda-Cook, 2012), and issues of choice (Wilkins & Wolf, 2011) just to cite a few of these studies. As Pezzullo argues, "This experiential approach to rhetorical and cultural analysis is, I believe, particularly useful because it provides the opportunity to examine a side of public discourse that tends to be marginalized in traditional written records" (p. 18). Food studies, of course, pose similar problems. Although the rhetoric/written artifacts surrounding the food and food politics are part of the persuasive message, so much of the food story is experienced. Hess (2011) writes that "'Text,' in these cases, does not only constitute the recording of speeches; rather, the text has become something living, breathing, and operating within unique spaces and received by particular audiences. In short, rhetorical scholars have turned toward *in situ* and everyday processes of textual production and reception" (p. 130). Thus, as Hess suggests, we took to the road to experience the food and to account for these very different types of rhetorical texts.

In our case, the experience of traveling through ten Southern states (Virginia, North Carolina, South Carolina, Kentucky, Georgia, Alabama, Tennessee, Mississippi, Louisiana, and Texas) and visiting more than one hundred restaurants (both fine dining and dive dining), roadside produce stands and farmers' markets, and gas stations and grocery stores was a necessary supplement to our understanding of Southern foodways. These experiences were recorded through extensive notes, gathered literature (menus and such), photography, and audio/video clips, providing rich written artifacts that could be analyzed. The fieldwork not only informed our reading of the kinds of standard rhetorical texts discussed above, but also served as rhetorical texts themselves. Middleton and colleagues (2011) explain that this kind of rhetorical research allows "critical rhetoricians to interrogate how smells, sounds, time, space, and other factors excluded by a focus on text or their fragments shape rhetorical experiences" (p. 396). Accounting for this kind of experience is important because it allows for an expanded understanding of what is considered rhetorical, although this type of research is more difficult to undertake than analysis of standard texts. As Middleton and colleagues (2011) conclude,

> Viewing rhetoric as a part of social practice . . . means that rhetoric is not constituted simply by texts or textual fragments, but through a combination of material contexts, social relationships, identities, consciousnesses, and (interrelated) rhetorical acts that produce meanings and that are co-constructed between rhetor, audience, and particular context. (p. 391)

Thus, our research includes these kinds of elements, providing a deeper understanding of the Southern food experience. In thinking through issues of race, class, and gender in Southern foodways, we account for not only written artifacts and oral histories surrounding Southern food, but also experiences in communities where we can see interactions and hear firsthand stories.

In many cases, it is the sight, smell, touch, and taste of the food that begins the experience, but it is also the conversations that are happening over the food and with the wait staff, the photographs hanging on the walls, the music playing in the background, and the neighborhood that contains the restaurant that add to our understanding of the food. As Edge (2013b) argues, "I learned that food offers entrée to talk of big-picture issues. Like race and class, gender and justice. Through the years, when I tried to tackle those matters head-on, I often lost an audience. But at tables piled high with country ham, buttermilk biscuits, and redeye gravy, I've marveled as all have leaned in close to eat, to talk, to listen" (pp. 4–5). The question of why Southern food may be the perfect rhetorical opening for these conversations is one of the central concerns of this book. We, therefore, incorporate these experiences into the analysis in order to account for the complete Southern food experience and to explore the rhetorical possibilities—as well as limitations—of the food.

SYNOPSIS OF CHAPTERS

This book develops the argument that Southern food is rhetorical by first laying out the theoretical and historical frameworks and then turning to specific food examples. Part one, "The Rhetorical Potential of Southern Food," uncovers the ways that food might act as a unifying force and explores the problems that the South faces with its relationship to the past. Southern foodways have the potential to help transcend past differences, moving us toward a shared experience. While food has the potential to emphasize shared experiences, there are obviously limitations to how much identification work it can do. This section, thus, tries to account for the rhetorical potential, while also noting the limitations. Chapter one, "Consuming Rhetoric: How Southern Food Speaks," details what we mean by the concept of identity and places our argument within the tradition of rhetorical scholarship. If rhetorical studies seek to understand how people are persuaded by messages, an identity based/constitutive approach argues that food can be considered a modern-day rhetorical expression of the South's complex racial, social, and cultural identity. In this chapter, we argue that Southern food is a constitutive rhetoric, creating a people based on the shared experiences through the food, as well as the narratives surrounding the food. Using food experiences, oral histories, and readings of various alternative texts, this chapter highlights the need to continue to move beyond "texts" to explore the rhetorical implications of "identificatory" experiences, such as food culture. We argue, for example, that crawfish boils, tailgates, and church suppers do just as much rhetorical work as a traditional printed text. We explore how identification with such Southern food cultures shapes discursive and cultural norms, that is, how we talk about and perform eating, socializing, consuming, and cooking. By showing how our identities can be shaped through sensory experiences (taste, touch, smell, sight, and sound) and memory during Southern food experiences, we continue to develop the line of constitutive scholarship that explicates how our identities constitute our practices. If identifying with the South through local food is culturally desirable, a different understanding of what it is to be Southern is possible. Celebrating Southern food creates a space for dialogue and therefore offers potential for changing the way we relate to each other, eat, and act as consumers. Southern food, then, influences how we view ourselves and can therefore influence our practices, which is to say how we perform our Southern-influenced identities.

That the local food landscape influences Southerners in how they define themselves is an example of how identities can be articulated through culture (Burke, 1950/1969). More than persuading people to select certain foods, appeals to "eat more Southern" reshape consumer identity by revising perceptions about food and creating an identity-constituting narrative (Enck-Wanzer, 2006; Tate, 2005). As legendary African American New Orleans chef Leah Chase observes, "everybody in the South eats the same things; we may cook a little different, but we eat the same things" (in Cole & Lewis, 2013, p. 80). Thus, food becomes a way to see some overlap between backgrounds when individuals seem divided by race, ethnicity, and class. Of course, many things still may separate Southerners (income, religion, education, music, etc.), but food can help cross those boundaries. Latshaw (2009), for example, suggests that ongoing embrace of regional cuisine "might be one of the few things that southerners of all races, ages, and classes lay claim to, have shared in the past, and still find commonality in today" (p. 108). This book, then, brings needed attention to how food rhetoric serves a constitutive function, an area that needs greater attention in rhetorical scholarship.

Chapter two, "A Troubled Region and Its Possible Culinary Fix," surveys the rhetorical problem that the South faces. The South has a complicated history marred by racial violence, segregation and discrimination, and economic inequality. At the same time, Southern culture has emerged out of this quagmire, developing from a mixture of racial and ethnic backgrounds, regional differences, and socioeconomic groups. Plagued by negative images of the region, it is difficult to be a Southerner of any background. Whether you are an African American with a family history haunted by racism and violence, a white individual with a family history of discriminating or tolerating discrimination, or a Mexican immigrant facing negative social outcry, feeling pride in the region can be troubling. Despite those conflicting identities, Southerners of all sorts continue to define themselves in relation to the region, embracing the duality of being both "Southern" and "American" (Burns, 2012). As one African American writer notes about embracing the complexity of Southern identity, "I'm Southern not because of living or not living in a certain place. It's because that culture has been nurtured in me, and I carry that wherever I go" (Penrice, 2012, p. 3). This chapter will explain the rhetorical problem that the reality-based and stereotypical images of the Southerner are all part of that identity. Finding a way to embrace a more positive and inclusive identity may provide a necessary route for recovering the Southern image and moving forward. We argue that the Southern food movement serves a constitutive function by helping to craft an identity based on diverse, humble, and hospitable roots that confronts a divided image of the South. This rhetorically constitutive work has the potential to provide an opportunity for strengthening relations within the South, as well as helping to repair the negative Southern image.

If part one describes why we should study identity through food and how Southern food itself serves a rhetorical function, part two, "Exploring the Southern Table," tells the story of the South's identities through the metaphor of a meal. The chapters trace Southern food identities starting with cocktails and other drinks (chapter three), main courses (chapter four), sides (chapter five), and desserts (chapter six). In each chapter, we compile evidence for the unifying and identifying potential of Southern cuisine through rhetorical analysis of printed texts, oral interviews, documentaries, cookbooks, traveler's accounts, literature, and fieldwork material. We also show how the rhetorical openings created by food may need to be supplemented by other societal changes in order to move groups of Southerners to better identify with each other. That is, we provide an example of how food is doing rhetorical work, while also acknowledging that it is not a cure all. Each chapter in the body of the book seeks to demonstrate how Southern food identities reflect larger race, ethnicity, class, and gender issues.

For example, chapter three, "Sipping on Southern Hospitality: Drink as Rhetorical Invitation," introduces the idea of hospitality in the South through an exploration of drinks. Although the idea of Southern hospitality is emphasized in stereotypes of the region, there is also some basis in truth. The offering of food and drink is a traditional symbolic gesture of Southern hospitality. Whether it is a glass of sweet iced tea, a powerful Sazerac, or a cold Shiner Bock, sipping a drink while settling into a conversation remains a way of life in the South. A Southerner is expected to be welcoming, inviting guests into his or her home (or other spaces) and plying them with food and drink in order to make them feel comfortable. It is within the first few minutes of entering into a Southern restaurant, home, tailgating tent, or event reception, for example, that the identity of the host begins to develop. The offering of libations sets a different tone than the offering of nonalcoholic drinks, given the lingering moral baggage surrounding alcohol. Appetizers, snacks, and finger foods begin the culinary conversation that will continue through-out the event. The idea of hospitality provides an example of what Kenneth Burke (1950/1969) describes as the principle of courtship—overcoming mys-tery or division by the "transcending of social estrangement" (p. 208). Food and drink can serve as a rhetorical opening for creating connections.

In a region marked by division, however, race, class, and even religious differences have historically complicated Southern hospitality, inviting some in while keeping others out. For example, the hospitality that is so symbolic of the region was (and still is, in some cases) limited to certain recipients for many years. Events and even homes remained segregated, and thus hospital-ity might only be extended to those who shared characteristics with the host. Religion also plays an important role in this part of the Southern food story, becoming a defining part of the contradictions in identity. Thus, the limita-tions of this part of Southern identity will also be explored in this chapter.

Chapter four "Turf Tussle: Uniting through North Carolina Barbecue," ex-amines how barbecue is a cultural institution that sends rhetorical messages about Southern history, gender, race, class, ritual, and fellowship. We rely on barbecue as a type of cultural synecdoche that continues to bring different types of people together, telling stories that simultaneously shape and express contemporary Southern identity. Barbecue may be a three-hundred-year-old Southern tradition that has been written about endlessly, but it remains a relevant and "good to think" way to understand Southern culture (Veteto & Maclin, 2011, p. 20).

When people declare a style of Southern barbecue to be the "right" kind, that tells you immediately about their influences and possibly their identi-ties as Southerners. If Southern food helps shape identity, barbecue pro-vides a perfect example of this process, because its rhetoric and ritual incite profound identification with regional styles. Tussling about which barbecue is best engages identity-forming behavior that serves a rhetorical purpose in gradually knitting groups of people together over their shared love of a particular food tradition. We explore how barbecue conveys identificatory messages of authenticity, masculinity, and rurality, showing how it stretches casuistically to still be descriptive of the South's character. Burke (1984) de-scribes casuistic stretching as "introducing new principles while theoretically remaining faithful to old principles," and we rely on this idea to see how (and whether) perceptions of traditional Southern foods like barbecue can stretch to broaden and deepen the narrative about the area (p. 229).

Chapter five, "Authenticating Southernism: Creating a Sense of Place through Food," then turns to the side dishes on the Southern food table, exploring the connection between the food and the region. Cornbread, grits, and greens are Southern food staples. We may choose these side dishes because of the flavors, but food choices are also largely historically driven by economic hardships, regional availability, and seasonal selection. "Making do" on what was available in the garden or with the cheapest ingredients stored away in the pantry was a defining experience for many families, but the taste for those simple foods has not left the Southern palate. Thus, the sides that accompany the entrees convey important information about Southern identity. The connection to the land and the seasonality of the food indicates a natural bond to place. That is, place affects action by limiting and influencing food choices, and choosing particular foods signals an understanding of the land. Often more than just an awareness of seasons, however, Southern cuisine also emphasizes frugality, highlighting the ability to depend on food grown in local soil or in areas considered to be "food deserts" (areas without options for fresh, healthy foods), in contemporary parlance. Whether Southerners eat these foods out of economic constraints or preference, the selection of seasonal and region-bound foods is a rhetorical deference to Southern roots based in humble, fresh, seasonal ingredients. The creation of these dishes is also an important tie to family roots, with families or even entire communities claiming to have the most authentic take on the food. The dish becomes a symbol of the person and his or her connections to the region. We will delve into the symbolism bound up in food through the concept of authenticity. Closely connected to Kenneth Burke's (1966) ideas about the human need for order, authenticity is one way that we both strive to maintain cultural order and show our allegiances to that order. Based on this desire for order and authenticity, we discuss the ways that this rhetorical work helps define the region.

Chapter six, "Nostalgia, Ritual, and the Rhetorical Possibility of Southern Baking," will explore the sweet ending to a Southern meal. From a dizzying array of cakes, to pies crowned with clouds of meringue, to the church-supper standbys of banana pudding and fruit cobblers, the South is well known for its desserts. These recipes may be recognized as traditionally Southern, but it might not always be clear how or why the Southern dessert tradition developed as it did and how it figures in shaping the identities of the region's people and practices. Desserts are viewed through a particular terministic screen where some imagine their great grandmothers patting out the pastry dough and setting up the tea table, quite literally existing in the kitchen, watching the outside world spin by. Burke (1966) reminds us that terministic screens direct our attention to certain realities and away from others, whereby we forget that baking constituted backbreaking, sweaty repression for certain groups of Southerners. This chapter argues that familiar Southern desserts may tie us to our pasts, but through certain types of nostalgia and ritual they also provide space to help change the South's narratives about race, gender, and community. Southern desserts are suspect in limiting women's subjectivities; they seem like time-consuming relics that worry modern health sensibilities with their Southern sweetness. They carry the weight of troubling African American history. Our meal ends, however, by investigating how these traditions might offer a taste of connection and resilience along with satisfaction.

Finally, the concluding section, "After-Dinner Conversation," provides closing thoughts about the rhetorical potential of Southern foodways. Chapter seven, "Redefining the South through Food," provides a reflection on what it means to be constituted in a particular food tradition and how food serves a rhetorical function in other parts of the country and throughout the world. Food may provide only one entry point into understanding culture, but this book argues that it is a central part of identity that has not been fully accounted for in communication scholarship. There are lots of arguments about the forces that shape who we are; throughout this book, we contend that when we eat the cuisine that has meaning for us as Southerners, we consume portions of our identities. Importantly, we argue that the boundaries of the region are stretched through its food and that expanding the rhetorical image of the region can do much to help redefine the South. Southern cuisine has the potential to cross racial, class, ethnic, religious, gender, and geographical boundaries, bringing a wide variety of consumers together to celebrate one thing. Southern food does not have to be—and never has been—*one* thing; in fact, it works more effectively rhetorically when defined more broadly. This boundary stretching allows for a more diverse understanding of the region when it pushes against the borders of foods and brings more people into the conversation. We show how the food of the South is changing as the population changes, with ethnic dishes making their way into the Southern palate. American culture is full of stories of how immigrant traditions changed traditional foodways, and the South is poised to become part of this larger story in more significant ways. Finally, this chapter considers the rhetorical possibilities of Southern food, arguing that although there is clearly a great deal of potential for using it as one of the tools to redefine the South, we must acknowledge its limitations. We want this to be a positive contribution to a study of contemporary Southern culture—one that offers up the potential of a future direction for actions that can be taken to help cure the region's ills. We realize, however, that there are many wrongs that must be dealt with, not only through a study of the culture and its history, but also through economic policy, political change, improvements in education, infrastructure work, and so forth. The rhetorical potential of Southern food is but one small part of the story of our shared past and future, but it is an important part, and it is a story worth telling. With this brief overview, then, it is possible to start the tour of the South through its foodways. Although we begin the discussion with a broader view of the rhetorical role of food in the South, we quickly turn to the food itself to build the argument for its regional rhetorical potential. The rest of the book focuses on those stories in an effort to cull out the ways that Southern food articulates a shared experience.

PART ONE

THE RHETORICAL POTENTIAL OF SOUTHERN FOOD

Figure 1.1 Weaver D's in Athens, Georgia

CHAPTER ONE

CONSUMING RHETORIC
How Southern Food Speaks

The scene at Weaver D's restaurant in Athens, Georgia, is just what we expected. The restaurant was made famous by Athens-based rock band REM after they named their album, *Automatic for the People,* for the owner's catch phrase. The cinderblock building, not far from the University of Georgia campus, is painted lime green and topped by a plain white sign announcing that this is "Weaver D's Delicious Fine Foods—'Automatic for the People'" (see figure 1.1). We are thrilled as we walk through the doors and find ourselves not only being waited on by Weaver D himself, but also getting "automatic'ed" (his famous greeting) by Weaver after ordering. The restaurant is simple. A small, one-room dining area is filled with long tables pushed together and covered with red-and-white-checkered tablecloths. After ordering at the counter, we head over to the kitchen window to stare down at the glorious sides—green beans, macaroni and cheese, greens, and squash casserole on this day—and make our selection. Decoration in the room is scant—a few signed REM posters, some framed newspaper articles, Whitney Houston albums hanging on the walls, a television tuned to *Judge Judy.* In short, everything about the place could be seen as mundane. And yet, walking through those doors, eating the outstanding food, and observing the other customers as they came in, ordered, and partook of that Southern food masterpiece was a bit magical for us. It was an enactment of all that we had been arguing Southern food could do. Our research unfolded before our eyes.

The food was good, no doubt, but there are better places to get Southern fare. We could have found better service elsewhere and certainly finer dining rooms in other locations. What made this restaurant different? The people. In a town, not unlike many Southern cities, that still faces de facto segregation in its neighborhoods, schools, and churches, the clientele was notably diverse. We sat next to a middle-aged black couple who prayed together before turning to their Styrofoam plates piled high with fried chicken and sides. Sharing the same table, we had a brief conversation about which hot sauce might make the best addition to the greens. While eating, we watched as a young black man, possibly a student, was welcomed by Weaver D and given his "usual plate." After that, a white family entered the restaurant. The parents, seeming a bit out of their element (perhaps visiting their college kids), tentatively ordered and sat down at the next table over to catch up with each other. Next came an older black man, still wearing his work overalls, who ordered his lunch. What brought this range of people together was the food. Although the interaction between the individuals might not have been significant, the fact that they were physically coming together in search of a common food created a moment of crossover between worlds. More than a brief shared moment in a fast food restaurant, this slower and homemade version encouraged people to pause. The food itself also served to connect people, as we discuss later in this chapter. The shared words, expressions of joy over the food, and quick smiles that were exchanged added something more to a feeling of consubstantiality. And this was not unlike the scene that we saw playing out in Atlanta's Sweet Auburn Curbside Market, Birmingham's Dreamland Bar-b-que, Memphis's Gus's Chicken, New Orleans's Dooky Chase, and many other places throughout the South. Food brings people together and is a significant part of Southern culture.

More than a passing fad or restaurant trend, the variety of ways that people seek to connect to the South through food-based experiences presents an intriguing question for scholars interested in constitutive rhetorical theory. In seeking to relate to, experience, or create this particular type of food, a desire to connect or to identify with this food culture becomes evident. In jointly celebrating Southern food, Southerners of all types have the potential to focus on commonality and shared ground—not the division that has historically plagued the region. The difficult past of the South does not disappear (Jim Crow, civil rights, and ERA, for instance)—nor should it—but a shared appreciation for Southern food provides a moment to experience what it might be like to come together in celebration of the region. This positive view offers new ways for people to relate to each other, to eat, and to act as consumers. Connecting with a Southern food identity, then, begins to constitute how we view ourselves and can therefore influence our practices, which is to say how we perform our Southern-influenced identities.

In this chapter, we argue that food is a constitutive rhetoric. We rely on various expressions of Southern food identity as explored through our rhetorical fieldwork in order to highlight the need to continue to move beyond "texts" to explore the rhetorical implications of "identificatory" experiences, such as food culture. This chapter highlights how identification with Southern food culture shapes discursive and cultural norms, that is, how we talk about and perform eating, socializing, consuming, and cooking. By showing how our identities can be shaped through the narratives that emerge from our sensory experiences, we continue to develop the line of constitutive scholarship that explicates how our identifications constitute our practices (Cooren, Kuhn, Cornelissen, & Clark, 2011; Cordova, 2004; Jasinski, 1998, 2001; Stein, 2002). That is, as we identify with particular characteristics and groups, we are then drawn to act based on those identities. If Southern food acts rhetorically, it sends a message that can help shape identity. This chapter will focus on how food communicates, while the rest of the book will explore what Southern food communicates and the types of identities that it might form.

In theorizing about the rhetorical, constitutive nature of Southern food, descriptions of such foodways and experiences help form our understanding of this function. In addition to examples from our field research, we rely on texts produced by the Southern Foodways Alliance (SFA), an institute of the University of Mississippi's Center for the Study of Southern Culture. SFA is one of the most important academic groups studying Southern foodways and has been called the most "intellectually engaged" food society by the *Atlantic Monthly* magazine (Kummer, 2005, para. 2). Importantly, the organization provides a collection of oral histories and films designed to capture the experience of Southern cuisine. By telling the stories of the people who have helped preserve and/or revive Southern cooking, the organization offers a compelling collection of the stories. These are rhetorical texts in that they tell a particular story of Southern food—in all of its complexity—and its place in Southern culture. The films do more than that, however. As John T. Edge (SFA, "An SFA Film Primer"), director of the SFA, says of its collection of almost ninety short films:

> We truly believe that these fried chicken cooks, these road crop farmers, these barbecue pit masters tell us a story about the South. We think these stories offer far more than just sustenance. We think they offer a way of thinking about race and class and gender and ethnicities—those deeply important issues that have long vexed and long defined the South.

Consequently, a look at some of the fieldwork examples that we collected, as well as a sampling of the SFA films, provides needed examples to explore the rhetorical nature of food and its constitutive possibilities. Indeed, Southern food and Southern food rhetoric such as the SFA's invite people to define themselves through the way they eat. We first frame the constitutive rhetorical tradition in terms of these identity-building properties. We then analyze briefly some of the examples from our fieldwork experiences and a selection of filmed SFA oral histories through five sensory experiences to demonstrate how food can serve a constitutive function. Finally, we argue that identification with these sensory experiences positions particular types of discursive and material action, particularly in the case of Southern food.

CONSUMING THE CONSTITUTIVE RHETORICAL TRADITION

Constitutive Rhetoric as Identity Building

Constitutive rhetorical theory illuminates how identities are formed, performed, and move us to action. This tradition moves beyond causality, where communication scholars look at how a message causes someone to act in some specific way, to understanding how discourse "makes something possible or creates conditions of possibility" (Jasinski, 2001, p. 106). Constitutive theory asserts that communication is ongoing and full of potential, symbolically creating and recreating our identities, social relations, events and experiences, ideas, feelings, and ways of expressing them (Craig, 2000). It is interested in the creation and negotiation of meaning in society (Craig, 2000). Constitutive rhetorical approaches help explain how these traditions continue to be culturally relevant and indicative of a region's people. As Cooren (2012) explains about the importance of understanding how communication creates culture, "for an accent or a language to live and exist, we have to make it live and exist in our interactions and discourse" (p. 6). Our words and actions not only embody our identities, but they also reify those identities. Constitutive rhetoric shows how things such as "attitudes, beliefs, traits, feelings, and emotions constantly invite themselves into our discussions through the way they animate us (in which case they are the ventriloquist and we are the dummies) and reversely, through the way we (willingly or not) ventriloquize them through our conduct and talk (in which case we are the ventriloquists and they are the dummies" (p. 10). The idea that identity is rhetorically shaped is not new, of course.

Maurice Charland (1987) is the seminal rhetorical theorist credited with arguing that a person's identity is shaped through persuasion leading to a collective identity that helps create social change. Building on Burke's (1950/1969) ideas about rhetoric's ability to engender identification, he argues that constitutive rhetoric facilitates the development of an identity committed to a particular cultural movement or societal possibility because it does more than address people; it attempts to remake them by replacing one reality with another. Identification, Burke argues, allows for a feeling of shared experience, thereby strengthening persuasive messages. By talking a person's "language by speech, gesture, tonality, order, image, attitude, idea, *identifying* your ways with his,*" the rhetor appeals to the audience and creates this sense of shared identity (Burke, p. 55; emphasis his).

The identity creation process is, in many ways, a performance. Constitutive rhetoric explains the ways in which discourse shapes identities because it helps uncover tendencies and possibilities in how the identities are formed without arguing that they are rigid or unchangeable. As a rhetoric of possibility, it allows for both the performance of a particular identity and the ability to ignore or challenge the offered subject position. Judith Butler (1990) argues, for example, that identities, and gender in particular, are not stable entities. Instead, she argues, gender should be thought of as a performance, as something that is "performatively produced and compelled by the regulatory practices of gender coherence. Hence . . . gender proves to be performative— that is, constituting the identity it is purported to be . . . There is no gender identity behind the expressions of gender; that identity is performatively constituted by the very 'expressions' that are said to be its results" (pp. 24–25). Butler's contributions to our understanding of performance have been widely used in the larger discussions about identity. Identity is constructed, according to Butler (1988), through a "stylized repetition of facts" (p. 519) or "an active process of embodying certain cultural and historical possibilities" (p. 521). Thus, the acts that we perform, the daily actions that we take, help form who we are. As Cordova (2004) notes, constitutive rhetoric "facilitates the performance of identities, not just their adoption" (p. 215).

Moving beyond identity creation and reaffirmation, however, the constitutive approach also explains how identities move us to action. Scholars employing this perspective are interested in how a metaphor, narrative, or other rhetorical device allows people to consider things in new or different ways and the ways in which "discursive practice shapes but does not completely determine the realms of the social, political, or economic" (Jasinski, 2001, p. 106). Constitutive rhetoric goes beyond identification because rhetoric is used in "constituting character, community, and culture in language" (White, 1985, p. x). It builds on Black's (1970) understanding of how rhetoric envisions an audience, as well as Althusser's (1971) work on interpellation and ideology. It is a rhetoric of socialization. In the act of addressing listeners (or in our case, those who experience Southern food), "an advocate's message awakens (or energizes) certain possibilities or a specific identity (or subject position) for that audience" (Jasinski, 2001, p. 107). Importantly, it is up to the listener to conclude a story once interpellated or identified, even though there is a type of forward movement or desired outcome offered.

Many recent constitutive studies speak to the power of these collective identities. Scholars have used the perspective to examine how political identities form (Cordova, 2004; Sweet & McCue-Enser, 2010); how women come to view themselves as mothers, employees, or both (Hayden, 2011); or how citizens come to feel attached to a particular national identity (Beasley, 2002; Stuckey, 2006). Many of these studies explore the strength of the collectivity, with Hayden (2011), for example, noting how a website devoted to women seeking to be good "aunties" to their siblings' children reinforces some harmful assumptions that underlie mothering, inviting these women to also define themselves through children. Another development in constitutive rhetoric seeks to understand how material realities create rhetorical opportunities that deserve our attention. Blair (1999), Greene (1998), and Jasinski (2001) all discuss this "constitutive materialism" whereby discourse "does more than describe the world; it creates what is real" (Jasinski, 2001, p. 119). As Selzer (1999) explains about this important line of materialist inquiry, "language is not the only medium or material that speaks" (p. 8).

As a largely celebratory discourse rooted in specific material practices (planting, cooking, eating), Southern food rhetoric provides the opportunity to build on these scholarly developments to explore the potential of a positive, affirming constitutive rhetoric, as well as the chance to further theorize the mediation between the material and rhetorical dimensions of experience. Indeed, Southern food is experiencing what Charland (1987) calls a "founding moment," when advocates try to "interpellate" audiences into a common, collective identity. National media, for example, talk frequently about the "Southern culinary revivalist" movement (Eddy, 2013, para. 2). Founding moments require that advocates negotiate paradoxical constraints in order to turn them into resources or opportunities to work toward a particular telos; it is in these moments that advocates need to "define away the recalcitrance of the world" and offer new, fresh "perspectives and motives" (Charland, 1987, p. 142). Through the creation of the SFA, the hosting of community and academic events, and the change in the way that Southern food is interpreted and created in homes and restaurants, as well as the perception of Southern food, it is clear that the Southern food movement is motivating this interpellation. If this founding moment is successful, Southern food and the rhetoric surrounding it will emphasize the history that Southerners share and encourage dialogue. This idea will be discussed more fully in chapter two.

Emphasizing commonalities is complicated by many factors and that is especially true in the South. There are multiple societal pressures pulling people to support different allegiances; and as Dubriwny (2009) explains, identity is not a "stable essence of self but a process of becoming through texts, discourses, and ideologies" (p. 108). These different cultural forces shape the formation of identity and must be "negotiated within a particular rhetorical culture among competing political visions, already constituted subjectivities, and material circumstances" (Tate, 2005, p. 27). Even if constituted, collectivities can shift and are subjected to power that is always both limiting and enabling (Drzewiecka, 2002; Zagacki, 2007). So, Southern food rhetoric may contain possibilities, offering adherents new ways to view their relationships to food and to each other, but it must first work to constitute a collective subject that challenges these divisive individual or class interests and concerns (Charland, 1987); therefore, in appealing to listeners, "advocates must consider competing worldviews . . . contradictions that arise between competing identities and the narratives that constitute them" (Zagacki, 2007, p. 273). Indeed, for a collective subject position to be able to challenge the South's racialized, classed, and gendered history is daunting, yet food seemingly carries this possibility. That is, we can celebrate our commonalities while sharing a culinary habit.

It is the stories surrounding food—the driving narratives—that seem to give food its rhetorical strength. Charland (1987) argues that constitutive rhetoric gives the illusion of freedom, which means that subjects are relentlessly driven to carry out or follow through on the narrative, what Zagacki (2007) calls "being constrained by the narrative telos of constitutive rhetoric" (p. 276). Scholars have examined the drawbacks of being locked into a particular narrative (Hayden, 2011; Stein, 2002); however, in the case of the collective subject position created by Southern food rhetoric, this process may be beneficial. An audience must be persuaded to accept the world created by the stories of Southern food, but if constituted, people may work to enact the narrative beyond sharing meals, positively altering relationships once the experience concludes. As Charland (1987) points out, "a narrative, once written, offers a logic of meaningful totality" (p. 141). Following the logic of the narrative in Southern food culture points to ways in which food, as a discourse, carries rhetorical force.

Narratives strengthen constitutive rhetoric in many ways. By employing a constitutive perspective, we are able to see Southern food as a story, or a narrative in rhetorical terms, which establishes relationships between or among things over a time period (Jasinski, 2001). These stories do more than serve an instrumental function; they contain constitutive or ideological rhetorical force that positions a culture's social world, making "its customs, traditions, values, shared beliefs, roles, institutions, memories, or language" become second nature to members of that culture (Jasinski, 2001, p. 398). Constitutive rhetoric, in the form of narratives or other texts, performs four functions that create lived experience. Narratives can constitute subjectivity, the experience of time and temporal experience, a culture's community and political norms, and finally, its language. Regarding constituting subjectivity, the food stories we share or tell about ourselves are constantly unfolding and changing, but "the way in which we organize, edit, and revise those stories help shape our identity, our sense of who we are as persons" (Jasinksi, 2001, p. 399). In reference to shaping the experience of time, "the meaning and significance of the past will be shaped by the narratives told about it" (Jasinski, 2001, p. 399) meaning, for example, that if a whitewashed version of Southern food predominates that ignores the contributions of black chefs and cooks, then that is the story we may come to believe. In terms of shaping political community and culture, narratives can tell the story of a community, what it is and what it is doing, "which is told, acted out, and received and accepted in a kind of self-reflective social narration" (Carr, 1986, pp. 149–50). This means, again, that if only nostalgic, mythic stories about the South are told, the community may remain resistant to change. Indeed, Jakes (2013) points out that constitutive narratives may exclude some from being part of a culture. For example, when Paula Deen tried to explain away racist behavior and comments she made to her employees, her narrative carried different constitutive force for different listeners, appealing to some and excluding others, performing a mixture of affirmation and subversion of particular Southern cultural norms (Jasinski, 2001). What some observers pointed out was that Deen built her culinary empire through historically African foods without paying homage to that history and the role that Africans, and later African Americans, played in creating a uniquely Southern cuisine. As culinary historian Twitty (2013) explains about this corrective reading of the Deen saga, "Don't forget that the Southern food you have been crowned the queen of was made into an art largely in the hands of enslaved cooks, some like the ones who prepared food on your ancestors' Georgia plantation" (para. 8). The Deen example helps show how narratives function rhetorically, working to "construct the social reality that constitutes the lived world of social actors" (Mumby, 1993a, p. 5); by extension, looking at the broader constitutive stories of Southern food allows scholars to see how people make sense of their lives, how they organize experiences and constitute their social world (Jasinski, 2001).

What is needed, and what we argue that food helps do, is to provide alternative stories that challenge a community's stock or received stories. As Lee Ann Bell (2010) argues, "stories have historically provided ways for people with few material resources to maintain their values and sense of community in the face of forces that would disparage and attempt to destroy them" (p. 16). In addition to sharing alternative stories, it is also important to examine underlying assumptions about standard narratives. Twitty's corrective reading of the Deen issue, for example, shows how stories propagate particular terms, values, understandings, and so on, that form a culture's language. In addition, reading food narratives showcases their other implications. That is, if we speak about food as a privileged resource that only wealthy Southerners can enjoy, it influences our behaviors and decisions. This might mean that we continue to eat at unhealthy chains rather than spend the same amount of money at a locally owned, culturally representative restaurant perceived to be "out of reach." If we don't hear the stories of Southern farmers more humanely raising beef and pork and learn that we can become part of this community through buying part of that animal with other families, the large-scale industrial farms of the South remain unchallenged.

Ultimately, what is important about studying Southern food narratives for their constitutive force is that they exist in many forms (independent discursive acts, embedded anecdotes, and the like), and regardless of the form in which they appear, they can be evaluated by asking who it is the story wants the audience to become. Narratives are where the public vocabularies develop that inform our lives (Dubriwny, 2005). As such, we are not merely applying constitutive theory to a new arena, which is exciting in and of itself, but we are going beyond application to viewing food itself as an ideologically, rhetorically powerful narrative. Scholarship in rhetorical studies has tended to focus on traditional texts, such as speeches, and is accused of "textocentrism" (Jakes, 2013, p. 319). Southern food narratives give us the opportunity to evaluate the rhetorical force of a variety of discursive and nondiscursive forms. If previous constitutive scholarship has explored how texts constitute identities and create and recreate culture, it is important to move beyond those written boundaries to explore these abilities in food, which, in the South, "isn't just the things we eat. Our food is experiences, history, heritage. It's as personal as the sound of our mothers' voices and as sweet as the smell of breakfast on a cold morning" (Purvis, 2009, p. 28).

One way to extend scholarly study of texts is by exploring how food narratives work through/with food memories. The memory of food can be a significant part of the overall experience, making the meaning of the food more explicit. Of course, what we eat is also a part of our daily activity. Aside from special occasions, the preparation of food also becomes a part of the experience. Family recipes and preparation tips can be a part of a person's memory, for example. As Cohen Ferris (2009) writes, "Food provides some of the strongest imagery in our personal and collective memory banks" (p. 14). How we remember our past has an effect on the way that we imagine ourselves and our society. As Phillips (2004) writes, "societies are both constituted by their memories and, in their daily interactions, rituals, and exchanges, constitute those memories" (p. 2). This is especially true with the memories that are created surrounding food experiences. Recreating a dish—from a family recipe or a collection of recipes representing a particular past—is recreating a memory.

Further, with the material nature of the food, the creator is also reading a visual message. As Barbie Zelizer (2004) argues, "Images are one such vehicle, the various forms—portraits, pictures, photographs, films—which constitute a cogent means of tackling the past and making it work for the present. But how we remember through images remains powerfully different from how we might remember the same events were images not involved" (p. 158). We argue that the material aspect of food can function in the same way that photographs act in stimulating and recreating memories. Zelizer (2004) writes that "images help us remember the past by freezing its representation at a powerful moment already known to us," (p. 158) and nothing acts as a snapshot as well as a food from the past.

Memory is thus a large part of the strength of food stories. As Jon Hotlzman (2006) explains, "What makes food such a powerful and diffuse locus of memory? The most compelling answer . . . is that the sensuality of eating transmits powerful mnemonic cues, principally through smells and tastes" (p. 373). The senses reinforce the experience, making the memory stronger, more powerful. Of course, not all Southern foods were a part of our own past experiences. Holtzman (2006) observes how ethnic grocery stores tap into a broader cultural experience and provide an imagined past for individuals. The emergence of the Southern food movement is a strong case study to see this in action. By crafting and buying Southern food, you are invited to participate in the shared experience of its past. Whether you are truly "of the South" or not, it is possible for food experiences to shape how you see yourself and others. Those experiences can, thus, develop strong memories related to identities, and the stories related to them—the narratives surrounding foodways—help shape who we are and how we see ourselves. Enacting memories of what we eat allows us to perform our identities and is played out in the narratives surrounding food. The next section will look more specifically at how the senses become a vital part of the food story.

Sensory Experiences as Rhetorically Constitutive

On a sunny day in June, we walked across the street from our hotel in Charleston, South Carolina, and into one chef's personal memory of the South. Sean Brock, executive chef of Husk Restaurant, has made national headlines for his commitment to preserving and honoring Southern ingredients in his establishment; as he puts it, "if it doesn't come from the South, it's not coming through the front door" (2014, para. 3). What is striking about Husk is its straightforward presentation of Brock's South that engages each of the senses. We didn't see faux *Gone with the Wind* décor, hear over-the-top Southern drawls, or taste plates piled with forgettable versions of stereotypical traditional Southern dishes like biscuits or fried chicken (although they are available at tourist traps close by); instead, we were amazed by how much every sensual element in the restaurant evoked Brock's particular vision of his upbringing. Brock's food looks back to explore the "realities" of Southern foods, not to "rediscover Southern cooking" (p. 4). The effect is striking. For example, we tasted a simple salad of heirloom tomatoes, dressed with olive oil and a touch of vinegar and sprinkled with bourbon-infused salt. Brock's version of a typical Southern dish took something familiar to a new level. This isn't "new South" dining where chefs take familiar Southern ingredients and use them in new or non-Southern dishes. Instead, Husk strives to take a memory a diner might possess about Southern food and/or the South in general and seemingly polish it or appreciate it in a new way. Diners hear country music in the background, but it is carefully curated, with the icons of the genre featured (Cash, Nelson, Strait). You might have heard the hype about Brock's insistence on using local ingredients, and then you see the supplier board when you walk in, listing each Southern purveyor's item's provenance, and you see the delivery cart in the back lot weighed down with local tomatoes. You smell wood smoke from the open kitchen. Even the restaurant's exterior is subtly evocative. We sat on the second-story porch staring at its ceiling (painted the traditional "haint blue" to keep the spirits away) and smelled the flowers of a giant magnolia tree and star jasmine growing down below. Husk's understated presentation of the "reality" of the South became more apparent as a horse-drawn carriage tour came by, its driver loudly laying claim to the building's "historic" and "traditional" virtues. Especially interesting in a city such as Charleston, what Husk does so well is that it doesn't paint a picture of the South in broad strokes, nostalgizing things that have become stereotypical of the region. Instead, it draws on all the senses to personalize and specify what makes the South distinctive according to one chef's vision, managing to cultivate personal memories of "your" South. We sat and talked about our memories of growing up in different regions of the South, what we ate, and why. We felt that Brock would say that he accomplished what he set out to do in hearing our conversation and watching us enjoy traditional Southern ingredients in presentations that highlighted their intrinsic value.

What makes this restaurant experience unique is the combination of all of the sensory elements. In addition to tapping into the memories and narratives surrounding the South, the food experience also "spoke" to us through sight, sound, smell, touch, and taste. The ability to explore the ways in which material practices/elements of culture carry rhetorical force, that is to read all of the rhetorical texts that were present in this experience, has thus far been limited in constitutive rhetorical theory. There is a need to broaden our understanding of constitutive rhetoric because sensory experiences help make up identity. Although previous constitutive rhetoric work has explored how narratives are the vehicles that make up audiences, we argue that narrative should be construed more broadly to encapsulate the variety of rhetorical experiences (Charland, 1987; Zagacki, 2007). Indeed, rhetorical critics have traditionally struggled with nondiscursive texts, despite Enck-Wanzer's (2006) call to incorporate more layers of understanding into our practice. While it is apparent with many texts that there is more to the story than mere words or visuals, it is often difficult to account for those aspects. Gunn (2010) has encouraged the field to explore voice; Goodale (2010) too argues we need to pay more attention to the aural along with the visual; and recently, Jakes (2013) considers the constitutive interplay between sound, embodied performance, and discursive speech acts in French protest songs. Thus, like these scholars, in making a theoretical argument for the constitutive nature of food, we argue for the need to account for multiple layers of meaning.

Food may appear to be too mundane a subject to be considered constitutive, but as Dickinson (2002) argues,

> The decisions we make, the actions we take, the conversations we have on this most mundane level are the warp and woof of who we are. Our identities cannot be said to exist outside of these little actions, these minute-by-minute performances. Rhetorical analysis of the everyday, then, seems to be a crucial activity for those of us determined to understand the material ways rhetoric constrains and enables our subjectivities. (p. 5)

If we are to account for the myriad rhetorical messages that we send and receive each day, food and foodways should certainly be part of that story. Eating, after all, is a daily ritual. And, although not all meals are symbolically significant, the day-to-day choices about the food we consume can become an important part of our identities. Moreover, food choices on special occasions (holidays, family gatherings, ceremonies, etc.) can be highly symbolic. Thus, attention to food as a rhetorical text brings a needed conversation to our discipline.

More importantly, the rhetoric of food—that is, consuming rhetoric—has the ability to create a strong reaction within the individual. As Ott and Keeling (2011) write, "[R]hetoric itself (not merely what it does) has concrete, observable, physical facets. Rhetoric directly engages our senses; we can see (images), hear (speech and music), and touch (memorials and museums) it. And when the way rhetoric *looks* or *sounds* or *feels* to one person is similar to the way it *looks* or *sounds* or *feels* to others, it creates substantiality" (p. 378). Adding the senses of smell and taste to the concept of memory through narrative means that the feeling of consubstantiality is even stronger. Consuming food—through all the senses—creates a strong shared experience that has the potential to help shape the identity of the individual. What follows is a brief account of the different aspects of food and the ways that food is rhetorical. We then theorize how identifying with these rhetorical experiences carries the potential to shape discursive practices. We use a sampling of our fieldwork experiences as well as the SFA's oral histories to provide examples of the constitutive nature of food.

Sound

As you step into Domilise's Po-Boys in New Orleans, you know you are in for a true Southern food experience. The po-boy might not immediately come to mind as a Southern food, but it originated in New Orleans, born out of necessity as an "on the go" meal for strikers, and has become symbolic of that region (Morago, 2012). Domilise's is one of New Orleans's oldest sandwich shops, serving the uptown neighborhood for more than seventy-five years (Massa, 2013). On a busy day, the sound of the restaurant will hit you before you ever enter the building. Sandwich seekers often queue around the ramshackle, one-room building, waiting in line to place their order with the staff standing behind the grill. The sound experience continues as you finally make your way through the door and into the small dining area. As you place your order, you not only look at the food being prepared, but you hear the chopping of the sandwich fixings, the sizzle of the frying oysters and shrimp, and the calling of customer names as the sandwiches are passed over the counter on their white paper plates. The sound of the preparation of the food itself becomes a part of the experience, but the conversations happening at the tables and the bar and even around the grill as orders are being made are highlighted. Domilise's, not unlike many neighborhood restaurants, is a meeting place for old friends and family. The chatter at and between tables is constant and gives the restaurant a vibrant feeling. The fact that the majority of the customers are clearly from the area also sends the message that this is a recognized and respected spot for sampling New Orleans cuisine. Beyond the experience of the newcomer, though, the conversations seem to be a part of the entire experience. Longtime customers are treated as family, and likewise, customers ask about staff members. In fact, our last visit to Domilise's occurred not long after the passing of "Miss Dot" Domilise, the matriarch of the Domilise family and maker of po-boys for seventy years. As we sat at the bar enjoying our lunch, concerned customers slowly came by to talk to the longtime bartender, to express their condolences, and to find out about the future of the neighborhood landmark. For repeat customers, this is more than a mundane environment; rather, this is a place to enjoy food that is made by loving hands.

Sound, although the least vivid of the senses related to food, is the first facet of food rhetoric. As with the Domilise's example, it is the sound as you enter the door that begins the food experience. Goodale (2010), arguing for including sound in rhetorical analysis, writes that it "adds another dimension to the study of rhetoric, complementing recent advances in visual rhetoric and the critical analysis of words that is at the heart of the discipline" (p. 167). Sound can simply serve to signal particular acts, as in the sizzle of a slice of bacon as it hits the skillet; it may even create a particular community environment, as in the ringing of the dinner bell; or it may provide a comforting environment "that surround[s] and protect[s] individuals against penetration from outside and the destruction of the self, thus helping to construct and preserve identity" (Goodale, 2010, p. 165). This last statement—that sound can help construct and preserve identity—is the most compelling argument when considering food rhetoric. That is not to say that every food-related sound serves this function, but even the least powerful of the senses (as it relates to food) can be a powerful component of the message.

There are many sounds that might be a part of our reaction to food. For example, the preparation of the food (the gathering and chopping), the cooking of the food (the sizzling and bubbling), the sounds of biting into the food (crunch, squish), and the reaction to the food (yum, ooh, ahh) are all sounds that become a part of the experience and memory. Perhaps more importantly, the conversations surrounding a meal or the memories of consistent conversations surrounding the preparation of a meal might also influence the overall experience. As with the Domilise's example, the sounds that surround ordering, preparing, and consumption are an important part of the food experience. Those conversations not only shape our experience, but also may have an influence on how we view ourselves. For example, the conversations at Domilise's confirmed the fact that many of their customers come there not only for the sandwiches, but also to be recognized as caring neighbors and community members. The use of sound in the Domilise's experience indicates that what we hear as we cook and eat is an important part of the message. The sounds of the preparation of the food act as the conversation opener, while the conversations surrounding the food provide context for the food conversation. Just as apparent, however, is the smell that accompanies the meal.

Smell

On a trip to Memphis, Tennessee, Ashli stepped off the plane and onto the jetway. Immediately, a very strong barbecue smell was pervasive throughout the concourse. The actual food court selling barbecue (an outpost of the well-known Interstate Barbecue) was located at the very end of the concourse, but passengers could smell it all the way down at the other end. Several passengers from the flight stopped once reaching the tiny counter to indulge. Perhaps they were visiting, sampling a taste of one of the cuisines associated with the city, or maybe they wanted a taste of home once returned. Memphis certainly wasn't alone in proffering the strong smell of barbecue to airline passengers. Passing through the Charlotte and Birmingham airports, there was the same whiff of barbecue from food court restaurants. In the way that the smell of other cuisines is associated with a particular region—the hot dog cart in Chicago, tomato sauce in Boston's North End, or Chinese food in San Francisco's Chinatown—the smell of barbecue helps define the South. The scent acts as a rhetorical marker, sending a signal that one has arrived in the region.

It is clear that smell adds yet another layer of meaning to experiencing food. As the smell of the cooking food or the food being delivered to the table dissipates into the air, all of those individuals in the surrounding area receive the message of the arrival of the food. Dickinson (2002) posits that the overall experience in a Starbucks coffee shop, for example, is created by the scent of the freshly roasted and ground coffee beans. The smell, he argues, becomes part of the message that Starbucks is brewing a natural product. That is, because the smell of the roasting and brewing coffee bean smells natural, the consumer is likely to accept the overall message that coffee—and the company that makes millions of dollars off of it—is natural. "In drinking the coffee," Dickinson says, "we hope to materially consume the naturalness that we have already consumed through sound, smell, and sight" (p. 16). Although touch, sight, and taste may be avoided or ignored, it is difficult to miss the smell of food. Thus, this sense allows for more far-reaching possibilities with its rhetoric.

Smell is also evocative of Southern identity in subtle but powerful ways. Of course, writers have long recalled the smells associated with the South, whether it is the smell of particular flowers, like magnolia blossoms or gardenia; the rich, fecund smell of agricultural fields; or perhaps less pleasant, the smell of paper mills or oil refineries along the coasts. It is possible to demarcate the region via the sense of smell and also to see how smell influences identity. For example, the South is known as a barbecue region, as evidenced by the scenario that opened this section of the chapter, with much written about its various styles, recipes, and restaurants. Barbecue is so associated with the South that parts of the region seem to permanently smell of woodsmoke and pork smoldering on the coals. But how is smell constitutive, beyond just helping to denote one part of the country from another? Marketers, of course, now rely on scent to draw in shoppers, working to cultivate a positive association or bring back a memory (Vlahos, 2007). Even realtors working to sell a home will bake chocolate chip cookies to help prospective buyers associate warm feelings or memories with a listing. Smell is considered to be one of our most powerful senses, capable of bringing back some of our earliest memories. Without it, eating loses pleasure, and foods become indistinguishable. Part of the reason that smell is an important component of the experience is because of the physical reaction that it can cause. Eckstein and Conley (2012) explain the process: "At the most abstract level, affect materializes consciously when the body 'bumps' up against an event or happening, like an aroma or a taste. When such an event occurs it forces the incorporeal parts of the body, namely consciousness, to become aware of the materiality of the body. It literally jolts the body into different positions and states of readiness" (p. 177). Thus, scent can awaken our understanding of our surroundings, causing us to read the situation in a different way or to have a more acute awareness of our surroundings. Smell is integral to the experience and, in turn, our memory of the experience. Our sense of smell, then, and the memories associated with these smells, begins to craft who we are. We associate particular smells with our existence.

In the SFA documentary *Saving Seeds*, for example, Kentucky heirloom tomato and seed farmer Bill Best introduces the viewers to the idea of an "authentic" tomato smell. Praising the "true" tomato, he denounces the tomatoes of the "mega markets." Describing a time when his wife "just had to have a tomato" and resorted to the market variety, Best explains the differences between the two: "We discovered that we couldn't eat it. It smelled like a locker room. So, I said, we'll feed some to our chickens so it won't be a complete waste. They turned up their noses at it. They refused to eat it. And I put one of my tomatoes in with our chickens and they will fight one another to get to it." Smell is a large part of the overall food experience, conveying information about the food and becoming a part of the overall reaction to the food. Tomatoes, a staple of many Southern summer diets, should have a particular smell in order to be authentic. And the documentary, in highlighting this description, implies that a good Southerner should be able to tell the difference between a "mega store" tomato and an authentic tomato. The idea of authenticity (an idea that will more fully developed in chapter five), although relevant to all of the senses, is particularly apparent with this example. Authenticity is judged, in this case, based on the senses—sight, smell, touch, and taste, especially. That is, the degree to which this food truly represents this region is judged by the senses, and not by any discourse surrounding the food.

Beyond the food's authenticity, though, the scent also adds to our understanding of the situation. The smells of tomatoes and barbecue in the earlier examples serve as symbols of the region. Smell, then, needs to be accounted for when "reading" the rhetorical nature of the substance. It becomes a part of the message that is created through the food, adding another layer of experience and meaning.

Touch

Walking into Gus's World Famous Fried Chicken in Memphis, Tennessee, diners are first struck by the restaurant's casualness. Located outside the tourist zone, diners enter a concrete/cinderblock structure containing pressed-tin ceilings, tables covered in red-and-white-checkered oilcloth, and an open, steamy kitchen, men working furiously at a deep fryer. This minimalist ambiance is of no concern to the diners. Families, businesspeople, hipsters, and groups of friends are too busy tearing into their chicken. Gus's chicken has the deep golden, slightly shimmery exterior, crust flecked with pepper look that fried chicken should have. It, like other fine examples of the genre, shatters upon a diner's touch. Bits of delicious crust (the whole reason some people even bother eating fried chicken) rain down when you take a bite or pick it up from the paper plate. When experiencing something like fried chicken, there is no space for formal social code. It's hard to be formal when pulling meat from bones, wiping greasy fingers onto paper napkins, or picking at what remains to get the last bite of crust (see figure 1.2). Other fried chicken shacks in the South don't even bother with tables. At Price's Chicken in Charlotte, North Carolina, diners place their orders (and God forbid they are on their cell phone when it is their turn), pay with cash, and cash only, and then take their chicken boxes to the street, where they dig in beside their cars or in the grass by the light rail tracks. All over the South, you still find places like these: informal, ramshackle gas stations, tiny storefronts, and regional chains that try to participate in the hands-on experience that is fried chicken.

Touch is clearly important in experiencing food. Whether it is someone selecting the freshest fruit by giving it a squeeze, enjoying the tactile nature of mixing together a type of dough, or even experiencing the sensation of warmth from holding a cup of coffee, touch cannot be removed from the sensory experience of food. There seem to be particular tactile experiences that are associated with Southern food culture, however, that help constitute an understanding of the region's people. We suggest that understanding these food encounters provides insight into some Southerners' informal, sociable nature.

In terms of a rhetorical component, touch has received more attention in recent years. Although rhetoric can appear to be merely symbolic, to add a physical experience is to emphasize its connection to reality. Carole Blair (1999) emphasizes two material aspects of rhetoric that help explain the role of food in creating meaning: touch and community. As Blair (1999) writes, "touch sometimes yields profound responses" (p. 46), as in tracing your

Figure 1.2 Gus's World Famous Fried Chicken in Nashville, Tennessee

fingers along the thousands of names on the Vietnam memorial, and part of the viewer's reaction might be to the physical exchange with the rhetoric. The symbolic nature of rhetoric emphasizes the appeal to the mind of the listener; however the material characteristic of rhetoric makes an appeal to both the mind and the body. Thus, touch becomes an important part of—an extension of—understanding rhetoric. By touching the food—gathering the ingredients, preparing it, and/or bringing it to our mouths—the feel of the food acts as a material facet of the experience and a physical reminder of the preparation. In many ways, preparation serves as a ritual, where cooks reenact important cultural, sometimes family, food practices.

Blair (1999) also raises the point of rhetorical places—and memorials in particular—acting as a gathering point for individuals. Memorials draw individuals in and attempt to shape their experiences. More importantly for this project, Blair writes that the experience can be "created in part by the presence of so many other people" (p. 48). Likewise, food events pull people together and craft an experience. This occurrence happens as families gather for daily dinners, as larger groups gather for celebrations, or as diners gather at a restaurant, as in the example of Gus's World Famous Fried Chicken. The table becomes a "communal space" (in Blair's words) and "that experience of the group's presence is significant, even if not wholly conscious" (p. 48). Thus, the physical nature of the rhetoric creates an audience for a common experience, and that group encounter is different than it might be if experienced individually.

The SFA film *Bowens Island* showcases the commonality that can be generated through a form of communal touch. Bowens Island is located eight miles from downtown Charleston, South Carolina, and has served as the site for oyster roasts since the 1940s, when the father of proprietor Robert Barber (the speaker in the documentary) bought the small, fourteen-acre island. Bowens Island serves as a communal gathering point, with families, friends, and strangers coming together to pry open bushels of steamed oysters, huddling over raw pinewood planks, often in the colder, rainy weather of oyster season. Viewers of the film see the patrons slice their oyster knives into the shells, the scrape of their blades slicing the oyster free, making quick dispatch of mounds of oysters as they stand together over the tables. The camera lingers on scenes of individuals interacting with the oysters, emphasizing the importance of feeling the food before consuming it. The tactile experience is, in many ways, as important as the taste of the oysters. Barber notes that this common experience—of standing together, working to open the oysters with one hand, a rag in the other, a cold beer by their sides—serves as a type of "fellowship." Prying open the oyster shells together is an important material part of the roast experience, as Barber explains: "We give you a knife, a rag, some cocktail sauce in a cup, and let you go at it." The hands-on experience is unique, he argues, because of its tactile properties: "when you're eating oysters, you don't just eat for five minutes and jump up and leave like fast food. You're going to be there a while and it's a great opportunity to converse and have fellowship." This type of tactile, material interaction is important in experiencing food. Indeed, months after viewing the SFA's film about Bowens Island, we experienced the communal power of touch for ourselves. It had been pouring rain on the way out to Bowens, and we were glad of the shelter of the damp cinderblock building. The servers dumped a huge pile of oysters onto the table in front of us, and at first, we just stood there eyeing it, nervously sipping our Solo-cup beers. We were a bit out of practice, so we asked the regulars how to proceed with prying open the oyster shells. The experienced shuckers came to our aid, showing us not only how to do it, but how to do it well, locating for us the best place on the oyster to slide in the knife. Soon, together with our instructors, we made quick work of our meal, feeling satisfaction in our newfound abilities. We continued to talk with our teachers, hearing about the best months to order oysters in the Lowcountry and quickly appreciating why people continue to come back to Bowens. Becoming one of many crowded around a table, knives working efficiently, meant that communal touch became a way to gain admittance to a culture.

Although it may be different depending on the type of food experience, touch is the stage of the experience where the food becomes more of a reality. Whether it is the physical manifestation of Southern characteristics (using informal, social settings with appropriately relaxed eating standards) or the physical coming together that Southern food inspires, this type of experience serves a rhetorical function by materially reinforcing the idea that food can bring people closer together.

Sight

The sight of the famed Doe's Eat Place restaurant in Greenville, Mississippi, would be shocking to someone unfamiliar with the history of the eatery. Dubbed one of "America's finest steakhouses" by The Food Network, Doe's displays a modest (to say the least) exterior (see figure 1.3). Walking through the restaurant's front door for the first time, we were shocked to discover that we were walking into the heart of the restaurant—the kitchen. To our left was the restaurant's impressive oven, displaying a row of thick, sizzling steaks. Standing beside the oven was one of the owners and the steak master, "Little Doe." That the food is so visible as you enter the restaurant is part of the experience. Wandering past the grills and ovens, customers grab a cold bottle of beer or some wine glasses to bring to their tables, clinking the glasses as they go. We then entered the prep kitchen. Here, Aunt Flo tosses the salads as they are ordered. Tables that are situated in this room have a view of the fresh cut fries sizzling in the iron skillet on the stove and the bread being sliced and buttered. This is a public restaurant, but it looks and feels like a home dining experience. The owners have intentionally left the building "design" as is so that customers are part of the food preparation experience. The sight of the food preparation and the food itself emphasizes its freshness and authenticity, demonstrating the importance of this component of the experience.

The visual component of food, thus, adds yet another layer to the message. Rhetorical critics have begun to account more thoroughly for the importance of visual rhetoric; whether the visual comes in the form of political cartoons (Edwards & Winkler, 1997), image events (DeLuca, 1999), government-sponsored photography projects (Finnegan, 2003), or iconographs (Hariman & Lucaites, 2007), images can have a significant impact on the viewer. As Olson, Finnegan, and Hope (2008) argue, "If we wish fully to understand the role of rhetorical communication in the United States, we should open ourselves up

Figure 1.3 Doe's Eat Place in Greenville, Mississippi

to the multiple and marvelous ways that rhetoric can be visual" (p. 1). This increased attention to the visual element of rhetoric is also apparent when talking about food. In the case of food, however, the reaction to the visual is more about the immediate image—the object as we actually see it—than a photograph. With food, we react to the visual cues that it sends. The food may look appealing or may be disappointing and off-putting. It might create a space for a visual memory associated with it. More than mere supplement to the message, visuals communicate meaning.

The experience at Doe's Eat Place provides a clear example of the visual component of the message adding to the food message. In this case, the sight of the food being prepared—both the food itself and the people creating it—adds to an understanding of the authenticity (in some cases) and the freshness of the food. That is, as many visual critics point out, the visual element can be a particularly powerful component of a message. Visuals can affect the way that we imagine ourselves (Atkins-Sayre, 2010) and others (Johnson, 2007). They can shape the way we remember (Zelizer, 2004) and the way we interpret experiences (Stormer, 1997). They can even encourage policy change, as the Slow Food movement did with its decision to plant an organic, sustainable victory garden in front of the San Francisco City Hall during its Slow Food Nation event (Stokes, 2013). Consequently, it is important that we would read visual elements and incorporate them into our understanding of a situation. In this case, the visual element of food adds to our understanding of how it communicates its authenticity and appealing qualities.

Taste

As we planned our summer travels across the South and dreamed of the wonderful meals that we would consume, several Southern staples came to mind. We looked forward to comparing barbecue across the regions; sampling tasty classic side dishes such as greens, squash casserole, and macaroni and cheese; and finding the best fried peach pie. We assumed we would stumble across an impressive array of road foods—fried chicken in Memphis and tamales in the Delta. What we weren't expecting, though, was one of the stars of the Southern food trip—salads. As we dined at many of the new Southern food restaurants, salads composed of ingredients that were fresh, local, seasonal, and basic were featured. Charleston's Macintosh offered up a watermelon panzanella salad with Geechie Boy's heirloom tomatoes, red onion, cucumbers, holy basil, and a raspberry vinaigrette. Atlanta's Miller Union served a field pea and peanut salad that was phenomenal, and Atlanta's JCT roasted beet salad included farm egg, fennel, fromage blanc, crispy sunchokes, chile oil, and a parsley vinaigrette. These were not your typical Southern salads, but they heavily featured Southern ingredients—field peas, peanuts, watermelon, and tomatoes. What was most striking about these salads was the explosion of flavors; the mixture of fresh, local ingredients emphasized the connection to the region. The flavors of the dishes spoke of the region, indicating the season, the quality of the land, and an understanding of how to best bring the ingredients together.

Taste is one of the most important sensory elements in food. Once the food reaches our tongues—after experiencing the sounds surrounding the food, the touch, smell, and sight—the consumption becomes a consummation of sorts. That is, it is a completion of the act of experiencing the food. More significantly, the consumption means that the food has now become part of our existence. Religious symbolism influences an understanding of this act, with, for example, the consumption of a symbol of Christ's body as a means to become one with the spirit in Christian communion or the Jewish ritual of Shabbat and consuming challah as symbolic of historical manna. Families and friends break bread together, sharing substance in order to symbolically strengthen relationships.

Writing, again, about the coffee experience, Dickinson (2002) notes that while the sound of the grinding beans and the smell of the roasting and brewing coffee is read as part of the message, it is the consumption "in literal, material and bodily ways—incorporating the coffee itself, an incorporation already made possible through the materiality of sight, sound and smell. Here, however, taste takes over, as do the sensations of viscosity, warmth, and the eventual bodily stimulation caused by caffeine" (p. 12). Thus, taking the food (or in this case, drink) into our bodies makes the message material. We go beyond merely symbolic. The taste of the fresh salad ingredients, for example, became a material representation of the idea that Southern food is tied to the land and driven by seasons. The fact that the South remains an agrarian-driven region is embodied in the dishes served in Southern restaurants and homes. In a brief oral history clip on "The Spoken Dish" web site (organized by the SFA), one person perhaps best describes the way that taste can create a strong experience:

> The lady actually took a bite of sweet potato pie, walked outside, sat on the swing. She didn't move for over an hour. She was like, "I have never in my life had something that brought me home." She had never eaten sweet potato pie before, but she said for one brief moment in her life, she felt the euphoria of what it would be like to actually have someone say "Come into my home. I want you to enjoy something."

The taste of the food, in this case, speaks to the person. There is an entire message—a feeling—relayed through the Southern dish. Consumption, then, brings together the other sensory elements—sound, smell, touch, and sight—and completes the experience, adding another level of meaning. Not only is the food then incorporated into the body, but tasting melds all of the sensory components of the (food) message into one complete experience. Although each of the senses was discussed here, it is really the combination of the senses that builds the argument for the rhetorical power of food. As Eckstein and Conley (2012) argue, all of these sensory elements can create "an acutely resonant, physically immersive experience" (p. 175). That experience can be moving in the way that a powerful speech can be. What we wish to explore more fully is *how* food speaks to us.

Sensory Experiences as Constitutive of Discursive Practice

Tying all of these concepts together, it is possible to see how food can act constitutively. Although many of the previous examples of constitutive rhetoric examine how discourse influences how we see ourselves and others, this project uses food experience as an example. Each of the sensory elements discussed in the previous section makes it clear how food can speak. That is, sound, smell, touch, sight, and taste all work to create messages about the food itself and also the people serving and eating it. It is the unique combination of all of these experiences, however, that gives food such a powerful rhetorical effect. If a food is symbolic of a region—and Southern food definitely falls into this category—then its symbolic message is expressed in all of these different ways. More importantly, if food is symbolic of a people or a region, then consumption of that symbol has even more meaning. The consumer is not only potentially symbolically touched by the meaning, but is also physically connected to the symbol. Eating becomes a type of ritual, a physical coming together of symbol and individual. Thus, "consuming identity" is possible through the experience of eating a food that is meaningfully tied to a region.

In this chapter, we have primarily focused on showing the rhetorical nature of food more broadly, although we have used Southern examples to bring this point to life. The rest of the book will focus specifically on what makes Southern food distinctive in its connection to Southern identity. The remainder of this chapter, then, will more explicitly discuss how food acts constitutively.

With the assumption that food is rhetorical, it is possible to conclude that sensory experiences and narratives help form a collective subject position seeking to animate specific desires and objectives (Charland, 1987; Cooren, 2012). In addition to studying the actual food and foodways as rhetorical texts, studying the rhetoric *about* Southern food provides scholars with another way to examine how identifying with a particular collective identity positions people "towards political, social, and economic action in the world" (Charland, 1987, p. 141). This positioning for action is an important tenet of constitutive rhetorical theory because if constitutive processes facilitate the "performance of identities, not just their adoption" (Cordova, 2004, p. 215), discourse warrants social action. Cordova (2004), for example, examines how rhetoric creates political identification *and* cultural changes, whereby identification with a document shaped a constituency whose performative demand was to vote for a particular political party. Like Jasinski (1998), he

agrees that constitutive rhetoric offers a range of possibilities that encom-
passes more than the formation of identity, such that our rhetorical choices
play a culture- and community-shaping, political norm-influencing, and
linguistic-crafting role.

Constitutive rhetoric is thus productive and generative (Giddens, 1984;
Jasinski, 1998; Stein, 2002), whereby what we call policies, laws, traditions,
and so on, are made possible through the indirect effects of "representation, incarnation, materialization" (Cooren, 2012, p. 6). Although discursive
practice cannot completely determine the realms of the social, political, or
economic, communication is not just a vehicle for ideas in a culture but
rather constitutes that culture's meaning (Mumby, 1989). We may communicate instrumentally to win resources and achieve goals, but in the process
we create cultural shifts and changes. The Slow Food movement, for example,
may have the instrumental goal of getting people to shop at farmers' markets, for example, but in communicating this goal, it may, along with other
movements and corporations, begin to influence broader communication
patterns and create audience expectations that they have farmers' markets *to*
frequent (Stokes, 2013). Carlo Petrini, founder of the Slow Food movement,
understood this power. By talking about consumers as "co-producers" in his
attempts to shift food discourse, he understood that audiences must first see
themselves in this role in order to create change by working together (Petrini,
2007).

Southern food rhetoric has an analogous possibility of creating or altering
discursive norms that exist in food culture; specifically, performing the collective identity encouraged through the food, rhetorical representations of
Southern food, and discussions about Southern food challenges the practice
of eating in two ways. First, rhetoric about food potentially alters the way we
talk about and experience the idea of what it means to eat. Similar to the use
of metaphor, constitutive rhetoric as expressed in the food rhetoric allows for
new conceptualizations, the ability to create connections between events and
people, and provides for narrative closure once identified (Jasinski, 2001).
In his discussion of the problems with "locker room" tomatoes in an SFA
oral history, for example, Best highlights the deficiencies of the modern industrial agricultural system in favor of one that creates real, satisfying food.
When Best notes that with "mega store tomatoes" "a lot of people just put
them on salads for some color and don't really expect them to be eaten," he
highlights all that has gone wrong in a system that ships green tomatoes
and then gasses them to change their color. Robert Barber indirectly does
the same in the SFA film with respect to oysters, pointing out the value of

Bowens Island's cluster oysters, discussing their unique "salinity, sweetness, and chew" compared to other kinds. Southern food rhetoric, as expressed in the SFA films and on Southern restaurant menus and web sites, may focus more on tasting traditional Southern foods, but in trying to get people to do so, it indirectly supports other food movements seeking to make changes to the dominant industrial agriculture system. Although it is possible to experience these foods in traditional supermarkets, there is an emphasis on going to the source of "authentic" produce—farmers' markets, small restaurants, farm stands, or even your own garden—in order to have the "full experience." Thus, engaging with Southern food rhetoric (such as the SFA messages) *and* eating Southern food encourages particular types of action.

Likewise, eating the foods celebrated by the Southern food movement not only encourages changes in *what* people eat, but in *how* they consume it. The Slow Food movement's idea that people gain more than nutritional benefits by slowing down and experiencing meals communally is also expressed in Southern food rhetoric. All of the films and experiences discussed in this chapter show the benefit of eating as a communal experience. Contrasted against an "eat and run," eat alone, and instant gratification American food culture, these films and experiences celebrate the benefits of creating community through what we eat. This reflects Blair's (1999) idea of the communal space creating a message. Robert Barber talks about the "fellowship" an oyster roast encourages. In doing so, his voice supports practices different than those encouraged by the modern food system. The films and experiences encourage eating seasonally, eating with strangers, and lingering for conversation. It is the rhetoric of the Southern food movement that reflects this message, but it is also the practices of Southern foodways that show a variance in the way that Southern food encourages individuals to experience food differently.

In this way, Southern food rhetoric may influence discursive practice in a third manner: influencing people's relationships with the South and with each other through food culture. Mumby (1989) points out that the constitutive process can produce and reproduce relationships of domination and power, but Cooren (2012) contends that we are not held hostage by the other voices/cultures/traditions we animate. These can be powerful, authoritative, or influential. Helpfully, Cooren (2012) theorizes the possibility of constitutive rhetoric through the metaphor of ventriloquism, whereby "people in interaction manage to act and speak for or in the name of specific beings to which they feel consciously or unconsciously attached, whether these beings be principles, values, beliefs, attitudes, ideas, ideologies, interests, organizations, etc." (p. 5). That is, if we are speaking in the name of the food-ways that the Southern food movement endorses, we are animated by it, led to do or say something (Cooren, 2012). In terms of enacting a collective Southern food identity, then, we can "ventriloquize" policies, ideologies, rules, norms, values, accents, and so on; indeed, "for an accent to live and exist, we have to make it live and exist in our interactions and discourse" (Cooren, 2012, p. 6).

This notion is important in considering the constitutive implications of a collective identity created by Southern food/Southern food rhetoric. We are able to pick and choose among the traditions that positively remake the present rather than condemned to continue the South's fraught past. Although this selective remembering is potentially problematic because of the traditions that might be excluded, there are also times when a shared sense of past can create positive change. Indeed, several of the SFA films and examples from our field research speak to this possibility of coming together through food, repairing relationships by moving beyond stereotypes and cultural distancing/isolation. Southern restaurants such as Athens's Weaver D's, Memphis's Gus's World Famous Fried Chicken, and New Orleans's Domilise's all bring people of varied background, race, ethnicity, and class together to celebrate Southern culture through its food; even if they don't know initially that they are connected, they are.

Southern food experiences often encourage interaction. At times, the Southern food movement and worshippers at the altar of Southern cuisine may make strong claims about the power of the region's fare, but our research experiences also supported the rhetoric. We actually broke bread (ok, crackers) with strangers at Bowens Island. We had conversations about fruit cobbler with storied cooks of varying socioeconomic backgrounds at farm stands. We marveled at how the performance of pouring a drink loosened an entire roomful of hotel guests in New Orleans's famed Carousel Bar. We asked for pound cake recipes and not only received them but also their stories and sometimes even a cake itself. In the South, some churches, neighborhoods, and schools may still be divided by color and class, but learning that you have dishes in common with other customers at the peach stand or gathering at the same restaurant to experience outstanding Southern cooking may help reduce this cultural distance. As a result, if Southern food rhetoric and Southern foodways locate the positive in a cuisine created from poverty, once used to divide races, and still frequently lampooned or misunderstood, then performing the collective identity created by Southern food rhetoric potentially serves to open dialogue between once-divided groups.

There are clearly historical obstacles in the South, including vestiges of overtly racist policies and violence, that are insurmountable by such constitutive rhetorical moves, but the fact that foodways and rhetoric about Southern cuisine hold some constitutive power is noteworthy. Ultimately, constitutive rhetoric scholars emphasize that "every rhetorical act is part of an ongoing, never finished discussion—an attempt to answer an 'unfinished call'—regarding everything from individual and collective identity, to political policy, to social norms" (Sweet & McCue-Enser, 2010, p. 605). In its founding moment, then, Southern food rhetoric begins to answer the call to bring people together through food.

The explosion of interest in Southern fare has had a significant effect on the culinary world. More importantly, the message of the Southern food movement has some important implications for the region and for all of those individuals who are open to it. It certainly takes more than the taste of a boiled peanut, a Southern-grown tomato, or a Southern peach to make someone Southern, but the sights, smells, touches, sounds, tastes, and memories that accompany that food create a compelling message. Food tells a story—it speaks to us and shapes who we are in many ways. The next chapter will look more specifically at the types of people that Southern food constitutes.

CHAPTER TWO

A TROUBLED REGION AND ITS POSSIBLE CULINARY FIX

Traversing the highways of the Southern states—from Virginia to the Carolinas, Georgia to Mississippi, and on down into Louisiana—there is no doubt that food plays a large part in defining regional culture. The fading signs of the barbecue joints, the decrepit catfish restaurants surrounded by hundreds of cars on a Saturday night, and the roadside produce stands populated by locally grown items all speak volumes about the region. Family reunions, wedding receptions, church socials, and even football games are planned around and often defined by the spread of food that appears on the tables. And there are, no doubt, recipes being used that are intimately tied to families, ingredients that are bound to the region, or meaningful cultural practices represented through the dishes. In each of these settings, food speaks; as Visser (1986) observes, "food is never just something to eat" (p. 12). That is, it sends a rhetorical message about the event, the larger region in which the event is taking place, and the cook and the local community.

This fascinating regional cuisine and a larger growing interest in food have led to a more organized effort to study and promote Southern foodways. The increasing popularity of Southern food results in part from the efforts of a "thriving movement of idealistic Southern food producers" (Moskin, 2011, p. 1), referred to as the "Southern Revival" (Ulla, 2012) or the "Lardcore movement" (Ozersky, 2010). This movement celebrates the South through food, seeking to "reclaim the agrarian roots of Southern cooking, restore its lost traditions and dignity" (Moskin, 2011, p. 2), and "tell the story of the South through food and drink" (Edge, 2011b, p. 21). In doing so, groups such as the SFA and others provide a pathway into understanding how food can be considered a modern-day rhetorical expression of the South's complex racial, social, and cultural identity.

Given the importance of Southern food to the region's culture, we argue, as expressed in chapter one, that Southern food and Southern food movement rhetoric serve a constitutive, or identity-building, function by helping to craft a Southern identity based on diverse, humble, and hospitable roots. This identity offers a hopeful alternative to those identities based on race and class divisions and regional stereotypes. Moreover, this constitutive work has the potential to open up dialogues in the South and create communities by considering the diversity of experience through the celebration of the food. We begin the chapter by discussing the identity problems that the region faces before turning to a discussion about the Southern food movement and its rhetoric. This rhetoric, with a focus on people, past, and place, helps emphasize shared substance and provides Southerners with an opening for dialogue by emphasizing that commonality, albeit with limitations.

THE TROUBLE WITH SOUTHERN IDENTITY

The ability to form even a temporary connection through food is important because the South struggles with its identity, especially considering its divisive history. Although race relations in the South have improved immensely in the years since the civil rights movement, the region continues to be haunted both by stereotypical images and by ongoing socioeconomic disparities. Much of what happens in the South is still read through the lens of the past; as Griffin (2000) argues, "In the South, to be sure, the past is not past, but even in America, the past is not even past, if the topic is the South" (para. 2). This continued focus on the racist and divisive South creates a sense of "two-ness," as Tracy Thompson (2013a) argues. That is, Southerners struggle with "how to express [their] deep love and respect for the South without pandering, apologizing, subscribing to racist delusions, or drinking anybody's Kool-Aid. These are pitfalls that have always faced any person who identifies himself as a Southerner" (p. 231). Although Thompson speaks as a white Southerner, her experience could be shared by Southerners of all racial and socioeconomic backgrounds because the region has been (and many would argue still is) largely defined by inequality. Struggling with the past is healthy for the region; indeed, it is better to question the past than to ignore it. The South's record of slavery, violence, racism, and discrimination should always be remembered as a part of our defining history. Many of these problems are not just in our past, however.

In reality, the South, like the rest of the United States, continues to face many issues of racial strife, including battles over the Confederate flag, apologies over slavery, and contemporary trials involving civil rights–era murders (Cobb, 2011). Even more troubling, the region continues to be plagued by racial violence (Schmidt & Apuzzo, 2015), controversial police profiling and shootings of African American men (Apuzzo & Williams, 2015), segregated schools (Carr, 2012), lower high school graduation rates (2012), and poverty levels that overwhelmingly affect the African American population (Macartney, Bishaw, & Fontenot, 2013). Although it is tempting to celebrate the accomplishments of the region in moving forward and taking action to rectify the wrongs of the past, it is also important to be aware of the disparity that continues to haunt the region, despite the ongoing persistence of racism nationwide.

Add to this history the negative image of the South in popular culture. Television shows such as the Learning Channel's *Here Comes Honey Boo Boo* and Arts and Entertainment's *Duck Dynasty* highlight "backwards" Southerners, playing up the stereotypes of the region and attracting a huge audience (AP, 2013). Celebrity Southern chef Paula Deen's use of derogatory racial terms and embrace of plantation-style celebrations certainly feeds into the larger stereotypes of the typical Southerner. As *Time* magazine's James Poniewozik (2013) wrote of the Deen controversy, "in one swoop, fairly or not, she single-handedly affirmed people's worst suspicions of people who talk and eat like her" (para. 9). Deen, along with other media-featured Southerners, the history of the region, and the questionable stereotypes forwarded by many "large scale, corporate projections of Southern cliché," all work together to create an overwhelming obstacle to changing Southern image (Allen, 2011, para. 2).

Given the stereotypes of the region as well as its troubled history, it becomes difficult for Southerners of many different backgrounds to celebrate the past because glorifying some experiences may ignore painful racial experiences. Likewise, embracing a Southern identity is problematic for many people. Thompson (2013a) speaks of a kind of "historical amnesia" that Southerners suffer from—a "disconnect" between history and how they see the region operating (p. 236). That amnesia may be self-inflicted, however, given the pain that is associated with the historical and contemporary division that marks the region.

The region itself is complicated. Although scholars agree that it is difficult to define the South because there are many interpretations, it is possible to paint a broad picture of the culture. Scholars agree that "the South" exists, although it is not monolithic, and much of it may be located somewhere between legend and reality. Several scholars argue that a quest for order, which is frequently divisive, is one of the key hallmarks of Southern identity and marks the region's distinctiveness (Cash, 1941; Hall & Wood, 1995; Watts, 2008). They point to the pursuit of the savage ideal, or "dogged resistance to change and obsession with order," as an important way of categorizing the region (Hall & Wood, 1995, p. 14). The loss of the Civil War and failure to attain the savage ideal still influence the region's history, because Southerners are familiar with scarcity and want, have experienced failure and defeat, and possess a tortured conscience, guilt, and tragedy (Vann Woodward, 1974). Degler (2000) also connects race, agriculture, and slavery/Civil War as key characteristics of the South's distinctiveness, agreeing that the ongoing focus on with order represented by these concerns can still be seen in the issues of secession, states' rights, and segregation. Even following the civil rights movement, these issues continued to cause regional fallout in terms of race, class, and gender. Watts (2008), for example, argues convincingly that the lingering quest for order creates and maintains division that plays out in contemporary debates over public space, cultural institutions, and politics. It can be seen in the debate over allowing women to enter Virginia Military Institute, which upsets the "proper" ordering of women and men in Southern society. It can be seen in arguments over whether a monument dedicated to African American tennis star Arthur Ashe on Richmond's Monument Avenue can join the shrine to fallen Civil War heroes. It can be seen in fights about removing the Confederate flag above the State Capitol building in Columbia, South Carolina. In each of these debates, Southerners still jockey for position within the social order, causing Watts (2008) to conclude that the South remains "in dialogue with itself and others" (p. 3).

Today's Southerners see diversity increasing in the region, with African Americans, Caucasians, and Latinos living and working together in greater proportions than other parts of the country (Watts, 2008). Indeed, between 2000 and 2013, the five states with the largest percent growth of the immigrant population were all Southern: South Carolina (99 percent), Tennessee (92 percent), Kentucky (86 percent), Alabama (85 percent), and Arkansas (82 percent) (Migration Policy Institute, 2015). Despite this increasing diversity, there is the lingering influence of Confederate baggage, such that old markers of Southern distinctiveness are still used to characterize the region, whereby Southerners are described as being "more conservative, more nationalistic, more self-identified, and more romantic than other Americans . . . less rich, less urban, less diverse demographically and religiously, and more likely to be black" than other areas of the country (Watts, 2008, p. 8). Hall and Wood (1995) elaborate on these tendencies, adding that Southerners are defined by a "reverence of loyalty, the power of evangelical hokum, the irony of the white man's world still holding on in a world ever more populated by people of color, by the ever waving banner of Southern pride" (p. 13). Generally, Southerners identify more with a feeling of closeness/affection with a regional group than with a particular geography of the South and may have a tendency toward politeness, friendliness, and a slower pace of life as a result of their history. Religion continues to be important, with 59 percent of Mississippians, for example, classifying themselves as very religious, compared to 40 percent of Americans overall (Roberson, 2012). Of course, over time, there have been slight shifts in some of these broad tendencies, although some whites may work to preserve past social hierarchy (Watts, 2008). However, Roberson (2012) notes that some Southerners have pride in the region that is tinged with a sense of shame for past sins.

Without this broad understanding of what "the South" is, it is difficult to understand how these qualities are expressed in Southern food. As we have seen, Southerners have multiple identities (ethnic, regional, gendered, classed) that are influenced by their past. Food practices challenge and maintain these identities, with "who prepares the food, serves it, cleans it up; where people take their meals, the shape of a table; and who sits and talks about what" all conveying roles, values, and ideas about gender, hierarchy, and power (Jones, 2007, p. 130). Therefore, scholars are correct in saying that transportation, urbanization, and market development were delayed in the South, leading to the persistence of a unique food culture (Engelhardt, 2011). Still, we must not deny the role that the South's history plays in forming this culture. Race, class, and gender continually "pushed against each other" in developing the cuisine (Engelhardt, 2011, p. 10). Just to provide a few brief examples, there is a clear connection between Southern division and class concerns with food. Southerners of lower income are likely to consume Southern food more often than non-Southerners and more privileged Southerners, "revealing a persistent association between the affordability/humbleness of southern foods items and economic or social disadvantage in the region" (Latshaw, 2009, p. 117). Indeed, the majority of poor and working-class Southerners remained hungry and ravaged by disease into the twentieth century (Ferris, 2009). Meanwhile, although the Southern food traditions that emerged during slavery ultimately came to "signify a sense of 'blackness' or cultural identity and heritage for African Americans" following the civil rights movement (Latshaw, 2009, p. 123), during that era, traditional Southern food served as a center for violent confrontations (at lunch counters and cafes) and a source of segregation (Cooley, 2015). The South's women, too, are of course influenced by the complex interplay of food and power. If we note that kitchen space and recipes are Southern women's domains, however, we also might overemphasize the connection to the home, ignoring Southern black women's experiences as domestics and cafe cooks (Ferris, 2009). Nevertheless, teasing out these distinctions is difficult and important, because as Edge explains, "especially in the South, the people who cooked dinner were women and they were black, and Southerners and Americans as a whole devalued the labor of women and blacks" (Dean, 2013, para. 12). Ultimately, then, it is important to recognize that "the intersection of food and history in the American South is about power. Those who control food—its quantity, its taste, its access—control everything" (Ferris, 2009, p. 13).

That food has been used as a source of power to divide Southern society also points paradoxically to its ability to serve as a source of identification and reconciliation among its people. Just as Watts (2008) argues that the debates about public space, politics, and gender in the South may serve to move Southerners away from old orders into a new order of identification, food similarly carries this possibility. Some Southerners may embrace Burke's (1966) definition of man with its emphasis on maintaining the status quo, but humans have the potential to overcome their propensities toward division. Importantly, Watts (2008) relies on Burke to argue that Southerners can "identify with one another while respecting the richness of the distinctions that continue to exist among them." That is, Southerners can agree that Southern food exists, "even if we fight over what counts" (Engelhardt, 2011, p. 7). We contend, in fact, that it is the "fight" over what counts that gives Southern food its rhetorical power. In this fight, there is the potential for different groups of people to accept each other and find consubstantiality. Whether they agree on the definitions or not, they are still having conversations. Like other debates, arguments over food point to ways that people who are typically oppositional may find common ground. Exchanging ideas about food helps allow people to see shared essences. Rhetorically analyzing acts of consumption, such as "choices of ingredients, suppliers, methods, cookware, dining companions and locations, stories, and even restaurants," provides us with a way to understand how Southerners might find these connections with each other (Brown, 2009, p. 94). These alternative forms of communication are more than instrumental, inviting Southerners to identify with certain subject positions and providing the opportunity to challenge the dominant divisive narrative of the South. Southern food may reflect its charged history "and clearly involves elements of inequality, but even so, it possesses a unique ability to unite wildly different kinds of people around visions of delicious, sustainable, and safe food" (Opel, Johnson, & Wilk, 2010, p. 251).

Indeed, the subject of food deftly addresses the South's troubled past, especially as it emerges in the recent Southern food movement. As SFA director John T. Edge (2011b) contends, embracing Southern food and drink is a way to take on this challenge of honoring positive elements of Southern history without glorifying or ignoring its past mistakes. Discussing the efforts of the chefs and others involved in promoting Southern cuisine, Edge (2011b) observes,

> I think these people see southern food and drink as representing our best selves. If you think about it, cultures create representations of who you are, whether it's the clothes you drape yourself in, the music you listen to, the food you eat or the drinks you drink—they tell the story of who you are. (p. 21)

And preserving and highlighting our "best selves" is an important cultural goal. Given the diversity of its roots, Southern food provides opportunities for dialogues and experiences shared across cultural, racial, and socioeconomic lines. Cuisine, perhaps more than anything else, opens up possibilities for crossing barriers; as Latshaw (2009) elaborates, "by framing Southern foods as something Southerners of all races, classes, and religions can claim and share, it seems natural that they could be used to find a sense of commonality or to ease into discussions of a difficult past" (p. 109). In Severson's (2012) words, "food, more than prayer, politics, or politeness, is the language of getting along" (para. 9). Given its abilities to highlight similarities, it makes sense that it would be used rhetorically to create identification.

FOOD MOVEMENTS

Why does Southern fare offer such a unique example of food as a rhetori cally constitutive element? Part of the rhetorical power comes from the meaning of food more broadly, as we argue in chapter one. Although not all meals are symbolically significant, the day-to-day choices about what we consume become an important part of our identities. As Dickinson (2002) argues, food is part of the "rhetorical analysis of everyday" that "seems to be a crucial activity for those of us determined to understand the material ways rhetoric constrains and enables our subjectivities" (p. 5). In making a theoretical argument for the rhetorical—indeed constitutive—nature of food and discussion about that food, the need to account for multiple layers of meaning is a primary concern, as we discussed in chapter one. As Kinsman (2010) explains, "Food fuels ideas, feeds minds as well as stomachs and is a catalyst for passionate dialogue about culture, economics, race, gender and, yes, the dishes themselves" (para. 14).

Not surprisingly, then, movements have developed around food and food-ways. It is important to recognize that the Southern voice is but one involved in the larger conversation about food culture in the United States. Whether it is called the sustainable food movement or locavorism, Americans seem to have a greater interest in sustainable food and healthier eating, judging from media coverage, cultural shifts, and business developments. The White House now has an organic vegetable garden planted on its grounds, the first time since Eleanor Roosevelt planted a "victory garden" in World War II. Organizations such as the Southern Foodways Alliance, Southern Food and Beverage Museum, Slow Food, Roots of Change, Sustainable Table, and Foodways Texas, among others, have begun to shift perceptions about food, with the ideas of the food movement, such as the importance of local, sus-tainable, nonindustrial food, and the benefits of home-cooked family din-ners, creeping into the mainstream. As preeminent sustainable food author Michael Pollan (2009) observes, "Americans today are having a conversation about food and agriculture that it would have been impossible to imagine even a few short years ago" (p. x).

Traditional methods of Southern cooking fit nicely into larger conver-sations about the benefits of home cooking, growing a garden, sharing a communal meal, and the like. Rufca (2010) points out the natural connec-tion between Southern revival and the sustainable movement, noting "one harmonious consequence of the slow and local food movement is that chefs and diners" focus on "local culinary bounty and traditions" (para. 1). The

Southern food movement introduces a new conversational thread to this larger trend, however. That is, in the South and increasingly outside of it, there is an emerging emphasis on celebrating the region's unique foods, traditions, and methods in enriching and developing our American food culture. Nicknamed the "lardcore movement" it has been called "locavorism on steroids" and seeks to do more than just join the farm-to-table movement (Ozersky, 2010, para. 6). Wanting to embrace the entire Southern pantry and change the "hayseed" image of Southern food, a group of chefs, activists, writers, growers, and organizations want to keep Southern traditions and producers alive (Moskin, 2011, para 1). They do not want Southern cooking to be represented by things like feedlot hams, cheap fried chicken, and faux Southern chains such as Cracker Barrel (Moskin, 2011) and have the goal of challenging Southerners "to recognize and embrace safe, delicious, locally raised fruits, vegetables, and animals" (Ferris, 2009, p. 32).

Although it may have things in common with the back-to-the-land movement, folk revival of the sixties and seventies, and today's farm-to-table/sustainable movements, the Southern revival/lardcore movement also involves giving more credit to the many influences that created Southern food. For example, one SFA symposium debated how much of Southern food culture could be attributed to black culture (St. John, 2004). Some chefs argue the debate is overblown, as Southern whites and blacks tend to eat similar things. Many restaurants in the South, serving either largely black or largely white clientele, offer fried chicken, green beans, black-eyed peas, cornbread, and sweet tea. Edge states that "when you say black folks eat chitlins, you start to get in trouble, because a food like that is totemic to white and black Southerners. Both see it as reaching back to the tough times they survived. Both see it as food imbued with meaning, and that doesn't go away" (in St. John, 2004, para. 15). Others argue that highlighting the roots of Southern foods is very important. During the civil rights movement, whites became less likely to acknowledge black contributions to Southern food; meanwhile, the term "soul food" gained traction in an effort to keep the spotlight on black efforts. Still others believe that just focusing on black contributions to soul and comfort food limits the understanding of other contributions to cuisine that African Americans have made (St. John, 2004). Chef Natalie Dupree revealed how difficult these conversations can be: "We've had shouting matches. I've been infuriated, because people have called me racist, just because I would say that something was White. It's taught me how emotional an issue this is" (in St. John, 2004, para. 26). Edge, though, sees the seeds of reconciliation in these debates, arguing that "by dealing directly with the issue of race and

Southern food, something like an understanding could be achieved" (in St. John, 2004, para. 28). Indeed, observers of the Southern revival believe the movement has great potential, as "the South today has just the right combination of climate, culinary skill, regional chic, and receptive audience" (Moskin, 2011, para. 7). Consequently, both the food itself and the movement that has emerged around it have the potential to reshape the region.

Southern Foodways Alliance: People, Past, and Place

We mentioned the SFA earlier in this book, but the contributions of the organization need elaboration, as it is the most noteworthy part of the Southern food movement. Created in 1999 as part of the University of Mississippi's Center for the Study of Southern Culture by Southern food enthusiasts from chefs to academics, the SFA has grown to a twelve-hundred-member-strong organization that has hosted numerous events and workshops; recorded more than five hundred oral histories; made more than eighty short films; and published numerous books, newsletters, podcasts, and magazines. Its work has been featured in more than three hundred articles, ranging from *Time* and *Fortune* to *CNN*. The group celebrates Southern food heritage by calling for a return to traditional, local, and healthy ingredients and seeks to "pay down debts of pleasure, earned over generations" by recognizing those who may have been overlooked in the popular narrative of Southern food (Roahen, Edge, & Southern Foodways Alliance, 2010, ix). The group has been called "highly visible and influential" (Glatz, 2011, p. 1) and credited with taking Southern cooking seriously while helping make it one of the most popular cuisines today (Maynard, 2012). The SFA uses food and drink as a lens to view life (Edge, 2011b), featuring the stories of Southern cooks, pitmasters, gardeners, and restaurateurs. In doing so, it tries to "evoke larger-picture American stories, ones that touch on race, class, gender, labor, change, and continuity" (Edge, 2011a, p. 51). If the SFA participates in the "foodie" culture that is part of the national zeitgeist, with more people cooking, seeking unique restaurant experiences, and the like, the group differs in some important ways. Going beyond exclusive restaurant experiences or rare and expensive ingredients, it goes a step further, using food to make an argument for a more inclusive society—one defined by the sustenance that is consumed by all, regardless of class, race, or background. The work of the group—its rhetorical creations, especially—is worth studying because of the way it endeavors to shape our understanding of Southern food and the people who produce and consume it. Through its rhetorical work, the

SFA attempts to craft the "cornbread nation"—people who are dedicated to the celebration of Southern foodways, but who are also committed to larger social justice issues.

If food provides a new thread on which to construct identity, the SFA's rhetoric provides the foundation on which to begin. John Egerton, author, activist, and creator of the organization, originally planned for a two-day discussion of Southern food when he called for the first meeting of the group. He wrote,

> The time has come for all of us—traditional and nouvelle cooks and diners, up-scale and down-home devotees, meat-eaters and vegetarians, drinkers and abstainers, growers and processors, scholars and foodlorists, gourmands and the health-conscious, women and men, Blacks and Whites and other identity groups, one and all—to sit down and break bread together around one great Southern table. ("SFA History," para. 4)

The group introduces its beliefs and attitudes very clearly in its statement of mission and values. Created in 2010, the document lays out the goals of the organization, providing insight into the influence that it hopes to have on its members and society more broadly (SFA Mission). More importantly, given the significance of the SFA to the larger Southern food movement, the group's mission statement and the works that it informs are worthy of analysis because of the commitment that the SFA members, restaurants, and groups affiliated with the movement make to that mission. This rhetoric, along with testimonies provided through its extensive collection of oral histories, recipe headnotes included in its *Community Cookbook*, and essays in its book series *Cornbread Nation*, also provides insight into how Southern food *itself* serves a constitutive function, as we argue in chapter one. Thus, as a first step toward understanding the Southern food movement, better understanding the ideas that guide the leading organization in the movement provides insight into the principles of those involved in reviving Southern food—the cornbread nation.

To help construct this positive alternative Southern identity that is diverse, humble, and hospitable, three themes emerge from an analysis of the SFA's rhetoric: the people, their past, and their place. That is, the organization emphasizes a spirit of inclusiveness, the importance of preserving a more nuanced Southern history, and enacting a pride of place that is welcoming and more open to progressive change. Within each theme, Southern food serves as the ultimate term (Burke, 1950/1969) or the ideograph that undergirds the

SFA's rhetorical appeals, and each theme tends to feature one of the three facets of the alternative subject position (diverse, common/humble, hospitable). These themes help clarify why the Southern food movement is able to invite individuals to consider commonalities and begin to embrace their Southern identities together.

The People: Telling the Stories of a Diverse South

The first emphasis that the SFA puts forward is a celebration of the people of the South and their food. The group attempts to create a "spirit of reconciliation" ("SFA Mission," para. 1) by telling the stories that emphasize the diversity of the region, recognizing forgotten (intentional or not) histories, and working to "sing the unsung" (SFA Mission, para. 5). Their rhetoric and the food that inspires it, in turn, brings people together. In order to accomplish this inclusiveness, the SFA argues that it is important to account for all stories in order to encourage people to come to the table together. It tells the story, for example, of people such as African American Henry Pettus, who did the actual labor and pit cooking of the barbecue used to designate white sheriff John W. Callaway "patron saint of barbecue" at the close of the nineteenth century. The SFA points to the importance of recognizing such people, arguing that "race has always been a subtext of barbecue. In much of the South, blacks traditionally did the pit-cooking while whites supervised" (Edge, 2011a, p. 51). Additionally, at a New South Supper event in Atlanta, the focus was on the stories of African American and women's roles in developing the food culture in that city. As the SFA director explained about the importance of this focus, "In the South, women have been left out of the conversation of food. African Americans have also been left out of the conversation of food. Arguably, so have new arrivals to this region. So we tried to build an event and a conversation that links those three" (in Endolyn, 2013, para. 3). This recognition of the different voices in their rhetoric as well as their actions (featuring those voices in events, for example) has made the SFA an integral figure in the Southern food movement.

The SFA, in acknowledging all these forgotten or overlooked voices, invokes the inviting imagery of a supper table and argues, "We share a common table with people of all races, genders, ages, and classes. We believe that there is knowledge, power, and beauty in diversity" (SFA Mission, para. 38). The imagery of the table affords an opportunity for informal discussion, a symbolic and physical coming together of a diverse group to share in a nourishing of the body. That nourishment comes in the form of both physical nourishment through the fruits of Southern fields and farms and also in the psychological nourishment of a shared identity achieved through food, the sense of joy that might be associated with the tastes of the South, and the possibility of forging a relationship through a shared table more open to a variety of community members.

This symbolism in particular highlights the constitutive nature of consuming Southern food. Breaking bread together builds bonds, and that shared sense of identity creates an opening for the articulation of Southern identity built around food. In fact, this appeal echoes the church as a primary locus of Southern food customs. Food in the Southern Christian church plays an important role not only in the sacrament of communion (bread and wine, the life of Jesus, the Last Supper), but also in Sunday afternoon church picnics (Egerton, 1993). Food becomes transcendent, a religious experience, and the strategy connotes "the mystical and the occult, the visionary and divine" (Evens, 1990, p. 590). Today, the religious overtones may be more symbolic than literal, but the dishes serve "as a kind of balm, proving that mistrust and social clashes fall away when people gather to eat" (Severson, 2012, p. 51). Recent racial tension highlights even more the need for the opportunity to break bread together, despite its limitations. In an oral history from the owner of the Pie Wagon, a Nashville "meat and three" (a cafe that offers customers a choice of one meat and three sides), for example, Dan B suggests how food can work in this way: "I mean it's, it's just a complete mixture of customers that come in. And there will be a group of painters, mechanics, body shop guys, and they're all in the same room, and they're all enjoying really good food and talking about things that cover all spectrums in society. And that's—that's really neat to see every day and to, to watch" (SFA, Pie Wagon). This location and its food bring diverse people together and provide a space for shared experiences. Likewise, in recording histories such as these and using them rhetorically to emphasize the diversity of the foodways, the SFA helps unite Southerners around a common food culture. Their rhetoric creates a sense of transcendence, a rhetorical strategy in which individuals and groups that constitute opposing or different viewpoints adopt "another point of view from which they cease to be opposites" (Burke, 1984, p. 336). To this point, the SFA proclaims, "We pitch a big tent under which all may gather to learn and cavort," arguing that it is important to treat with respect "the dishwasher as well as the chef, the migrant farmer along with the farm CEO" (SFA Mission, para. 31 and 79).

This spirit of inclusiveness in the SFA mission statement calls forth Martin Luther King Jr.'s idea of the "beloved community," a concept that he used to inspire the continued fight for civil rights, in that the group is designed to "foster a South where all are welcome and all are valued" (SFA Mission, para. 50). King's beloved community was a "vision of a completely integrated society, a community of love and justice wherein brotherhood would be an actuality in all of social life. In his mind, such a community would be the ideal corporate expression of the Christian faith" (Smith & Zepp, n. d., para. 2). The SFA's spotlight on inclusiveness, reconciliation, justice through food-related actions, and an emphasis on community all seem to fit with King's vision. Edge (2011b) speaks to this point when recalling the SFA's oral history work on Georgia Gilmore, a 1960s Montgomery, Alabama, cook fired for testifying about the bus boycotts. With King's help, Gilmore opened a backdoor restaurant serving both black and white customers, forming what Edge calls a "kind of clubhouse of the Civil Rights Movement" (p. 20). In the SFA's work in sharing these stories, food becomes a way to think about issues of race and class; that is, the SFA enacts a part of the civil rights movement. Although this claim seems lofty, both proprietors and patrons express this belief in various oral histories. The group calls Gilmore's legacy restaurant "a modern day incarnation of the Civil Rights Movement ideal of the beloved community," and a patron feels this connection, remarking,

> Now, I will say when you go to her place, aside from the fact that her food is quite good, you do have a sense that you are participating in that great arc of what the boycott and other Civil Rights things were about…Martha Hawkins (the current owner) is not simply running the café, she's building the community. (SFA, Welcome Table)

That community—with an emphasis on the diversity of the people—is the result of the food that brought them together. Similarly, Leah Chase notes that her New Orleans restaurant was a movement resource: "We cooked; they ate; they planned, then they went on" (SFA, Leah Chase). These civil rights discussions show how Southerners physically and symbolically come together to create a shared sense of identity based on a shared meal.

Even without specifically connecting to the belief that they are extending the civil rights movement, several proprietors/vendors in the oral histories believe their restaurants help build community, noting, for example, "It's—this idea that a restaurant is more than just a place you eat it's—a kind of community center" (SFA, Chuck's BBQ), and speaking about the Greenwood, Mississippi, farmers' market, "Well I think it's meant a lot, as far as bridging the gap between the racial community. I mean we have, you know, black farmers, white farmers, you know, both. And I think it's a community builder" (SFA, Spooney's Barbecue).

Reading through the SFA's oral histories and other rhetorical documents reveals how Southern food provides an outlet for connection between different groups of people, but observing this possibility firsthand speaks to its rhetorical power. During many of our experiences traveling and documenting Southern foodways, we witnessed how food can have this "community-knitting together" power. Having breakfast at Evans Fine Foods in Atlanta demonstrated how food crosses racial, class, and gender lines and can act as a community builder. Evans has been open since 1946 in the East side of Atlanta, close to the Decatur, Emory, and Druid Hills neighborhoods. What becomes apparent immediately upon entering the strip mall eatery is its comfortable, familiar, "honest" feel. Laid out diner style, dated teal booths line the red walls. The hanging menu boards feature moveable plastic letters, and handwritten signs hang beside them. Servers, mainly waitresses, wear casual pants and polo shirts and seem genuinely interested in their tables. Black and white staff and clientele chat easily, and it is possible to overhear snippets of conversation about family goings-on, teasing between a black woman and her white server, and hearty greetings to patrons who have been coming in and ordering the same things for years. There is nothing trendy on Evans's menu; it announces firmly that it uses margarine instead of butter, allows no substitutions for the grits that come with breakfast entrees, and its jellies come from a foodservice truck. In an age when trendy restaurants try to create the Evans-style authenticity, often veering into hipster parody, what is striking about Evans is the way its simplicity fosters conversation. This is a dining experience that encourages interaction by virtue of staying out of the way of its patrons and not working too hard to force an agenda or particular way to enjoy its foods. Evans is not self-conscious in the way that some contemporary restaurants can be, earnestly informing diners of the welfare of its animals or the provenance of its products; it just simply "is." As a result, you can feel the comfort that patrons share as they eat their breakfasts, and this comfort works to seemingly build community between the residents of the neighborhood.

This Atlanta diner, as well as many other Southern restaurants and homes, creates a needed space for cooperatively eating and enjoying common foods. The veneration of Southern history is extended to all of those involved in forming the foodways of the South; it is a recognition of *all* of the people. Moreover, the food of the South is diverse. Consumption of that symbolic embodiment of the South also has the potential to create a sense of shared substance. If food can act in a constitutive manner, consuming multiple and diverse flavors through foods with strong cultural and historical roots calls forth a common identity. To identify as a Southerner or to relate to Southerners through the food provides a unique rhetorical tool for bringing people together. As the creator of the Crescent City farmers' market puts it, "All Southerners have a desire to reconnect with food. It's more than nourishment. Food is where we meet to build trust and community" (Street, 2012, para. 2). Through the discursive emphasis on recognizing all Southerners (both past and present), as well as the act of coming together (physically or metaphorically) and eating at shared tables, a common, more diverse identity is put forth.

The Past: Preserving Southern History through Humble Foods

The SFA also emphasizes the importance of remembering and celebrating Southern history but is careful to acknowledge the region's difficult past. In the group's words, they "share freely a people's history of the South" by exploring Southern foodways (SFA Mission, para. 7). Although the story of how Southern food has emerged and so heavily influenced the region and the people is not an easy story to tell, sharing the sometimes troubling/troubled food history is important because, as the SFA argues, we "leverage that past for our future" (SFA Mission, para. 91). Finding a way to save a history that might be lost to shame, while acknowledging reasons for that shame, preserves a vital part of the Southern narrative. The SFA acknowledges such difficult histories/realities in its statements, but it does so in the service of greater understanding as in the following example: "We embrace Southern history, the realities of the Southern present, and the opportunities for Southern futures . . . In other words, we don't flinch from talking about race, class, religion, gender, and all the other biggies" (SFA Mission, para. 11). These stories are worth telling, the group argues, because it is through this understanding of Southern foodways that we learn "the stories of our region." And a focus on this shared history allows for individuals to rise to a level of understanding. By focusing on a common food history, food becomes the value that allows the organization to recover a more nuanced understanding of the South's past. Celebrating the common history of Southern foods becomes an avenue for opening up discussions about a shared but difficult history.

One way that the SFA rehabilitates the past is by illuminating the shared race and class history of common Southern foods. The group explains that humble greens have been part of a variety of Southern tables, for example, noting that "greens have long been integral to, if not the centerpiece of, Southern meals. Simple, nutritious food that transcends race and class, greens are as likely to appear on a plastic folding table as they are a polished mahogany sideboard" (Roahen & Edge, 2010, p. 67). Thus, even though the different groups that comprise the South have different historical realities, food is or can be the common denominator among them. Legendary African American chef Leah Chase observes that "everybody in the South eats the same things; we may cook a little different, but we eat the same things" (in Cole and Lewis, 2013, p. 80). Egerton (1993) agrees when writing about the role of Southern food during segregation: "Segregation may have kept black and white Southerners from eating together, but it could not keep them from eating the same things, and for the most part they did" (p. 34). The SFA helps illuminate these culinary connections between groups.

For example, in several oral histories, the group discusses the shared consumption of tamales (meat wrapped in masa dough and steamed or boiled) among Hispanic Americans in Texas and African Americans in Mississippi. An observer watching the two groups craft the tamales in similar but unique ways notes, "Beyond the ethnicity and geography and spoonfuls of cayenne, the two rooms possessed a beautiful interchangeabilty" (Bruce, 2010, para. 3). Whether discussing tamales or other humble Southern foods like spicy fried chicken, it is the comfort, ease, and relatable nature generated by these foods that may invite identification among different groups of Southerners. The owner of a hot chicken place in Nashville notes in an SFA oral history the cross-racial pull of his product, recalling, "But people from all walks of life come here and a lot of them have—they—they'll tell you the story of how they grew up on this chicken, their parents took them" (SFA, Prince's Hot Chicken). Similarly, an owner of another Nashville meat and three remarks, "And I express soul food really being something that—that makes you feel comfortable, that brings you back to a time regardless of the—the type of food being prepared. But it makes you—if it makes you feel good, then it's soul food, you know" (SFA, Pie Wagon). In each case, the humble dishes on offer create a sense of comfort and stimulate a food-based nostalgia. What the SFA does, then, is make these shared food commonalities more explicit, asking audiences to build from them in order to encourage understanding. The organization argues, "We set a common table where Black and White, rich and poor—all who gather—may consider our history and our future in a spirit of reconciliation" (SFA Mission, para. 1).

Additionally, the act of recreating historical pieces of the South through the food of the region provides a powerful and material way to reify the importance of a more nuanced history of the region. Many of the group's events, oral histories, interviews, and various publications focus on offering this more honest and forthright history. For example, unlike mass media outlets that celebrate National Barbecue Month without paying homage to any African American pitmasters, the SFA features them in documentaries, oral histories, and the like (Miller, 2012). Another example of this kind of work appears in the SFA *Cornbread Nation* book series, where an author discusses the story from a slave narrative in which Mrs. Flint, a mistress in a big house, spits into the leftovers in the kitchen so that the black cooks could not eat them (Harris, 2012). By helping Southerners learn these stories of their food, teaching them how to locate the ingredients that will best recreate a recipe, how to prepare the dishes, and then discuss and consume these foods, the understanding of foodways helps build a fuller understanding of the region. Edge explains in an interview that "keeping Southern food traditions alive is one way of connecting regular folks with their history . . . and with the importance of providing 'teaching moments' to people who craft policies. When people are eating, they're not thinking about what keeps them apart, but linked by the food that connects them" (Center for a Better South, 2011, para. 2). The SFA, then, argues that we recreate a shared and diverse history by crafting and consuming Southern food.

This recovered and reconfigured history allows for a rearticulation of identities. By acknowledging past and current racial and class divides, but also focusing on shared substance through foodways, individuals are invited to couple this complicated past and present with a more promising future. A complex and honest understanding of the history of the region and its people makes it possible to bring multiple strands of identity together in order to offer a shared Southern identity, despite other differences. In this case, a celebration of Southern food allows for a transcendence or safe nostalgia, a recognition of the shared components of the Southern experience. As Severson (2012) puts it, Southern food is the "great equalizer, the common ground in a region still working to repair the scars left from slavery and the Jim Crow era" (p. 50). Those scars affect Southerners directly through relationships, and this effort to restore a positive Southern history opens up possibilities for finding common ground.

As we wrote about the possibilities of finding bright spots in the South's history through the SFA's work on sharing common foodways, it became hard to overlook the observations and contributions of Leah Chase, the proprietor and chef of Dooky Chase in New Orleans. We had the opportunity to visit the restaurant on a research trip and witness how putting the focus on food helps bridge the gap between black and white by emphasizing shared enjoyment of tastes and experiences. Dooky Chase is not located in the French Quarter or Garden District, but it is instead a fixture of the African American Treme neighborhood. The restaurant has survived in various iterations since 1941, serving as one of the only places in New Orleans during segregation where civil rights leaders could openly discuss strategy (Dooky Chase). Closed for two years following Hurricane Katrina, New Orleans residents rallied behind Ms. Chase to reopen the restaurant. Many political and cultural luminaries, including President Obama, have enjoyed her cuisine over the years (Dooky Chase). Though its history is colorful, Dooky Chase could be mistaken for any Southern neighborhood joint. The humble cinderblock structure opens into an elegantly decorated and inviting dining space with important examples of African American art lining the walls; the staff is dressed in white button-down shirts.

The food quickly takes center stage, however, keeping the experience from feeling stuffy or formal. Down the center of the restaurant sits a long buffet filled with Southern specialties such as ribs, fried chicken, greens, gumbo, and sweet potatoes. We watched as tourists, businessmen, neighborhood residents, and college students filled their plates, all enjoying the food and returning for more. Patrons chatted with servers about the history of the restaurant, and the servers took obvious pride in their employer and their city. The restaurant's simple presentation of foods and the friendliness of the servers seemed to invite conversation. We talked about how the sweet potatoes had more cinnamon than what we were used to, how the ribs had more of a tang than what we had experienced in Memphis, and how the fried chicken ranked among other versions we had experienced during the trip. In noticing these differences, it became clear how food can act as a way to reflect on differences and similarities in family food traditions. Instead of customers being threatened by differences in culture, the traditional food at Dooky's (and indeed at restaurants like these throughout the South) invites people to savor, take stock, and perhaps see that "their" version of a dish has much in common with someone else's. Experiences such as this, which can be recognized by many Southerners, show how Southern food can act as an equalizer, celebrating the diverse history and foodways of the South.

The Place: Reenvisioning Southern Pride and Hospitality

With recognition of the diversity of the Southern people and their shared, often humble past, the SFA also has as its goal developing a way to embrace Southern pride by celebrating the place. Nostalgia surrounding the South can craft a sense of identity because "nostalgic sentiments serve as unifying narratives that mask various tensions and hierarchies" and "manufacture unity and wholeness for order's sake" (Von Burg & Johnson, 2009, p. 353). Nostalgia can be problematic, however, because it is "rarely concerned with moving forward and with positively reconstructing the past" (McPherson, 2003, p. 10). There is a danger in falling victim to this problem when discussing food, as "a great deal of contemporary food writing is so thoroughly soaked in nostalgia," but the SFA is careful (Raskin, 2011, para. 3). The organization provides an outlet for inclusively reminiscing over the past, arguing that we should celebrate the region, but we should do so "thoughtfully and oftentimes critically" (SFA Mission, para. 90). It acknowledges that "our South reflects contradictions and contains multitudes" (Roahen & Edge, 2010, p. xiv). Indeed, the SFA's work often pierces through troubling bits of nostalgia, making apparent the role of race, class, and gender in Southern foodways.

Importantly, the SFA envisions an active pride that engages but transcends such troubling memories: "We promote pride of place, and encourage local communities to invest in cultural richness through fieldwork, events, and volunteer opportunities. We serve as advocates for economic and cultural heritage development" (SFA Mission, para. 15). It is a South that recognizes the troubled and painful past, yet celebrates the region by thinking about the future Southern community that is possible through the recognition of similarities that might come about through the food movement.

For the SFA, Southern pride must involve a particular kind of action that a focus on hospitality provides. One observer remarks about this characteristic of Southern identity that "what we prepare, and how we do it, in lovingly generous, belt-busting proportions—may be our region's finest recipe" (Cross & Street, 2011, para. 1). Many of the SFA oral history interviewees express pride in their ability to welcome people through food and celebrate their ability to connect people this way. David Swett of the Nashville meat and three expresses this sentiment: "Everybody is welcome; everybody feels comfortable. You can find former Senators, Presidents sitting at the same table as guys who work hard every day for a living" (SFA, Swett's). Food is celebrated as being a social, group activity for people to experience. As an SFA member explains, for example, "Barbecue is a reunion, a party, an opportunity for everybody to come and join in and enjoy each other's company" (Fertel, 2013, para. 7). Another restaurateur interviewed by the SFA notes that creating connection through hospitality is the entire point of her business: "People come to my restaurant to fight loneliness. The restaurant pays my bills, but more importantly, gives the comfort of human relationships" (SFA, Mama Dips).

In this case, the act of hospitality with/through food provides a way to create relationships. This hospitable *place* is made possible through Southern food. Many interviewees express this belief in the importance of creating connections through sharing their food. For example, a former leader of the Chicago chapter of the Negro American Labor Council describes a soul food restaurant in this way: "You could get that good food at home . . . But it was the camaraderie that attracted you. It was the conversations and the owners who knew you by name and came out to talk to you. It was the history and the pride that you could touch and taste and feel" (Trice, 2011, para. 8).

From a rhetorical perspective, the byproduct of taking pride in offering hospitality is that Southern restaurants give the opportunity to build connections through sharing food. Instead of trying to connect to a mythic and exclusionary nostalgic "moonlight and magnolias" past, eating together becomes the way of finding what you have in common, regardless of your cultural or racial background. As one patron of a soul food restaurant featured by the SFA explains, "it really goes to the heart of what we have in common. I mean a lot of us love that kind of food, it doesn't matter what race you are, so you really do see a little bit of everybody there" (SFA, Welcome Table).

The SFA uses oral history as a rhetorical vehicle to show how food becomes an entry point into learning about others. As Howard Shinn of the Buford Highway farmers' market explains, "food is a great way to experience another culture. It's not very risky. . . . It can be a singular experience, it can be a social experience and it can be something you can share and talk about and enjoy" (SFA, Buford Highway). Ultimately, the group shows how hospitality provides the ability to form an understanding of the South's people as patrons share food.

If the SFA uses interviews to illustrate how food can serve as an avenue into getting to "know" the South's culture, the physical act of eating at particular Southern restaurants highlights similar possibilities. When we went to Doe's Eat Place in Greenville, Mississippi, on a hot July night, we experienced firsthand the connective power of Southern hospitality. Wendy had made an offhand call to the restaurant before we arrived, asking if we could speak to a family member about the restaurant and its role in building Greenville's community. We were pleasantly surprised that Charles Signa, son of the original Doe's owner, not only agreed to speak to us, but sat with us for several hours talking about the restaurant and making sure we had our fill of its delicious, James Beard Award–winning food. In a way, Doe's shouldn't be considered a particularly Southern restaurant. As Charles explained when we asked him what makes his food "Southern," he said, "It's not really Southern food. When I think of Southern food, I think of cornbread." We asked him why he thought his was a Southern restaurant, and he summed it up this way: "People keep coming here because we're different. You can get this food anywhere, but it's different here." And he was right. The steaks, salad, broiled shrimp, and tamales might be available at many restaurants in the Delta and throughout the South, but the Doe's experience is singular—a perfect example of the hospitality that makes the region distinctive. Where else could Charles hop up in midsentence, slice, toast, and butter bread for us (all two steps away from our table) and then sit back down, with the conversation not missing a beat? He brought almost every single item on the menu for us to sample, even offering a few "experiments" that his brother was testing in the steak-grilling room next to ours.

Doe's is the kind of place that exists because it offers a unique, hospitable experience, seeking to give diners something special, yet comfortable. It survives and grows through word of mouth, not because of foodie culture; in fact, it thrives despite it. If the Signa family can run a restaurant since 1941, weathering racial strife, economic challenges, and culinary changes, it is because of its atmosphere and genuine warmth. It is clear that the servers, regulars, and owners care about each other; as Charles tried to explain to us, "It's just different in the Delta. We're friendlier." We kept thinking about Charles's statement in the days to come on our trip. Of all the areas of the Deep South we visited, the Delta did stand out. In a region down on its luck in many ways, the residents' pride was evident and infectious. People wanted to talk to us; they wanted us to see what was special about their area. And through welcoming, delicious, incredibly friendly experiences like eating at Doe's, we did—albeit as white, middle-class women.

This example perfectly illustrates the Southern characteristic of hospitality. In featuring stories of welcoming, the SFA can assist Southerners' desire to connect to more positive associations of place. The organization again taps into the spirit of transcendence, attempting to show how a hallmark of a region coalesces into something community building and affirming, arguing, "We know where the food we share comes from, who prepares it, and how it can tell stories of our region" (SFA Mission, para. 33). In recording the oral histories of everything from barbecue shacks, to farmers' markets, to meat and threes, the organization seeks to ensure it records a variety of stories of food and place to thoughtfully represent the region. It explains that it "tries to bridge that gap between oilcloth and white damask tablecloth" (Edible Nation, 2011, para. 5). Indeed, the "place" of the South features importantly in the SFA, with its presentations and plates benefiting from context, such that "meals and menus at events are built sourcing ingredients, cooks, and chefs who are pertinent to the event dialogue" (SFA Mission, para. 27). Food has been a large part of the pride that develops around the South, but such actions celebrating a broader, less nostalgic understanding of that food allow for a pride in the South that is less tainted by troubled history and more welcoming. And for many in the oral histories, the time is right. The SFA helps this active, more progressive pride to be expressed by recording these stories and by encouraging Southerners to buy local produce, cook regional recipes, eat at Southern-grown restaurants, and participate in the Southern food movement in other ways.

THE CORNBREAD NATION: OPENING SPACE FOR DIALOGUE

This movement, one very much grounded in constitutive rhetorical tactics, calls for followers to enact their Southernness (whether they are truly Southern or not) by consuming and embracing Southern food; symbolically sharing a table with a diverse crowd; reaching out to community members and inviting them to take the same rhetorical steps; and finally, investing time, money, and effort into restoring the South in a number of ways. Food, as we have demonstrated, is the rhetorical force driving this movement, used to get to "conversations about race, class, gender and other aspects of who we are as people and more specifically southerners" (McLaughlin, 2011, para. 3). As market owner Harold Shinn points out about food's role in creating cultural understanding, "you can read about it, you can smell it but hey ultimately, you just have to eat it and you have to eat a lot of it to understand the variances and nuances" (SFA, Buford Highway). The cornbread nation is crafted through a celebration of the food of its people, their past, and their place.

A study of SFA rhetoric shows the possibility of Southern food and food rhetoric as a way to open up dialogue and emphasize shared backgrounds. It also provides new ways of talking about rhetoric. The rhetorical function that food serves in constructing a more positive and broad-appealing Southern identity is an important part of understanding how to create the space for finding commonality in the region. The work of the SFA shows one way that individuals might negotiate the troubled Southern identity, embracing some parts, while also acknowledging problems with traditional conceptualizations of the Southerner. It provides individuals one way to fold diverse individual and family histories into a celebration of Southern identity. Importantly, the

SFA's message is also reflected in other Southern food organizations (such as Texas Foodways), restaurant menus, and farmer's market web sites. As the Southern Food and Beverage Museum in New Orleans proudly says of the role of food in that city following Hurricane Katrina, "it is food that delivers the biggest message in New Orleans . . . giving the crowd something to smile about." Not far from the museum, the Crescent City farmers' market brings farmers and community members together: "By providing a forum where consumers and producers come together over food—a powerful cultural common denominator in the New Orleans region—the Crescent City farmers' market promotes good health among citizens, greater social interaction between communities and sustainable economic development" (Who we are, n.d., para. 2). This general idea of food bringing the community together is frequently found in farmers' market literature and other organizations dedicated to Southern foodways, demonstrating the SFA message.

The SFA illustrates how to confront difficult issues of race and class by reflecting the characteristics of Southern food. If Southern cuisine is marked as being diverse, humble, and hospitable, the SFA is symbolic of that cuisine in its values. The organization emphasizes the importance of recognizing diverse histories and backgrounds, just as Southern food is a conglomeration of flavors and histories. Rather than waxing nostalgic, the SFA is humble in its approach to Southern history, relying on simple foods to help recognize past mistakes and move forward with those mistakes in mind. The SFA also emphasizes the importance of openness and inclusiveness through its focus on hospitality, a sharing of culinary experiences. It shows how being hospitable means inviting people to experience a South more open to difference and more willing to accept the possibilities made available when broadening the popular/traditional story of the region. While the historical Southern table might have been segregated, the vision of the new Southern table crafted by the SFA is open, honest, and committed to equality in a number of ways.

We are not claiming that all Southerners are ready to embrace the diverse, humble, hospitable identity offered by the SFA's rhetoric, nor are we arguing that every person connects with the food, but that it makes a strong case for how food provides the framework for this possibility. What is unique about this case study, then, is that it shows how food can open discursive space between people. It is the rhetoric that allows these identity characteristics to be enacted. While we may intuitively recognize that food is a way to find common ground, this study makes explicit how the rhetoric surrounding the Southern food movement turns food into a strong rhetorical force. And we certainly need a reminder of this force now, as stories about the South continue to feature news of racial prejudice and injustice. Food offers us hope that a better story can be told.

When we argue that Southern food and the surrounding rhetoric have the ability to unite people, we are arguing that the food acts symbolically. Although SFA events and actions may indeed physically bring together a diverse group of people, it is the acts of sharing, cooking, consuming, and celebrating Southern food that form a commonality. As Draper (2013) writes, "Food brings you to the table. It's the invitation, the connection point, the way to get the conversation started. From there, stories about who we are, where we come from, what's important to us rise to the surface" (para. 6). Food provides more than just the start of a conversation, however; we argue that food is also a *part* of the conversation. The constitutive nature of Southern food and the rhetoric that surrounds it can act on several levels, overtly celebrating culture ("I created my grandmother's deviled eggs"), implicitly celebrating ("Let's have a Southern church supper"), or just reaffirming Southern culture through its foods (buying locally produced products). Sharing foodways, and then studying, celebrating, and encouraging those shared foodways, symbolically unites people, potentially overcoming perceptions of difference and division. And as Charland (1987) argues, the ability to overcome these *perceptions* is necessary in order to "define away the recalcitrance of the world" and act in ways that support this subject position in today's South (p. 142). We must first believe we share foodways before we are willing, for example, to share meals with people different from us.

Of course food is not a cure all. It cannot heal the wounds caused by past racial strife and class division. As Watson (2009) argues, "There's more to southernness than food, of course, and even Mama's biscuits can't blot up all the tangled leftovers from history and popular memory" (p. 2). There are always dangers in reminiscing over troubled times. Painful memories beg to be forgotten by some, but they are impossible for others to forget. Claims over traditions are muddled by a diverse cast of individuals involved in that history. Without careful construction, the rhetorical move of celebrating Southern food risks being called into question for proposing a postracial take on the South, blending all food experiences into one experience and dropping out all of the historical struggles and inequalities connected with those foods.

And yet, given the choice between hiding away traditions because of the painful past or recovering and embracing those traditions in the interest of positive growth, celebration seems to be the best choice. Clearly, racial inequality persists, and the SFA as well as other Southern food movement groups must continue to be mindful not to gloss over these inequities in its work. Indeed, as the SFA is made up primarily of academics and Southern chefs, cooks, and food writers, it must be vigilant in comprehensively drawing attention to the unsung heroes of Southern culture whose work may have been overlooked due to racial prejudice. However, our close examination of the SFA's food rhetoric shows an organization committed to celebrating individual contributions, recognizing inequalities, and placing the food stories within the difficult narratives of the past.

The SFA and other players in the Southern food movement may just provide some of the needed ingredients to craft a Southern culture that can look back in recognition of the past, but also move forward with a better vision of what the region is and what it can become. The SFA provides one example of taking the rhetorical possibilities of Southern food to enact change. Those possibilities extend far beyond this one organization, though. The remaining chapters of this book turn more specifically to Southern food and the kinds of rhetorical work that it does. Moving through the courses of a Southern meal, we explore the ways that the food itself acts to constitute a people.

PART TWO

EXPLORING THE SOUTHERN TABLE

CHAPTER THREE

SIPPING ON SOUTHERN HOSPITALITY
Drink as Rhetorical Invitation

Sitting down to enjoy a drink at the top-floor bar in the Charlotte, North Carolina, Ritz-Carlton, we were prepared for a delicious concoction. The Punch Room had just opened the previous week, and "Head Mixologist" Bob Peters was already receiving a great deal of attention (Wile, 2015). What we were unprepared for, however, was the combination of dazzling bartending performances and a heavy dose of cocktail history and education. As our mixologist artfully carved the lime zest, put in dashes of this and that, vigorously shook the cocktail shaker, and poured the drink into a glass with a flourish, it was clear to us that the offer of a drink—the crafting of a drink—can be an art form, a performance. Of course, drinking sometimes gets a bad name in the South, from watching stumbling celebrants on Bourbon Street in booze-laden New Orleans, to an excess of brown liquor at SEC tailgates, to the raucous St. Patty's Day party in Savannah. The performance, the history, and the simplicity of the symbolic offering can be overshadowed by the desire to drink for the sake of drinking.

But to Terry Jordan, a longtime bartender and now restaurant manager in Hattiesburg, Mississippi, Southern drinks are about much more than "just getting drunk" or performing the part of the bartender; instead, they are about "relaxing, taking time, slowing down." In fact, a cold glass of sweet tea on a hot day, a hot cup of coffee on a cold day, or even a much-needed glass of water can create an opening for conversation. Southern drinks are about sharing stories and building relationships. In a good Southern bar, Terry says,

> You learn a lot about people when you . . . if you sit and watch and just
> listen . . . You hear a lot of interesting conversations. You see the start of a

relationship just budding from "Hi, how are you doing?" to . . . "I do." You know, you see all of that in between. You see courtship, you see things fall apart in a relationship. You see million dollar deals done right before your eyes . . . But yet you still treat it all the same. You know, you feel joy for people, sorrow. And all of that does go into the drink.

What is striking about how Terry describes the bar is that his custom- ers—many of them his friends now—describe this same sense of relationship building in describing his skills (see figure 3.1). Yes, the drinks themselves are impressive, but he is also careful to create a particularly welcoming environ- ment in his bar. He creates that sense of Southern hospitality through drink. "That's what I think southern drinks are all about," Terry claims:

> It's hospitality in a glass. It is something you can take your time and sip and slow down the day. No matter which drink you choose to make. It can be a glass of sweet tea and it's still just as good. It can be the water from the springs of Columbia and if you pour it just right for somebody you start a conversation and that's the best thing in the world.

Hospitality is central to any stereotypical image of the South, and many in the area do embrace this welcoming rhetoric, helping the region live up to the stereotype. The cocktail plays a significant part in that image of hospital- ity. Although the origin of the cocktail is disputed, it has long been a part of Southern tradition, with New Orleans claiming to be at the center of that history. Whether at a restaurant, in the home, while tailgating, or at other events, the offering of a drink is a symbolic gesture of Southern hospitality. As Onorato (2008) writes, "When we think of Southern hospitality nowa- days, we conjure up a scene of gracious folk sitting on the veranda in the shade of a magnolia tree, sipping a concoction of bourbon and mint from a silver cup while black-coated servants tend to their needs" (para. 1). Perhaps Onorato's description best captures the stereotypical, plantation-type setting of this imagery, both emphasizing the idea of an open society—opening doors and welcoming others in—and an exclusionary society at the same time. And yet, Southern hospitality is not necessarily a concept or set of behaviors that is tied to any one class or race. Instead, it is a Southern char- acteristic that can be interpreted and enacted in many ways. As John Egerton (1993) argues, "Whether in the home or in public places, the food traditions that had become a part of the Southern culture by the 1940s could be sum- marized under a single descriptive heading: hospitality" (p. 38). The South is certainly not the only region that is welcoming, nor do all Southerners live up to the stereotype. However, as we argue in chapter two, the Southern tradition of providing food and drink as a way to welcome others, smooth over problems, ease pain, and celebrate is one of the defining characteristics of the region and its people.

These kinds of offerings are fraught with contradictions, however. The idea of hospitality provides an example of what Kenneth Burke (1969) describes as the principle of courtship—overcoming mystery or division by the "transcending of social estrangement" (p. 208). Food and drink can serve as a rhetorical opening for creating connections. In a region marked by division, however, race, class, and even religious differences have historically complicated Southern hospitality, inviting some in and keeping others out.

This chapter examines the topic of the rhetorical possibilities of drink by exploring the concept of Southern hospitality through the example of the Southern cocktail hour and the possibilities of this symbol as a marker of the region. We put forward two arguments: that hospitality, although problematic, is a type of discourse indicative of the region and that food and drink play a role in that discourse. We begin by discussing the role of drinks in Southern culture, before turning to concepts of courtship and hospitality and the rhetorical role of that offering in defining the region.

COCKTAIL HOUR IN THE SOUTH

The idea of cocktail hour in the South brings forth images of offerings of drinks on the veranda, porch, or patio. Typical Southern cocktails tend to be light and juice based, crafted to ward off the heat. As Terry Jordan argues, Southern drinks have "to be full of sunshine. Lot of cheer. Lot of joy. It's gotta reflect how we live with the sun." They are "full body, fruity, that gives you a ray of sunshine, that gives you a little positive attitude. A little sweetness on the tongue, but yet a little bitter on the back end." In the end, Terry explains, the Southern drink is "welcoming. To me, if I make one, it's opening myself up, putting myself on the table. That's what a southern drink is to me."

Whether this offer of a drink takes place in the home, at a reception, in a tailgating tent, or in a restaurant, the cocktail is an important part of the foodways of the South. Obviously hospitality can be extended in many other settings and with other offerings, but Southerners tend to take great pride in their alcohol-based creations.

Figure 3.1 Terry Jordan, master mixologist at Patio 44, Hattiesburg, Mississippi

The history of the cocktail changes, depending on who is telling that history. New Orleanians claim that one of the city's pharmacists, Antoine Peychaud, who was famous for his bitters, was the creator of the first cocktail in the early 1800s. His bitters, at first sold to settle the stomach, were occasionally mixed with brandy in order to make the concoction more palatable. As they tell the story in New Orleans, Peychaud and other area bartenders then began serving similar drinks in a *coquetier*, or a French egg cup, and the word "cocktail" came about as a variation of that word (Thompson, 2005; Wohl, 2012). The Museum of the American Cocktail (part of New Orleans's Southern Food and Beverage Museum) emphasizes the importance of the drink to the region, although the museum does not claim that New Orleans birthed the cocktail. One museum placard argues, "While other places can lay claim to definite milestones in the life story of the Cocktail and the spirits it contains, no place has embraced it as passionately as New Orleans."

David Wondrich (2007) tells a different story, however, concluding that cocktails were a creation of the North, not the South, crediting famous American bartender "Professor" Jerry Thomas with the spread of their popularity. Talk to a Londoner and you receive yet another take on cocktail history. Brown (2012), writing in the *Telegraph*, traces the roots of most of the American drinks and, indeed, the early bartenders to London.

Figure 3.2 Oldest surviving bar in the city, Southern Food and Beverage Museum, New Orleans, Louisiana

The true origins of the cocktail may never be determined, but Southerners certainly claim the inventor title and argue that they are indeed the perfectors of the concoctions. Enjoying a drink at the oldest bar in New Orleans, currently housed in the Southern Food and Beverage Museum's restaurant, Purloo, we asked the bartender where she stood on the matter of the origins of the cocktail (see figure 3.2). She brushed the question aside, saying that she was less concerned about the history ("I don't think it's necessary to take claim over something") and more concerned about making people happy with her concoctions. "In the end, I'd rather be giving someone something they want to be tasting." The drinks on the menu, however, were all based on historical recipes. The South's beverage offerings have become as much a part of the story as the foodways.

There are several Southern drinks that have become particularly symbolic of the region. The mint julep, created with a mix of bourbon, simple syrup, and mint, has become the "most celebrated and romanticized" of the Southern drinks (Egerton, 1993, p. 211). Most associated with genteel Southerners sipping the drinks on the veranda, the mint julep is generally held up as an example of the exclusive side of the South. Although it is a drink traditionally linked to events such as the Kentucky Derby, it is also the most stereotypical symbolic drink of the region, often used to place a "Southern stamp" on an event and to show some knowledge of traditional Southern drinks. The drink is cliché, but "along with white columns, moonlight, jasmine, and magnolias" it is "part and parcel of the patrician southern myth" (Harwell, 2007, p. 198).

The Sazerac is yet another drink that claims its roots in the South. Created in the 1850s in New Orleans, the drink has become closely linked with the iconic Southern city and was declared the official drink of New Orleans by the Louisiana House of Representatives in 2008 (Egerton, 1993; NPR, 2008). New Orleanians often claim that the Sazerac was the first cocktail created, although Wondrich (2007) denies that claim. Made with rye whiskey (or cognac, originally), absinthe, and bitters, some would say that the drink is known more for its symbolism of the South (and New Orleans in particular) and for the performance of the drink (discussed later in the chapter) than for the flavor. As Egerton writes, the "Sazerac cocktail, after 130 years, is still a sweet sip of New Orleans history" (p. 214).

Whether you are drinking a Ramos gin fizz in a New Orleans bar, a Bloody Mary while tailgating at an LSU game, an old fashioned in Louisville, or a Hurricane while surrounded by tourists at Pat O'Brien's, many Southern cocktails are designed for slowing down and sipping. As Terry argues, "Drinks in the South are made for conversation. No matter if you go to discuss what's in it, why you drinkin' it. And if it's a long drink—most of our drinks are big—so it takes a little while to drink . . . You take your time to drink it. You want to sit back and enjoy it."

Aside from the cocktail, alcohol more broadly has a longer history in the region. Although wine and beer were consumed in the South before the Civil War, they were not necessarily popular or widespread until after Prohibition (Taylor, 1982). Virginia saw some of the earliest beer and wine production, with English influence on the colonies. Whiskey was also available before the Civil War, but saw more booming sales with Prohibition. Of course, the bootleg industry surrounding whiskey during Prohibition was a part of Southern history. James Crow, a Kentucky physician and chemist, was one of the earliest and most successful whiskey distillers. His creation led to the Kentucky variation of whiskey—bourbon—becoming one of the most visibly Southern drinks (Egerton, 1993).

Bourbon deserves its own examination, consequently. No other liquor finds its way into traditionally Southern cocktails more frequently. Walker Percy (1991) poignantly writes of the brown liquor that it connects the drinker to the South in a vivid way: "The joy of Bourbon drinking is not the pharmacological effect of C_2H_5OH on the cortex but rather the instant of the whiskey being knocked back and the little explosion of Kentucky U.S.A.

sunshine in the cavity of the nasopharynx and the hot bosky bite of Tennessee summertime" (p. 103). Percy is not alone in viscerally connecting the drink to the South. That is, in large part, because of the way that the "brown-hued elixir" has worked its way into Southern culture. As *The Southerner's Handbook* (2013) explains, "It would be a challenge to find a Southerner without a good bourbon story. If it's not your libation of choice, your father drank it, or your mother cooked with it, simply calling it whiskey, or your grandfather had a secret eggnog recipe calling for bourbon poured with a heavy hand" (p. 119). This Southern tradition of bourbon thus weaves its way into family stories.

Beer is also a large part of the Southern foodways story. In fact, the South has seen an increase in microbreweries in recent years thanks to loosened alcohol laws and successful business models in the region (Pramuk, 2015). Although there are numerous Southern suds, Spoetzel Brewery, the maker of Shiner beers, successfully helped bring Southern beers forward. Established in 1909 in the tiny central Texas town of Shiner, Spoetzel primarily supplied surrounding counties until the 1990s when a successful marketing campaign helped it grow to the fourth largest craft brewery in America (Rienstra, 2013). Driving into the small town of Shiner—population just over two thousand—it is apparent that the local beer is a large part of the culture. Almost every business in town features a neon Shiner beer sign. On the brewery tour, it is clear that community members not only founded the business, but also contributed to its continued success of, with many of its 125 workers coming from Shiner and the surrounding area (Rienstra, 2013). During Wendy's tour of the brewery, an eighty-year-old Shiner man was celebrating his birthday with some of his family and friends and reminiscing about all of the community members that he recognized in employee photographs hung on the walls. It is not only the local resources (artesian springs) but the local people that make the beer "of the land."

Of course, it is also important to point out that sweet tea, one of the most popular nonalcoholic drinks in the South, is also associated with the region. As Egerton (1993) points out, "With iced tea especially, there is a distinct Southern accent; people in the region drink it the year around, whenever and wherever food is served, and have done so with increasing regularity since ice became generally available in the late nineteenth century" (p. 205). The drink itself is connected to the region, but the offering of sweet iced tea as an alternative to alcohol is also an important story of food and drink in the South. As Glock (2013) argues, "sweet tea means something. It is a tell, a tradition. Sweet tea isn't a drink, really. It's culture in a glass. Like Guinness in

Ireland or ouzo in Greece" (p. 106). As will be discussed later in the chapter, religious and/or moral restrictions on alcohol (not to mention Prohibition-era restrictions) made this nonalcoholic alternative an important part of Southern hospitality.

The drinks themselves are not necessarily the main part of the story, however, although the region is proud of its libations; instead, the rhetorical symbolism often comes about through the *offering* of the beverage (or food, as is also often the case). That offer is one motivated by a symbolic and experienced commitment to the image of hospitality, a concept that has an important rhetorical meaning in the region.

COURTSHIP AND SOUTHERN HOSPITALITY

The idea of Southern hospitality grows out of a desire to create a sense of identification with others. As humans, we are inherently drawn to finding commonalities with others and communicating in order to discover and/or create those identifications (Burke, 1969). This is all created, according to Kenneth Burke (1969), as a way to develop a sense of order. Thus, our motivation to persuade, to create identification, is driven by our desire to create an ordered world. As Burke argues, identification is the key to persuasion, writing, "[W]e must think of rhetoric not in terms of some one particular address, but as a general body of identifications that owe their convincingness much more to trivial repetition and dull daily reënforcement [sic] than to exceptional rhetorical skills" (p. 26). Despite this desire to connect, however, we also constantly encounter division. As Burke argues,

> In pure identification there would be no strife. Likewise, there would be no strife in absolute separateness, since opponents can join battle only through a mediatory ground that makes their communication possible, thus providing the first condition necessary for their interchange of blows. But put identification and division ambiguously together, so that you cannot know for certain just where one ends and the other begins, and you have the characteristic invitation to rhetoric. (p. 25)

Thus, we are drawn to look for ways to use symbols to join together.

Burke (1950/1969) turns to the idea of courtship, defined as "the use of suasive devices for the transcending of social estrangement" (p. 208), to bridge this gap. It is what he terms "mystery"—the division between people—that leaves us with a sense of unease and draws us to look for ways to overcome the estrangement. Courtship is typically imagined to be persuasive action between love interests for the purposes of romantically winning someone over. In this case, however, Burke is imagining differences between classes in his examples—the division that comes about through social differences. Paradoxically, Burke's idea of mystery places a certain amount of power with the individual who remains mysterious—the person who benefits from the separation. As Ramage, Callaway, Clary-Lemon, and Waggoner (2009) explain, "This 'courted' audience thus yearns to transcend the gap of social estrangement to unite with the persuader, while the persuader 'coyly' maintains that distance and thus captivation and power" (p. 201). Consequently, we find a way to court the other person, to smooth over that divide, to soothe that sense of unease, while also attempting to maintain a sense of mystery or control.

Courtship, however, requires a certain amount of risk. As Szczesiul (2007) argues, the site of hospitality is the "threshold between differences, the site at which boundaries are both crossed and maintained" (p. 138). In practice, the guest is not always raised to the level of the host, meaning that the ethics and the practice of hospitality often differ. These politics of hospitality influence how we define the threshold and "negotiate borders between ourselves and those we deem foreign or strange" (Szczesiul, 2007, p. 139). True hospitality is about risk, because if we welcome only those we know, or those who are like us, it is not hospitality.

That balance between the known and the unknown, comfort and mystery, identification and division is clearly evident in the idea of Southern hospitality. Dating back to the creation of the Southern colonies, hospitality was an important part of the culture, according to historian Cynthia Kierner (1996). "Southerners were not unique in offering hospitality," she writes, "but their willingness to give sustenance, shelter, and entertainment to all ranks of invited and unexpected guests served practical as well as recreational ends in their rural societies" (pp. 451–52). Given the long distances between households and the lack of inns along the way, it was often a forced need to provide hospitality in the South.

On a basic level, then, Southern hospitality is a broad concept that generally involves offers of interpersonal warmth, a feeling of being at home and comfortable, a sense of family and friendship, and the ability to treat people with respect (Hemenway-Forbes, 2007). Southern hospitality has also been an important vehicle for self-definition among Southerners, standing "as an image of regional pride, exceptionalism, and superiority" (Szczesiul, 2007, p.

140) and providing "ideas of home and community, relations with outsiders and strangers, the sense of a distinct regional identity and regional pride, the image of an agrarian lifestyle of leisure, the rise of travel, tourism and hospitality industries in the post-bellum and modern South, and social hierarchies of class, gender and—perhaps most subtly—race" (Szczesiul, 2007, p. 140). This discourse allows the South to define itself in particular ways, in that "The South *is* what the North *is not*, just as the *North* is what the *South* is not" (Szczesiul, 2007, p. 129).

Although hospitality in general is a significant part of the Southern persona, drink plays a large symbolic role. Egerton (1993) explains the importance of food and drink to an understanding of how Southerners attempt to bridge a gap between individuals and define the culture:

> The tradition of hospitality, of serving large quantities of good things to eat to large numbers of hungry people, of sharing food and drink with family and friends and even strangers, proved to be a durable tradition in the South, outliving war and depression and hunger. Hospitality could be extended over an elegant and sumptuous dinner, an intimate private party, a picnic for the multitude, or a simple meal of cornbread and beans. It had as much to do with table talk as it did with the food, though the talk would often be about the food itself, or about great meals of the past, or great ones still to come. (p. 38)

Of course, some types of hospitality could only be extended by people who had the means to do so, because entertaining on a grand scale takes a certain level of understanding, time, and wealth to extend. Still, one of the markers of Southern hospitality in general is that it knows no class barriers, such that if the offerings are meager, they might have even more meaning on the part of the host. Despite "class status" then, Southerners often find a way to send this message of hospitality to others, acting as a "threshold symbol" and inviting others in.

It is important to recognize hospitality as a discourse, with the potential for creating a sense of inclusion, but also exclusion. Southern hospitality functions as a "meaning-making story" that is told and retold in the South and beyond, reaching mythic dimensions, even though the actual practices upon which the myth is based went out of fashion as early as 1800 (Szczesiul, 2007). Gray (2002) contends that Southern hospitality is not "fake" but "fictive" in the sense of it needing to be discursively maintained, the process imbuing the South with a particular character. Thus, the region is contrasted often with "northern reserve, aloofness, or haughtiness—a general lack of hospitality" but as such becomes a single South divorced from the history of slavery (Szczesiul, 2007, p. 130). Further, because Southern hospitality is in many ways performative, not necessarily associated with original practices, its expression may not be genuine, instead serving as "a masquerade, an agreed-on social fiction, albeit a powerful one with material effects" (McPherson, 2003, p. 150). A performance based on insincere, surface-level emotions, for example, might help reinforce the genteel Old South mystique of "moonlight, magnolias, and manners," where, instead of breaking down some barriers and making a more welcoming environment, race, class, religion, gender, and other divisions are left purposefully intact (McPherson, 2003, p. 150). Thus, Southern hospitality, although it does much to create connections between people, comes with its own set of limitations; it can be accused of being superficial.

Whether read as a false or sincere performance (and noting the concept's limitations), hospitality has served several functions historically. First, opening up one's home, inviting in guests, and offering up food and drink is a way to display wealth and to show social dominance. Hosting became "an indicator of wealth and cultural attainment" (Kierner, 1996, p. 452). Not unlike Burke's (1950/1969) idea of the negative side of courtship—where it both brings people together and separates them—hospitality has the potential to separate the receiver from the giver. A second performative aspect is allowing a public display of Christian virtue. Many Southerners "regarded it as the duty of men and women to offer food and shelter to those in need and as the responsibility of elites, in particular, to assist their community's less fortunate members" (Kierner, 1996, p. 455). Thus, generous offerings can be interpreted as symbolic ways to enact a felt Christian obligation to care for others. Given the importance of religion to the South (Thompson, 2013a), it would not be unusual to see signs of this public display of virtue. Finally, gender performance is another aspect that influences our reading of Southern hospitality. Although hosting is not necessarily bound to gender roles, it is certainly a part of the story. As Whitelegg (2005) writes, "Being a good hostess was a central part of southern hospitality and a key component of being a good southern lady" (p. 12). Both male and female Southerners have historically performed this role, but as Kierner points out, men were often the hosts of public events, while women provided the domestic-oriented events. Both used the acts to communicate a message, whether the image of the patriarch or matriarch. Hospitality can speak a number of different messages, then, but not all of them are inclusive.

The promise of Southern hospitality, for example, is not always implemented in practice or is implemented in problematic ways. It may encourage hostility and even violence toward those who may be marginalized or "othered" by the concept. Newman (2000), for example, argues that while certain audiences were being *courted* to see Atlanta as a thriving global city in the 1970s, the focus on the city's "hospitality," particularly during a violent era, served to promote, justify, and secure differences among the city's largely African American inner city residents and its more white suburban dwellers. White Southern hospitality, then, masked the strife within the city while presenting a pretty face to outsiders. Similarly, the discourse of Southern hospitality cultivates behavior at a more micro, individual level. Cohen, Vandello, Puente, and Ratilla (1999) explore the region's relationship with violence, suppressed emotion, and an over-reliance on norms of politeness. Frequently, Southerners are taught to be polite and tread lightly with others in order to act in accordance with these norms. Cohen and colleagues (1999) argue that enacting them masks negativity and keeps parties from working out their differences before it is too late.

Although there are possibilities for the symbolism of drink to play a part in welcoming people, it is also important to note the rhetorical limitations of the symbol as well as the larger concept of hospitality. In theory, the idea of Southern hospitality is inclusive of all people. Southerners pride themselves on being friendly and welcoming, and, in many ways, this is true. Of course, the flipside of inclusion is exclusion. Or, in Burke's (1950/1969) terms, identification also includes division. Southern culture includes a long history of eating, drinking, and "visiting," in Taylor's (1982) words. Southerners place great value on opening up their homes and welcoming individuals in to eat, drink, and socialize. At the same time, that open-door policy is not always extended to all. "In addition to the color barriers imposed by race," Taylor writes, "people of definitely lower social status were not invited to visit, and they did not come" (p. 132). Indeed, Southern hospitality has historically been limited by racial exclusion, often "read" as Southern white hospitality. Although there is nothing inherently raced about hospitality, it did/does take a certain amount of income, a particular space, familiarity with some cultural standards and etiquette, and so on, to make an offering that was/is socially acceptable. Racial lines were some of the hardest to cross with hospitality. There is a difference between front porch hospitality and welcoming people into the home, for example. Architectural barriers were even a part of the design of many plantation estates (Ferris, 2014). Although times have certainly changed in the South, there are still lines of division that are not regularly crossed. Thus, Southern hospitality is sometimes only extended so far. More broadly, however, it serves several rhetorical functions, from inclusion to exclusion, becoming a central part of the Southern identity. Whether it is to welcome a certain group or dismiss other groups, food and drink have continually been a part of that message.

DRINK AS RHETORICAL INVITATION

With the centrality of food and drink to Southern culture established, it is important to examine what these symbols mean. Clearly, one of the primary functions of initial offerings of food and drink is to open up lines of communication; to invite individuals to enter into a conversation; and if only a temporary relationship, to put people at ease in relating to one another. In particular, we argue that food and drink can be used to create a connection, to create a sense of identity and identification, and to perform culture.

Creating a Connection

There is no denying the fact that the cocktail is a significant part of Southern culture. The offering of a drink as a way to welcome visitors into the home is one of the most vivid examples of Southern hospitality. This is the first sign of, as Burke (1950/1969) describes it, the attempt to create a sense of courtship—closing the distance between the visitor and visited. As Wondrich (2007) writes, "A proper drink at the right time—one mixed with care and skill and served in a true spirit of hospitality—is better than any other made thing at giving us the illusion, at least, that we're getting what we want from life. A cat can gaze upon a king, as the proverb goes, and after a Dry Martini or a Sazerac Cocktail or two, we're all cats" (p. 10). In this case, "getting what we want from life" is creating a sense of belonging, of bonding with the host, of creating identification between individuals. There is, of course, the most obvious type of bonding brought on by the effects of the alcohol—creating a sense of relaxation and decreased concern over social estrangement. As Link (2014) explains, once the bourbon or scotch has been flowing for a bit, "there's always a tipping point, a graceful exit of formality before the booze kicks in and leads to long conversations where you make lasting connections with the other guests" (p. 32). The symbol of the drink rhetorically works beyond the physical reaction, then.

The offering of a drink is a way to welcome someone into your home (or whatever is serving as the symbolic home at the time—tailgating tent, reception location, etc.) and provides a symbol of the host. In other words, the chosen drinks of the host speak to that person, providing some insight into who they are and how they view the event and the relationship (more about this later in the chapter). Consequently, the initial offering is, in many ways, a meaningful and symbolic one.

Another rhetorical aspect of the offering of drinks in the South is the communal message that is sent through the sharing of a drink. Wondrich (2007), for example, talks about the change that occurred over time when transitioning from very traditional social drinks such as punch (made in large batches and served in a bowl) to the more individualized cocktail. Punches were traditionally served at social meetings and celebrations, bringing people together around the bowl and encouraging people to "stay a while." As Wondrich writes, "At its peak, the ritual of the Punch bowl was a secular communion, welding a group of fellows together into a temporary sodality whose values superseded all others—or, in plain English, a group of men gathered around a bowl of Punch could be pretty much counted on to see it to the end, come what may" (pp. 66–67). The transition away from punches occurred around the time that America began its industrialization, around the turn of the nineteenth century (Wondrich, 2007). America was becoming a "go-ahead country" and thus individual cocktails meant that there was less of a long-term commitment to the group (Wondrich, 2007, p. 67). Although the drinks changed, the symbolic coming together and enjoying a drink together still remained.

Similar to this shared cocktail experience is the traditional Texas beer hall. The scene of years of weekend and holiday dances, weddings, receptions, parties, and even church services, dance halls in central Texas were lubricated by a generous amount of Lone Star and Shiner beer. With the influx of German and Czech immigrants, the scene, cuisine, and language in the area started to change in the mid-1800s. Gruene Hall, in Gruene, Texas (just north of San Antonio), for example, has gathered Texans together for more than 130 years (see figure 3.3). As McLeod (2010) writes, "Historic dance halls were not invented by the German and Czech immigrants; they were just perfected in the farming communities of Central Texas. Among the rich legacies of these early Texans were sausage, Shiner beer, and barnlike dance halls" (para. 1).

Although the crowds have certainly changed over the years, Wendy was able to experience this scene. On a Sunday, with a free show scheduled to start that evening, an assortment of locals and tourists gathered. Gruene

Figure 3.3 Gruene Hall in Gruene, Texas

Hall offers a very modest bar at the front—only bottles of beer and wine are available. Lone Star, Shiner Bock, Dos Equis, and Corona (as well as some of the standard national beer brands) were available, but Lone Star was, by far, the favorite of the crowd. Beers in hand and finding a spot at one of dozens of worn down picnic tables, some settled in to listen to the band. Others found their way to the dance floor and did their part to smooth the floors that were now butter soft after decades of dancing. Young and old, biker and hipster, rural and urban—all were brought together in this unlikely building in the middle of the Texas hill country. Sitting next to us was a family—a husband and wife and her father. Later, an older couple joined us, asking us to snap their photo. It is not the beer that has helped this dance hall maintain its bustling atmosphere or that created the perfect mingling space, but the drinks are a part of the experience that creates an odd, temporary bond between an eclectic group of people.

As in this case, drinks are ancillary; that is, they are not necessary, but add something special to the moment. Thus, when the host offers and the guest accepts a drink or when two strangers grab a beer and sit down at a shared table, the two are making a commitment to create a temporary bond. Both are committing to spend a certain amount of time together. In general, then, one of the rhetorical functions of drink is creating a connection between people, inviting a relationship, if only temporarily.

Creating connections through alcohol can be particularly complex in the South, however, because of the difficulty for some (often Protestant) to reconcile their religious beliefs with their enjoyment of alcohol. A personal experience illustrates some of this complexity. A new, chic bar opened up in Hattiesburg, Mississippi, a project of the local celebrity chef. The bar, filled with modern furniture and low lighting, sells itself on Southern-inspired craft drinks with inventive ingredients. As we walked into the bar one night, we noticed tables with young couples and a table with what appeared to be a family of two older people and perhaps their adult children and their spouses. As we entered the bar, they were enjoying some wine, but about an hour into the experience, they received food at the table. As the server walked away, the family members joined hands and said a lengthy and audible prayer before beginning their meal. This scenario seemed symbolic of the region, perhaps especially to Wendy, having grown up in a Baptist-dominated small town in Texas; it reflected the complicated history that some parts of the South have with alcohol and religion.

Although religious beliefs are a driving force in the region, and many religious (primarily Southern Baptist) Southerners frown upon alcohol consumption, it has always remained a staple in many Southern households and  restaurants. As John Egerton (1993) writes, "True to its schizophrenic nature, the South somehow managed to lead the nation in bourbon manufacturing, moonshine making, and temperance fervor; even now, some of the region's most famous whiskeys are legally manufactured in counties where their sale is prohibited by law" (p. 30). Social and religious prohibitions against alcohol did not exist until the nineteenth century. Before then, followers of all kinds of religious denominations "imbibed freely and frequently—at barn raisings, sheep shearings, horse races, weddings, even funerals" (Egerton, 1993, p. 202). Thus, the South has had periods of time when alcohol was a fundamental part of the culture, but it has also seen limitations to its use. In fact, restrictions on alcohol sales are still most stringent today in the South (Wheeler, 2012).

Part of the reason that the family's choice to mix religion and drinks struck us as odd, then, was because of their violation of the historical public division between alcohol consumption and religion in some parts of the South. In fact, "sin taxes" (taxes on alcohol) and other restrictive laws that make it difficult for breweries to exist still prevent Southern crafters from flourishing in some states (Pramuk, 2015). While in this situation, alcohol and religion mixed very naturally for that family, there is certainly a history of the South having a complex relationship with alcohol. Although in the

S chizophenic
Nature

bar scenario, the family might not have meant to send a rhetorical message about their personal beliefs, there was a message afoot. There was acceptance in that space at that time for combining two important characteristics of Southern culture—religion and appreciation for food and drink.

Despite this example, there is still a certain amount of shame for some people, even today, in entering a liquor store in small Southern towns. As Miles (2013) writes, "In a region dominated by Baptists, drinking carried, at best, the tinge of scandal, and the risk of eternal damnation, at worst. Gusto was required to overcome that hard-shell resistance; every drink mattered because, well, that drink might actually matter" (p. 72). The biases of the past continue to influence behaviors today. At Southern family get-togethers, it is not unusual to have a closet somewhere in the house or an ice chest in a truck with the hidden alcohol supply for those "in the know." And at public events, flasks and cups designed to mask the true contents of the cup can be commonly seen (although this might also be attributed to open container laws). One person even told us that her mother, afraid that some might question her moral fortitude, never acknowledged having a "church key," used to open beer cans before pulltabs. As Taylor (1982) writes, "In a survey taken in the late 1960s, two-thirds of the southern Protestants questioned stated that they were tee-totalers, and almost half of them favored the restoration of national prohibition. Some of these people, of course, 'vote dry as long as they can stagger to the polls'" (p. 155). In these situations, the consumption of alcohol might undermine the person's religious and cultural identification, threatening their social standing, or at least other people's understanding of that person. Additionally, the continued existence of "blue laws" (laws restricting the sale of alcohol on Sundays) is a noteworthy example of the lingering signs of the struggles that the region has with its understanding of alcohol. Thus, the significance of religion and its historical rejection of alcohol still has some influence over the way drinks are "read" by others in the South. Cocktails can unite, but they can also sometimes divide.

Identity

The offering and selection of drinks can also communicate something about individuals, even when unintentional or misread. This initial message about identity, although surface level, becomes a part of the courtship because it appears to say something about the person. For example, offering or choosing a local beer might be due to taste or could signal a sense of pride of place. Texans might select a Lone Star or Shiner beer to signal their state loyalty.

The offering of an expensive bourbon has the potential to speak to the person making the offer as well as the way that person perceives the other.

Bourbon, in particular, offers a rhetorically rich Southern drink example. McKeithan (2012) talks about the ways that the symbolism of bourbon changed over the years. In the beginning, it was a sign of basic Southernness—a connection to the region. It was a drink that the "common man" would enjoy. At that time, moneyed Southerners might turn to European imports such as scotch or cognac to emphasize their wealth and their separation from the "common man." Today, however, bourbon has experienced a renaissance, with a wide selection of fine varieties manufactured and savored in the South. To know your bourbons is to show your Southern authenticity. And, in this case, "bourbon remains a piece of masculine identity that southerners can 'put on,' much like overalls, a seersucker suit, or a North Carolina twang" (McKeithan, p. 8).

Aside from the public side of drink choice, consumption of the drink can also affect identity by emphasizing particular connections. As McKeithan (2012) points out,

> "Knocking it back neat" serves a transportive function, immersing the Bourbon drinker in the rich cultural imagery of the American South: woody, sunny, and romantic. The hot bite of the Bourbon sensuously connects the body of the drinker to nation, region, and locale, enjoining his experience with those of imagined, historical bodies, soaking up space and place in the slow burn of what appears to be an endless southern summertime. (p. 6)

It may be unusual to ascribe so much meaning to a drink, but the visceral connection that bourbon in particular creates serves as a strong example of this kind of rhetorical force.

On a recent trip through Kentucky, Wendy experienced firsthand how a drink can be so connected to place. Traveling the "bourbon trail" in the middle of Kentucky, our three-day excursion allowed for tours of five different distilleries. Although each was different in some ways, themes emerged from hearing the stories of each of the distilleries and products. Through each of the tours, there was a strong emphasis on the region. Although bourbon does not have to be made in Kentucky, almost 95 percent of it is because of the unique qualities of the land ("What Is Bourbon Anyway?" 2013). Kentucky bourbon calls forth the unique water flavor found in Kentucky, a taste that is created by the state's limestone. Most of the distilleries use corn and rye

Interesting

Figure 3.4 Bourbon barrels at Buffalo Trace Distillery, Frankfort, Kentucky

Regional

Familiar

that have been grown in Kentucky, in many cases just a few miles away from the distillery. Many of the casks for the bourbon are created by hand in the state's small towns. The rickhouses—the warehouses that store the barrels while the bourbon is aging—are historical sites at many of the distilleries, with some dating back to the late 1800s (see figure 3.4). The distinct four seasons that can be found in Kentucky also play a vital role in creating the bourbon. Aside from the ingredients, the makers and distributors also tie the drink to the region. Most of the master distillers at the major companies have connections to the same families. On our tour through the Jim Beam distillery—the largest distributor of bourbon in the world—our tour guide, for example, was from the Beam family. All of the distillery guides, though, expressed pride in the Kentucky product, describing how important the production was to the community.

Whether it is an offering of bourbon, beer, or sweet tea, the choice has the potential to speak to identity and how individuals perceive the situation, as well as help to build a group identity. Terry tells the story of post-Katrina Hattiesburg, Mississippi, for example, and the emergence of the "grapefruit something" as a drink. Using the ingredients that he had available, his creation became a shared drink experience, with people (in some cases) escaping their storm-damaged homes to join together, share stories, and sip on a drink. He still gets requests for that drink, with bar goers remembering the circumstances of the "grapefruit something." Although that experience—and the accompanying drink—might only be one small part of an identity that they embrace, that drink can be a part of that story is noteworthy.

Performing Culture

Another rhetorical aspect of cocktails is found in the creation of particular drinks. Although not all Southern-created drinks call for such elaborate steps, many of them are defined by the performance of the creation. In this case, knowing how to make particular drinks becomes a performance of culture. That is, the creator must be familiar with the history of the mixture and know something about what the culture expects out of the creation.

One example of this type of culturally significant drink is the Sazerac. The history, described earlier in the chapter, only tells a part of the story of the drink. To see a Sazerac being created in a traditional New Orleans bar, for example, seems to instantly connect you to a regional history. The Sazerac Bar, now located within New Orleans's Roosevelt Hotel, but originally located on Royal Street, has a proud history of creating traditional Southern cocktails and has been called the "drink's cradle and headquarters" (Wondrich, 2007, p. 200). On a recent visit to the bar, Ashli ordered a Sazerac and then sat back to watch the creation. The bartender pulled out two squat glasses, chilling one by filling it with ice and saving one for the main ingredients. Pouring in Sazerac brand rye whiskey, Peychaud's Bitters (the local creation mentioned earlier), and some simple syrup, the bartender then set that glass aside to pick up the other, toss out the ice, and dash some Herbsaint (a modern variation of absinthe) in the chilled glass, swirling it around, and tossing out the remnants. He then strained the contents from the first glass into the chilled glass and topped it off with a twist of lemon. We were told that the bartenders go through extensive training before they start mixing the drinks, and a historical understanding of the drinks seems to be a part of the training.

Similarly, the Ramos Gin Fizz has a long history in New Orleans (see figure 3.5). Henry Ramos, a saloon owner in New Orleans, is said to have created this drink in the late 1880s. The recipe was closely guarded for many years, and people "flocked in droves to down the frothy draft" (Egerton, 1993, p. 212). The creation of this drink is just as storied as the Sazerac. Because it is a frothy drink, it requires a great deal of hands-on time. As Egerton describes the historical creation of the drink, "The corps of busy shaker boys behind

Figure 3.5 Bartender making a Ramos Gin Fizz at the Sazerac Bar, New Orleans, Louisiana

the bar was one of the sights of the town during Carnival, and in the 1915 Mardi Gras, 35 shaker boys nearly shook their arms off, but were still unable to keep up with the demand" (p. 212). Again, in the Sazerac Bar, Wendy ordered a Ramos Gin Fizz and watched as the bartender crafted the drink. He chilled one glass while mixing the ingredients for the drink in a metal shaker. Gin, simple syrup, and lemon and lime juice went in first before adding in egg whites, heavy cream, and orange flower water. The key then is to shake the ingredients until they become extremely fizzy, and our bartender did not disappoint us with his shaking skills. After adding a little soda water to the chilled glass the bartender then did a high pour from the shaker (lifting it up several inches from the glass) and topped it off with a little more soda water before presenting it with a flourish.

Although the performances may change slightly, the recipe and the general assembly of the drink prohibit too many changes. The drinks themselves become an enactment of culture, requiring the maker to be familiar with the historical drink, to locate the ingredients, and to be able to craft the drink in the way that others have done for years. Additionally, the performance invites communication about the history of the drink and, thus, the culture. As we argue in chapter one, the making of certain recipes can be a performance that helps to create or reinforce a particular identity. In this case, the drinks form a symbolic connection to the past and the culture.

All three examples of how cocktails serve a rhetorical function help to explain the role that drink might have in communicating a particular message. In this case, drink can serve the purpose of creating a message of hospitality, thus opening up lines of communication.

CONCLUSION

Although the Southern relationship with drinking is complex, it remains a significant part of the food and drink story of the region and certainly a part of the hospitality aspect of the South. Miles (2013) writes that "where Southerners differ—and where they excel—is in *how* they drink: zealously, ebulliently, loquaciously, impiously. One could lay reasonable credit to the environment, I suppose: When it's 98 degrees outside, a drink is not merely a drink, it's the sensate equivalent of a winning lottery ticket" (p. 72). Whether it is a mint julep, a Shiner Bock, a Coca-Cola, or a sweet tea, the symbolism of offering a drink in the region means something noteworthy.

The larger argument that we make is that food—and Southern food in particular—can act rhetorically. Although food and drink are often accompanied by other discourse that frames the message, they can also communicate a message on their own. In the case of drinks in the South, the message of hospitality and identity is complex. Not only do offerings of drinks send an initial message of welcoming and serve to connect people in the face of separation, but they also say something about regional identity. As an opening to the communication act, then, the first offering of a symbolic welcome through the drink can set a particular tone. The drink breaks the barriers set up by alienation, allowing courtship, or bringing people together, to take place. Whether through the chemical effects of lowering inhibitions or merely the gesture of sharing, this offering invites conversation, and that invitation, in turn, can serve to bring people closer together.

The offering is even more meaningful, however, when it underscores a sense of shared history through ritualistic performances of the creation of the drink or drinks that are *of* the region. This is partially because the drink can serve as a symbol of the identity of the host, emphasizing his or her likes and dislikes, regional affiliation, class, gender, and so forth. What we choose to serve can be read as a rhetorical message about the host. The performative nature of some drinks confirms that identity even more if its creation requires a certain amount of understanding of its history and/or the steps in creating it. Making a Sazerac at home, for example, most likely requires someone to have read about or witnessed the creation of the drink. Thus, the performance of the cocktail feeds into a larger history of drink creation in the South.

Although Southern hospitality is a regional identifier, there is also the flip side of hospitality in the form of division and limits, as we have emphasized. Offerings of food and drink are limited in their ability to overcome a sense of estrangement, for example. "Front porch hospitality"—the idea that Southerners create a sense of welcoming right from their porch—is both a symbol of openness (opening up the front of the house to all) and a limitation (inviting people only as far as the porch and keeping them out of the "heart" of the house). As Beckham (1989) writes, "Southern porches have traditionally been transition spaces between indoors and out where marginally welcomed guests could be entertained without violating the sanctity of the home. The races could comingle when necessary or desirable . . . Much of the Southern reputation for southern hospitality must emanate from the ubiquitous porch" (p. 515). Thus, not only does the offering of food and drink speak, but the location of that offering is also a factor in its interpretation.

Offerings can also lead to rejections. An offering of beer might be rejected by someone who eschews alcohol for health or religious reasons. In that case, the estrangement has to be overcome in other ways. It is also important to account for food's role in communicating hospitality. Because the offering of food can be such an important symbol in the South, it is often difficult to reject it. A specially baked cake, a slow-cooked brisket, or a jar of preserves might be a particularly meaningful symbol of the Southern host's identity or the perceived relationship between the giver and receiver. For example, Wendy doesn't eat red meat, which often made for uncomfortable moments at many of our stops since she was conflicted over whether to smile and accept the offering of meat or to politely refuse the hospitality. One stop in particular, though, put her in the awkward position of having the host offer up every type of meat on the menu. Although Ashli frantically agreed to sample all the meat on the table (while we were left alone), we both knew that the symbolic offering of the host's family recipes meant that a rejection of the offering would be very symbolic. Food also offers particularly poignant performative moments. Recreating a beloved family dish for the first time connects generations. Creating a dish from an old cookbook or using a recipe that has strong connections to the region allows an individual to enact his or her Southernism. The offering of that dish, then, can be an enactment of a regional belonging or attempt to identify with a region, and the hospitality becomes even more symbolic.

In the end, the idea of Southern hospitality is certainly flawed, but there is no denying that the offering of food and drink—especially in the South—is filled with rhetorical meaning. When Ashli first moved to Charlotte, her new neighbor knocked on her door, bringing in a basket of chicken salad, fruit salad, pimento cheese sandwiches, and a gallon of sweet tea. That the offering came from Harris Teeter, the regional grocery store, did not lessen its meaning, providing sustenance as she painted and cleaned; more importantly, it made her feel welcome and comfortable despite knowing no one in the city. The following week, when the same older couple mixed gin and tonics on their patio and shared stories of neighborhood antics they had seen in their 40 years there, Ashli knew they were in the right place. The drinks and cocktail nibbles said come in, stay a while, get to know us. When those neighbors moved recently into a retirement home, Ashli and her daughter brought over homemade chocolate chip cookies to the new family. The people were different, but the message was the same. Welcome.

With the opening of the door through the offering of food and drink, it then becomes possible to continue the conversation over the rest of the meal. The next chapter will move beyond the initial rhetorical meaning of the meal and delve more specifically into how food speaks a certain message.

CHAPTER FOUR

TURF TUSSLE

Uniting through North Carolina Barbecue

Last summer, I (Ashli) had two disappointing barbecue meals. To my astonishment, I simply didn't enjoy my beloved barbecue at two very famous restaurants in Tennessee and Alabama. The more I thought about it, the more puzzled I became. The patrons around me clearly enjoyed their meals. The quality of the pork was good. The prices were right. The answer finally dawned on me once I went back out for barbecue in my home state of North Carolina. Nine months pregnant, I left Lexington's Honeymonk's stuffed and happy, with more barbecue to go and my sweet tea freshly refilled. It occurred to me that what I had eaten elsewhere simply wasn't "my" barbecue. The sauce was different; it was too sweet, too thick, and overwhelming. The bread was wrong; instead of coming on a plain white squishy hamburger bun, this white (still squishy) bread had crusts. The meat was not pulled enough, so the texture seemed off, with dense pieces of meat in every bite. It was too smoky. And why wasn't the slaw red? As I drove off with my bag of goodies, munching all the way back to Charlotte, I had my barbecue epiphany. I could speak the code of "Q" well enough to know that unless it was western North Carolina barbecue, it just wasn't "true" barbecue to my childhood-conditioned palate. I knew just enough to speak the language of barbecue, and I could now hold forth with true believers and heretics alike about why western Carolina has the best. As I later argued about it with a dyed-in-the-wool Memphis-style fan, it became clear that we had more in common than our appreciation for smoked pork. When we North Carolinians debate the merits of eastern or western barbecue, and Memphis fans argue with South Carolina natives, we all still find common ground enjoying pork on a plate. As we square off, our porcine preferences form a bizarre type of communion.

Schizophrenic Nature??

We become united, identified, by our love of pork and barbecue culture in the South.

More than a meal, barbecue is a celebratory culture with a long history and ongoing expression in the region. This is one food tradition that "makes the South the South," so much so that "to be a Southerner is to love barbecue with very few exceptions" (Auchmutey, 2007, pp. 22, 5). Of course, not all Southerners enjoy traditional barbecue, so they revise it to better reflect their lifestyles (vegan, kosher, etc.), but barbecue remains a three-hundred-year-old cultural tradition (Moss, 2010; Reed & Reed, 2008; Veteto & Maclin, 2011). Outside of joints ("restaurants" is too formal), barbecues are still held to celebrate football season, to serve as church fundraisers, and to rally the politically faithful. This storied tradition continues to bring different groups of the population together: "to 'cook a pig' in the South has always implied a special occasion, a gathering of the community" (Pollan, 2013, p. 46). Barbecue remains a distinctive culinary event where people linger around a pit or cooker for hours; as one observer puts it, "I've never seen a crowd gather around an oven to watch a cake bake" (Pollan, 2013, p. 84; Sampson, 2007). Today, travelers to the region can experience barbecue and participate in the local culture, with barbecue offering "a sense of place and history that you could taste" (Pollan, 2013, p. 46). Traditionalists argue that competitions, television shows, and chain restaurants dilute the spirit of the barbecue craft. The cuisine has been written about endlessly. Still, there is something important left to say. Barbecue is "good to think," providing insight into regional identity, authenticity, and consubstantiality (Veteto & Maclin, 2011, p. 20).

Barbecue is cultural synecdoche; indeed, it is difficult to overstate the importance of the food in the South's culture because it sends rhetorical messages about Southern history, gender, race, class, ritual, fellowship, "belongingness," and nostalgia (Egerton, 1990; Fertel, 2011). In this chapter, then, we do not add to the history of barbecue, weigh the merits of various cooking styles, or crown one region as king of the cuisine. Instead, we argue that barbecue tells stories that simultaneously shape and express contemporary Southern identity. Someone might write about fried chicken or other popular Southern entrees, but when she declares a style the "right" kind of barbecue, she immediately speaks to her background, upbringing, and expectations; in other words, she tells you a lot about her identity as a Southerner. All cultures have foods intimately tied to them, but barbecue speaks loudly: "Barbecue . . . is coded with insights about the nature of relationships among all who participate in this immensely social, inclusive food event" (Nolan, 2011, p. 54). If Southern food helps shape identity, barbecue provides a perfect example

Individuality w/ the collective

of this process, because its rhetoric and ritual incite profound identification with regional styles, leaving those who do not appreciate a particular variant to champion their own. Tussling about which barbecue is best engages identity-forming behavior that serves a purpose in gradually knitting groups of people together over their shared love of a particular food tradition. We contend that Southern food generally serves a rhetorical purpose, but pork is powerful, and when building community in the South, "barbecue is the food with arguably the greatest potential to do that" (Boorstein, 2004, p. 7; Fertel, 2011; Smith, 1984, p. 209). Even as people insist that *their* barbecue is the *only* barbecue, their playful barbecue boasting binds the Southern diaspora together; and as patrons wage rhetorical war, the South is drawn together by this most essential entrée.

Whereas in other chapters we have looked at broad categories and regions of Southern food, here, North Carolina barbecue is an appropriate "text" for study because lots of North Carolinians eat it, with those who do not still surrounded by its culture. We first contextualize North Carolina barbecue, because what counts is interpreted differently throughout regions of the state. Then, by exploring how barbecue conveys identificatory messages of authenticity, masculinity, and rurality, we show how it stretches casuistically, adapting and changing, to still be descriptive of the South's character. We rely on the notion of casuistry because barbecue manages to keep its familiar essence while subtly incorporating different contexts and expectations. We draw on these frameworks to go on a sensory tour of the state's traditional barbecue joints, contemporary festivals and competition circuits, and new restaurant interpretations, comparing the types of identities that are expressed along the way and exploring what they mean in understanding the nature of the South today. More are admitted to the fold as knowledge and appreciation of barbecue grow throughout the South and around the country with the various expressions of barbecue helping to explain how traditional Southern entrees in general may stretch their meaning (through different reparation/cooks/audiences), and still invite people to come together and find common ground through food. Throughout its history barbecue has provided a place for Southerners at a (perhaps fitfully) shared table, and today's barbecue encourages lots of different people to find a seat.

ANSWERING THE RHETORICALLY FRAUGHT QUESTION: "WHAT IS NORTH CAROLINA BARBECUE?"

North Carolinians will tell you, first off, that barbecue is a noun, not a verb. It is something you eat, not do. Beyond this broad definition, interpretations splinter. In trying to offer a succinct description, one pitmaster suggested that barbecue was "the mystic communion among fire, smoke, and meat in the total absence of water" (Pollan, 2013, p. 67). For many North Carolinians, though, barbecue means pork; indeed, "nowhere is the love of slow-cooked pork, smoked for half a day over chips of oak and hickory, greater than in the state of North Carolina" (Buncombe, 2005). North Carolinians' tendency to mean pork when they say barbecue descends from several historical traditions. Historians note that slaves, who had watched Caribbean Indians cooking over fire, brought the barbecue tradition to the region in the 1800s. In the South, pigs were cheaper to raise than cattle and became dominant, so much so that "meat and pork are synonymous in the south" (Pollan, 2013, p. 46).

Although other Southern states have entrenched barbecue traditions, North Carolina's developed in a way that smoked pork became favored by individuals both black and white, rich and poor. Barbecue remains a "democratic" meal available to most, with the typical cost of a barbecue sandwich less than a McDonald's Big Mac (Pollan, 2013). Georgia, Virginia, and South Carolina had more aristocratic histories but North Carolina's comparative lack of a planter class made barbecue a signature food, with agreed upon "good" barbecue places visited by all, even before passage of the Civil Rights Act. Of course, the South's troubled history prevents any claims that barbecue traditions are untouched by racism. Barbecuing was another African and Native American technique adapted to plantation life (Opie, 2008), and enslaved people were made to work the pits, with Warnes (2008) contending that "barbecue symbolizes America's record of savagery and oppression" before the Civil War (in Browning, 2014, p. 10). Serving as one of the strongest contributors of the false "moonlight and magnolias" image of slavery and the South (remember the barbecue scene in *Gone with the Wind*?), planation-wide barbecues were in reality "safety valves" that served as means of slave control (Moss, 2010). Indeed, barbecues were not held for relaxation during the antebellum period but functioned as incentives for collaborative work needed during the busy harvest season (Moss, 2010). Though the bringing in and harvesting of various crops did provide occasion for blacks and whites to work and eat together, barbecues were frequently segregated, with long tables laid out side by side for each race, enslaved black men serving as the cooks (Harris, 2011). After the Civil War and the great migration of blacks to the North, barbecues became some of the most important social events for African Americans (Moss, 2010).

Even today, the legacy of the tradition's racist elements persists, and scholars continue to debate barbecue's role in racial reconciliation. You still hear that the "best pitmen were black," for example, and until recently, some called black pitmasters "pit boys" (Pollan, 2013, p. 47). Others contend that barbecue restaurants are less segregated than other parts of Southern society, with those types of restaurants frequently being more integrated than neighborhoods or places of worship (Pollan, 2013). Even Warnes (2008), with his condemnation of the racial history of barbecue, grants that today's practice of the tradition can serve as an equalizer, going so far as to call barbecue "color-blind," and a "post-racial cultural practice in which cultural fusions and connections continue to occur even in situations of acute racial division" (in Browning, 2014, p. 11). Optimistic observers claim that barbecue "drifts across class and racial distinctions like the sweet vapors over hickory embers" (Auchmutey, 2007, p. 22) and helps bridge "deep racial divides" (Veteto & Maclin, 2011, p. 4). We remain cautious, however. Edge warns that we need to be careful that the "back door" patronage of whites to black-owned establishments in early parts of our history might be better understood as a "culinary equivalent of a booty call . . . less of a cultural product and more as an ephemeral indulgence, entered into lightly, exited from easily" (in Veteto & Maclin, 2011, p. 44).

The issue of race and barbecue, then, remains complex. If the historical and cultural legacy of barbecue is complex, so is its culinary execution in North Carolina. Americans typically think of heavily smoked meat and sweet sauce when they think of barbecue, but North Carolina's version is idiosyncratic. Like other Southern barbecue traditions, North Carolina's typically starts with pork, fire, and smoke, but what happens in each microregion of the state varies greatly. The basic facts of North Carolina barbecue are these: there is eastern or western North Carolina barbecue, with an imaginary "gnat line" dividing how the meat is prepared in the region of sandy soils of the east from the rockier soils of the west (Franzia, 2005). Reed (2004) likens this intense regional variation to that of Europe: "Southern barbecue is the closest thing we have in the U.S. to Europe's wines or cheeses; drive a hundred miles and the barbecue changes" (p. 78). Eastern barbecue tends to be a bit less smoky and is sauced with a thin vinegar and red chile pepper sauce; western has a bit more smoke, and sometimes its similar vinegar-based sauce may include a bit of ketchup or tomato. Garner (1996) calls the differences between the regional sauces "a distinction in search of a difference," and laughs, "That's it. That's the big difference all the shouting and arguing is about" (p. 25). What might seem to be minor variations on a general theme calls forth fierce loyalty. Western aficionados, for example, decry the east's version of barbecue as too mild, preferring the smoke and spice afforded by their preparation method. Easterners rebut that western and other barbecue variations distract from the taste of the smoked pork, arguing, for example: 'To me, the difference between these versions and real [eastern], traditional [N]orth Carolina barbecue is much like the difference between a woman masked by makeup and a lovely, fresh-faced young girl" (Garner, 1996, p. 39).

Despite these arguments, "enthusing about 'that great barbecue place' is one of the honest pleasures of life in North Carolina" (Garner, 1996, p. xxvi). Barbecue's humble roots and complex history, in particular, may allow patrons to sit down together, argue a bit, and learn about each other as they indulge in their favorite North Carolina barbecue style.

BURKE AND "TURF"—IDENTIFICATION THROUGH DIVISION

Burke (1973) helps shed light on how worshipping at a particular church of barbecue draws you into a broader community of fellow parishioners. His take on identification through division, along with the idea of casuistic stretching, is useful in understanding how identification with particular foodways works generally, as well as in specific cases such as barbecue; after all, "no other foodstuff has contributed more to the formation and delineation of diverse Southern identities" (Veteto & Maclin, 2011, p. 5).

As we have discussed previously, identification moves away from explicit forms of persuasion to broader, subtler forms of connection like those forged through food. We may have physiological natures that prevent us from fully understanding each other, but food is one material substance used to create, maintain, and solidify social relationships (Mintz & Dubois, 2002). Two people may identify simply by some principle they share, identifying with another by thinking that they also belong to a particular group or appreciate a certain idea or object, connecting through congregation. But, as Burke (1973) and Carlson (1992) point out, congregation and segregation go hand in hand, with division serving as a type of invitation to social action, making it difficult to know when division ends and congregation begins. When we join a congregation, for example, we imply that we differentiate, or segregate, from something else. In fact, in order to identify with someone, you must divide from someone else: "Identification is affirmed with earnestness precisely because there is division. Identification is compensatory to division" (Burke, 1973, p. 267). Burke (1973) argues that saying what we are "against" also helps establish identification, especially if enough people agree with us. This identification through antithesis is the "most urgent" form and "clearest instance" of congregation by segregation, whereby union occurs by some shared opposition (Burke, 1973, p. 268). Understanding these types of identification allows us to see deeper into the rhetorical situation, because we better understand the "integrating force" of external foes (Burke, 1973, p. 269). As such, using identification as a lens allows investigation into how different "sides" of an argument may find resolution, such that we find a way to understand the rhetorical significance of "the state of (barbecue) Babel after the Fall" (Burke, 1950/1969, p. 23).

Indeed, identification forms a supportive structure so that we can be divided from one another over our disagreement about which barbecue region is "better" or "more authentic," yet still come together over the overall importance we place on barbecue in the Southern food canon. In fact, Reed (2004) suggests that Southerners should unite under a flag with a dancing pig and fork and avoid the connotations of hate symbolized by the Confederate flag. Although barbecue "pits community against community" these disagreements "reflect and reinforce the fierce localism that has always been a Southern characteristic, the 'sense of place' that literary folk claim to find in Southern fiction" (Reed & Reed, 2004, p. 82). Despite regional differences, then, barbecue is the thing that unites Southerners against "outside forces" (Veteto & Maclin, 2011). And, in the case of North Carolina, debates about barbecue are not just stylistic; "they are fundamental to the identity formation, providing us with a way to bond over saying 'to heck with what outsiders think'" (Garner, 1996, p. 18; Veteto & Maclin, 2011, p. 5). We thus have the potential to become consubstantial, fully identified with each other over this substance, and as a result, continue to fortify identification as we unite against those outsiders who believe "that barbecue is what you do with hamburgers and hot dogs on the grill" (Leeman, 2014). Southerners may frequently reinforce their community by emphasizing the differences from their approach to barbecue from outsiders; similarly, outsiders may derive knowing satisfaction from mocking or "otherizing" those who become so vehemently protective of a regional foodstuff (Veteto & Maclin, 2011). As Scott and Rushing (2014) write, "Southerners love barbecue, but the 'tenaciously regional' methods of preparation and flavor profiles create allegiances and animosity within the region itself. A southerner can tell you which barbecue he/she prefers, and more importantly, why. Given the local differences in the final product, talking about barbecue might be more 'southern' than the barbecue itself" (p. 150).

The intense loyalty to particular barbecue traditions provides a lens into understanding how we use exclusion to knit those closer to us more forcefully, particularly in a still ostracized and stereotyped South. Because we exclude those who do not share our appreciation for a type of barbecue, we exalt those of us in the inner circle. That is, those who appreciate "correct" barbecue form part of a group of people who "get it" (vinegar and all). In the case of North Carolinians, barbecue boasting serves to "buck up" against a culture that has "sometimes been characterized as impoverished and unsophisticated by mainstream America" (Garner, 1996, p. 18). Much like an inside joke in a sitcom, regional barbecue lovers are made to feel connected because they understand a tradition's appeal. Sometimes this "inclusion through exclusion" is problematic, as when restaurateur Maurice Bessinger flew the Confederate flag at his Piggie Park barbecue eateries throughout South Carolina. In other instances, rhetorical exclusion serves a more positive identificatory purpose. Southerners who come from the towns "outsiders" sometimes mock, for example, might find a reason to feel pride, as "rating barbecue is all tied up in traditional values and pride of place—as well as a sort of reverse snobbery . . . the best barbecue will probably be found in or near one's own hometown" (Garner, 1996, p. 17). Interestingly, though, those who come to love barbecue as adults or who are from nonrural traditions may still find consubstantiation with those for whom small-town barbecue is a way of life. As Garner (1996) explains, "suburbanites who discover barbecue later in life have the pleasure of choosing from among various ready-made, secondhand rural identities. Settling on a favorite style of barbecue can be as much fun as dressing up in boots and a cowboy hat or developing a Southern drawl" (p. 18). Identification by antithesis seems to allow this flexibility, in that as long as a newcomer shares contempt for the style scorned by those "in the know," they become part of that particular barbecue community. This search for the ultimate rural barbecue tradition can make for some seemingly strange bedfellows at a local barbecue joint, with young hipsters decked out in plaid shirts and skinny jeans discussing the virtues of pit styles with the Carhartt old timers who've been eating this way for decades. Nevertheless, both share in the pleasure of understanding "their" style.

Being able to try on barbecue identities to see which one best fits also provides the opportunity to understand how casuistic stretching is connected to identification. Burke (1984) describes casuistic stretching as "introducing new principles while theoretically remaining faithful to old principles," a process of "removing terms from an accepted context and moving them into new territory" (Carlson, 1992, p. 21). It is through these metaphorical extensions that language stretches a particular frame of reference, with the new context "borrowing" respectability from the established context, such that city folks can become part of the rural barbecue tradition, women can become famous pitmasters, and immigrants can adapt the cuisine to fit their home cultures (Carlson, 1992). Casuistic stretching is at work in to-day's barbecue culture in at least two ways. First, by allowing those who did not grow up with a certain type of barbecue into the fan club, we become consubstantial with those who self-identify with barbecue culture; second, by granting that notions of traditional North Carolina (and other) barbecue can stretch and still be called barbecue, we allow these new expressions to further draw in new and different audiences, restarting the identification process. In this way, we use barbecue as the example of how (and whether) perceptions of traditional Southern food can stretch to broaden and deepen (and make more inclusive) the narrative about Southern food (Burke, 1984). From a rhetorical standpoint, it matters less if barbecue or other traditionally Southern entrees become less "authentic" as they are enjoyed by more people and in different iterations; instead, what matters is that people are drawn in to *talk* about the barbecue with each other. Similarly, it does not matter if the ongoing use of down-home imagery used in barbecue culture is no longer authentic; what matters is that it may put people at ease, so they will open up in today's fast-paced, disconnected world. A barbecue joint's folksy nostalgia invites people to let down their guard, relax, and perhaps strike up a conversation. What we seek, then, is to see how barbecue remains relevant without becoming something else entirely and losing the soul of its original greatness. So we set off across North Carolina to test our theory.

CONGREGATION AND SEGREGATION THROUGH RHETORICAL AUTHENTICITY, MASCULINITY, AND RURALITY

As we traveled through North Carolina, we found that barbecue invites peo-ple to identify through three rhetorical themes: authenticity, masculinity, and rurality. To varying degrees, these themes worked either to knit people more tightly together by showing them how they were unique or simply opened the doors wide, inviting all who entered to connect on the basis of their appreciation for the North Carolina barbecue tradition. Rhetorical congregation was clearly evident and held invitational possibilities, using themes of authenticity and rurality to send messages of accessibility and comfort, while barbecue's macho legacy complicated connectivity in its modern interpretation on the barbecue circuit.

Authenticity

Food and travel writing's endless debate about which barbecue is most authentic may drive readership, but often it does not account for the rhetorical power embedded in these claims. The difficulty with authenticity arguments is that they do not turn on the basis of facts or evidence, such as which documented form of barbecue is the oldest, but they have an emotional, individual quality, whereby what can be most authentic to someone is likely what they first experienced or ate as a child. One way to consider authenticity, then, is as a rhetorical device that invites connection through remembrance. As Mississippi chef John Currence explains, "authenticity" for native Southerners can mean foods of their childhoods. This tendency applies especially when talking about barbecue, because "everybody has an opinion on what barbecue is supposed to taste like. It tastes like what you originally tried in the beginning when somebody told you that was barbecue, so you compare everything to that taste" (*Richmond Times Dispatch*, 2008, p. 1). Ashli's experience this past summer illuminates the tricky nature of authenticity claims: "authentic" barbecue for her is sneered at elsewhere, as fans from different traditions decry the vinegar with which one area insults great pork. As a result, Pollan (2013) argues that the ongoing debate about "the most authentic barbecue" or the quest for authenticity in general "is a fraught and often dubious enterprise, and nowhere more so than in the American South in the time of acute gastronomical self-awareness" (p. 30). Today it is popular for patrons, restaurants, and chefs to claim that theirs are the most authentic examples of a Southern food tradition, but Pollan (2013) asks astutely, "Can authenticity be aware of itself as such and still be authentic?" (p. 71). Therefore, although the search for the most authentic Southern barbecue is likely to resemble the quest for Atlantis, it does serve a valuable rhetorical function, knitting together groups of Southerners. Others might insist that it is the quality of the pork or the restaurant's history that makes it most authentic, but in North Carolina, practices, place, and proprietors most signaled authenticity, creating consubstantiality over shared barbecue enjoyment.

The specific practices used in creating North Carolina barbecue challenge some of the tenets one usually hears about what constitutes authenticity, but we found them to appeal broadly to many customers. At many Southern restaurants, authenticity can mean using local indigenous ingredients, but in barbecue, we found it was as much about the process and how ingredients were prepared as the ingredients themselves that signaled authenticity (Egerton, 1990; Fertel, 2011). Authentic North Carolina barbecue requires smoke and time. Smoke, in particular, is considered to be essential, acting as the most prominent signifier that you are about to experience the "real deal." Though the smoke level varied between the stops on our tour, its presence was undeniable, serving as the "common thread" between different establishments. Even before we ate, smoke spoke; the crackle of logs popping in our ears, and the smoky heat of the pits on our skin served to elevate the sensual pleasures of the eating experience. Smoke infused meat, sauce, and sides, offering variations on a theme. At Jack Cobb and Son, for example, the suggestion of smoke in the meat complemented the velvety collards and simple boiled white potatoes. At B's, the vinegary, slightly sweet but hot sauce punctuated the smoky meat, while at Grady's, smoke was faintly detectable in everything from the meat to the butter beans. Sides heightened the importance of smoke by offering balance, either fanning the flames of heat and spice or offering brightness and richness to the pork. Slaw's cooling feature was a common denominator, and other sides provided different counterpoints to the smoke, the tang of vinegar in collards, the crunch in cornbread or fried okra. Sides offered the palate brief respite from smoke: the smell of smoke, cords of woods, smoky pits, and clouds of smoke surrounding the pits across North Carolina.

It did more than offer a pleasing taste to our palates and familiar sounds to our ears, sending a message of connection and familiarity. It combined with ingredients to form a cooking ritual that can be detected and appreciated by diners, inviting connection. In fact, the search for the woodpile outside a joint's doors is one way North Carolinians come to believe they will experience "authentic" barbecue, and yet the reliance on this smoky ritual connects North Carolina's traditions to other regions and to other times in our collective food experiences. From the distinct smell noticeable from the parking lots to the ordering counters, smoke calls up memories of campfires and woodstoves, tying a modern iteration with a powerful primal one: "It is a powerful thing, the scent of meat roasting on an open fire . . . We humans are strongly drawn to it" (Pollan, 2013, p. 39). Whether emanating from a backyard cookout or from a ramshackle barbecue joint, smoke suggests that a group is present, as one does not typically associate smoke with singularity. Smoke, then, is the ritualistic presence in the barbecue tableau, its omnipresence recalling kinship and community. The search for smoke becomes a symbolic search for an authentic communal dining experience.

If the ritualistic preparation of North Carolina barbecue sends a message of familiarity, the element of place, specifically the décor and overall dining experiences, heightened welcoming identificatory possibilities. Reed and Reed (2008) define authenticity through issues of place. The place of North Carolina barbecue is signaled largely through extremely casual décor and a warm, comfortable dining experience that invites interaction. Restaurants feature porcine and "farm implement" themes, a staple in barbecue restaurant decorating generally, and most we visited had golden-toned pine-paneled walls and either bare or red-checkered tablecloth covered pine tables, many of which were communal. The joke goes that if a Carolina barbecue place does not have a cartoon-style pig as part of its signage or decor, move on, it is not the "real deal." Adroitly capturing this "Barbecue Primitive Style," Smith (1984) notes that barbecue eateries are identified by "torn screen doors, scratched and dented furniture, cough syrup calendars, potato chip racks, sometimes a jukebox, and always a counter, producing an ambiance similar to a county-line beer joint . . . Everything in a barbecue joint, including the help, should be old" (p. 213). Most restaurants were "pay-at-the-register" type places with boxes of Peppermint Patties or other "old school" candies (melt-away mints, Chiclets-style gum, Chupa lollipops) for sale by the till. The search for these place-based markers of authenticity serves a rhetorical purpose. Through their casualness, diners may not experience the anxiety that fine dining sometimes causes and feel relaxed enough to "put their guard down" and interact.

In fact, along with the decor, we found the layout, employees, and general operation of these traditional places to encourage easy interaction. Without exception, the waitstaff were informal, gladly describing the menus and usually taking orders on old-fashioned notepads. The waitstaff were not alone in their friendliness and relaxed manner. One hushpuppy cook, for example, asked me where we were from and was amused by our trip focused on "driving around eating barbecue." Her genuine friendliness put us much at ease, although we were the only white faces in a black-owned and patronized establishment. Most staff chatted with regulars in this way, especially at the very brisk takeout and counter-service areas.

The general operation of many barbecue places further facilitated a level of interaction not seen as frequently in other dining establishments. The tables outside of the takeout areas turned over quickly, and people popped in to pick up their takeout order, encouraging an easy give and take among people.

Figure 4.1 Busy cashier/
counter area at Wilbur's
Barbecue in Goldsboro,
North Carolina

During an extremely busy Sunday lunch rush, for example, we watched the constant action of the counter crowd, casual in their jeans and pullovers, brush past the impeccably dressed church crowd, waiting patiently for tables. Patrons would call out, "Hey Wilbur, how you doin'?'" as they walked by the owner. Ashli took a picture to try to capture the intense level of activity unfolding, but a static picture did not do it justice. Little old men stood by the cash registers chatting and laughing (see figure 4.1). We listened as the owner chastised several waiters, figuring out how to meet the demands of the crush of diners on the fly. As the weekend wore on, we noticed this interactive pattern at every stop we visited. Easy exchange of pleasantries, talk about what to order, and nods and smiles from patrons as they waited for tables or for their carryout orders. Nothing felt forced; everyone felt part of the busy scene. The places were populated by a mix of ages, races, and incomes.

The places better characterized as barbecue "joints," with walk-up, "concession-style" counters, offered a similar level of interaction that was rhetorically significant, symbolizing the potential of community. At evocative B's, literally in the middle of an agricultural nowhere, a white family with

Figure 4.2 B's Barbecue,
with its simple storefront, in
Greenville, North Carolina

teenagers, a single black man, and an older white lady stood outside the order window, all talking to each other to figure out what was left to order at 2:00 p.m. on an October Saturday (see figure 4.2). Although the staff was clearly busy wrapping up a day's work, we were told "of course" we could look in the pit. At Jack Cobb and Son's, this swirl of interaction continued, with patrons chatting as they took their meals back to their cars or homes. Gospel music played in the background, while the all-black staff waited on a mix of white and black customers, trucks and Mercedes lined up in the parking lot. An older black man sat on a bench, watching the parade of diners go by and simply taking in the scene. All these joints offered less of a division between the "front" and "back" of house, to use restaurant terms. This spatial layout complemented what was observable in conversation; that is, instead of kitchens that diners do not see, staff trained to focus on the food, and/or a lengthy eating experience, barbecue's open "kitchens," socially focused waitstaff, and quick eating times encouraged people to interact with each other. Writing about "shade tree barbecue" in Texas, Walsh (2012) explains,

At first I thought it was strange to be eating barbecue with the trunk of my car as a table and traffic whizzing by. But then I started to contemplate the purity of the experience. The smoker was sitting right in front of me. I didn't have to ask what kind of wood was used. It was in full view in the back of the pickup. And there weren't any assistants or waitstaff to filter my questions. There was just me and the barbecue man. (p. 208)

The experience of barbecue *became* the rhetorical potential of barbecue; that is, the removal of physical boundaries encouraged the absence of social, communicative ones.

Eastern North Carolina proprietors of barbecue straddle the line between place and practice, further cultivating congregation through allegiance and admiration. These proprietors' authority afforded a degree of distance that inspired reverence in the way a minister might among his flock or simply invited connection through warmth and dedication. Authentic barbecue men (and on this trip they *were* all men) do not stand back and watch employees handle the day's demands; they are actively involved, nay dominating, forces of nature who convey an air of efficiency and almost paternal level of responsibility for their places. Authenticity in barbecue men, as Fertel (2011) describes it, means that "an authentic pitmaster not only controls the smoking process with fire but also smells, looks, and talks the part, exuding what can only be called barbecuity" (p. 102). And how.

Mr. Wilbur Shirley, of Wilbur's Barbecue, is a perfect example of barbecuity that cultivates reverence and connection. When Ashli called Wilbur's earlier in the week to set up an interview on a Sunday, for example, the waitress who took her call scoffed and said that "Mr. Wilbur" would be entirely too busy to speak to her during the Sunday lunch rush. Ashli thought she was just pushing off her request until she saw the scene for herself later that week. Mr. Wilbur *never* stopped moving the entire time we were there. He was in constant motion so that we couldn't even get a picture of how busy he was. He was involved in everything from bussing tables, to sorting out staffing issues, to greeting customers, to settling bills. He was rolling silverware and cleaning the counter. He was easily doing all these different things at once with an air that was a bit intimidating, even though he was a tiny octogenarian, dressed in brown polyester suspenders and pants. This was a man too busy to be trifled with. We understood why the waitress had shrugged off our request—it was clear the waitstaff tried to do everything in their power not to bother him, their leader, so of course, a customer would understand why conducting an interview during Sunday lunch was not an option. Nevertheless, it was clear that Mr. Wilbur had a devoted, respectful following among his customers, the dedication to his craft inspiring loyalty.

Though Mr. Wilbur had an intense energy, other owners evinced this level of engagement with their businesses, sending the message to diners that they are taken seriously, that their experience matters. The proprietors' performances signaled to customers that they were in the presence of authentic North Carolina barbecue. The owner of Jack Cobb and Son, for example, was a middle-aged or older black man who, like Mr. Wilbur, was extremely busy fulfilling large takeout orders on a Saturday, but waited on us with a friendly and curious manner, wanting to know where we were from. Similarly, Mr. Grady represented the quiet, almost-fatherly stewardship of his family's establishment. He spoke so quietly I had to strain to hear him, but what he said could epitomize the role of modern owners in traditional barbecue restaurants, whose level of devotion to their craft in turn facilitates a kind of trust among their patrons. Mr. Grady started cooking hogs when he was ten years old and had to have back surgery from hauling all the wood he uses to smoke his pork. He talked about the hours it takes to cook his hogs and the constant supervision it requires. In talking to Mr. Grady and others, the importance of dedication to the craft and responding to the community becomes clear. To a person, these proprietors' "all-hands-on-deck" devotion to their restaurants engendered trust, loyalty, and respect on the part of their customers. Their activities helped set the stage for diners to interact and communally enjoy their experiences.

The point is, then, that the proprietors were different, the establishments varied, and the food changed slightly depending on where we were, but overall the message stayed the same: Come in, eat, feel comfortable, be a part of *this*. Enjoy our community and take it with you back to your house or car. The elements of practice, place, and proprietors worked together to tell people they were experiencing authentic eastern North Carolina barbecue. Of course there are other messages that barbecue sends and other places to consider, with authenticity's complex, evolving nature presenting other instances of what can be considered real. Still, these elements were so pervasive that tampering with this "formula" presents rhetorical challenges for those seeking new ways to stretch barbecue, something we encountered when we attended a barbecue competition.

"Authenticity"

Pit Masters Masculinity 2 'Mastery'

Barbecue competitions are frequently covered in travel and food literature and have become popular ways to generate revenue and build community for small Southern towns and cities. They too need similar rhetorical attention, because if rhetoric of eastern barbecue joints coalesced to send a message of welcome, comfort, and trust, entering the world of barbecue competitions sent a different, regimented, more divisive message. Indeed, the idiosyncrasies appreciated in the traditional barbecue community are cause for point deduction in competitions, with detailed rules governing cooking methods (teams can use gas grills or fires made from wood pellets), presentation (lettuce, parsley, and cilantro are the only acceptable garnishes), and sauce (teams are allowed only to "stripe" a line of sauce across the meat). The Eastern Carolina Barbecue Throw Down stood out during our barbecue tour for offering a sense congregation for the competitors but division for everyone else. Arriving early to Rocky Mount following a day of comfortable and welcoming eating experiences, we found that because barbecue drew largely on the trope of masculinity during the competition, it lost much of its ability to cultivate community.

Cooking with fire remains a male-dominated enterprise, and this legacy continued at the Throw Down. The first thing we noticed about the competition area was its masculine appearance. Smokers, tables, and awnings were all filled with lots of "tough" imagery: Harley-style motorcycles, black leather, red and orange fire imagery, fierce-looking pigs. We saw only men cooking at the competition tents, practicing their craft on different kinds of elaborate smokers: tube styles, chest styles, all large enough to require huge pickups or even a horse trailer to tow them. Our initial male-dominated impression turned out to be typical in this area of barbeculture.

Several scholars argue for a lingering primal, ritualistic connection for male dominance in competitions. Along with the primal connection to fire, Pollan (2013) muses that the issue of control (over fire, over nature, over many things) influences every part of barbeculture, warning that "those of us who do it should probably count ourselves lucky Freud isn't around to offer his analysis of exactly what it is we're up to" (p. 31). Similarly, Deutsch (2011) contends that barbecue, for men, is "something to be mastered." (p. 117). While some might share this essentialising, ritualistic view, Croke (2009) notices a paradox in this "preordained" connection because in other contexts the responsibility for cooking falls to women. Men participate in special occasion cooking and maintain patriarchal authority, because barbecue is typically

Competitions → Masc.

done in the public sphere and day-to-day cooking in the private sphere of women (Croke, 2009). This tradition extends into chef culture today, where male chefs wield their authority over other men in the professional kitchen, while a pitmaster "adapts to harsh realities and survives" (Croke, 2009, p. 120). So although barbecue is not inherently male in today's world, it "reflects a specific interpretation of masculinity that is distinctly class-based, pragmatic, and frontier-oriented" (Croke, 2009, p. 120). Indeed, _Barbecue Pitmasters,_ a television show in its fifth season on Destination America, captures this masculine ethos, wooing potential viewers with the claim that these men are "part chef, part athlete, and part five-star general." In Rocky Mount on that October day, evidence of this persona was on full display.

Although some tents gave off a tough, masculine chef/competitor vibe, others seemed to serve more as an outlet for male socializing. In fact, some view barbecue as an outlet for modern men in modern U.S. life, providing a "much-needed release and the chance to cut meat, chop wood, brandish knives and generally get back in touch with their masculinity" (Browning, 2014, p. 11). Barbecue perpetuates the division between traditional female-dominated activities and male-dominated outdoor activities, whereby "when the hearth moves outside, it moves into male territory" (Browning, 2014, p. 3). As barbecue has gone from community-wide slow roasting of animals over wood coals to largely gas-grill fired patio "barbecues," this shift "should get rid of notions of manliness, but our culture still clings to it" (Browning, 2014, p. 6).

Competitive barbecue culture represented by Rocky Mount's event seemed to evince both of these theoretical groundings. As Elie (1996) muses, "To an extent women don't barbecue because men do barbecue" (p. 70). This was our experience. We simply did not see any women cooking at the Throw Down. This observation mirrors the competitive barbecuing world, where roughly less than 5 percent of teams have a head female chef, with women serving more as tasters, meat trimmers, and presentation artists, assembling the boxes for the judges (Deutsch, 2011). Not only were women relegated to support roles in the competitions, they are largely relegated to different spheres outside of it, literally and philosophically. Elie (1996) argues that men cook for culinary events like weekend breakfast while women do the rest of the work of cooking, with one woman explaining why women don't often compete: "They really don't have time. Because they're busy taking care of children. And a house. And everything else. And cooking because they have to and not because they want to" (Elie, 1996, p. 135). The physical layout of the festival itself not only evinced this philosophy at work; it created two separate spheres, with the competition area set aside from the rest of the Throw Down. While one part of the street featured local vendors and a bandstand where people were milling around, the competition tents sat apart, and within them a distinctive, somewhat closed culture. A grassy field was lined with competitive booths, all decorated in individual, masculine styles. Beside them, rows of large RVs, trucks, and vans stood side by side, with living areas created by tarps, chairs, tables, and coolers, and many with a dog. As we strolled past the little RV village and back over to the competitive tent area, it became clear that the competition area existed in its own little universe.

Fortunately, we arrived at a peak cooking and presentation time, and the competitors were all very busy, giving us a chance to experience the way that the Throw Down served as a closed outlet for male socializing. The men were very serious in their work. One tent kept curious onlookers at bay, for example, by a sign that said not to talk to them between the official cooking/presentation time of 11:30–1:30 p.m. Concerned he was getting in the way, Ashli's husband walked back to the main festival area to look around. Ashli then was a woman in a sea of mostly retirement-age men, and to her amusement, teams began talking to her. Wandering around, men would just hand her something to try—a rib here, a piece of pork there—and food led to a conversation. The first team representative she walked by handed her a rib without her asking, waiting on her reaction. He talked to her about how he catered for all kinds of corporate clients, showcasing Guarente's (2003) finding that competitions are as much about client entertaining as they are the barbecue. Walking by another table, a team member commanded her to "pick up that camera and take some action shots of us," telling her which photography angle to use. She was rewarded for her work with some samples. One team, after noticing Ashli looking at the "don't talk to us during peak competition time" sign, tried to explain the way their little subculture worked. "No one wants to talk during that time," he said, because they are focused on competition, but, he noted, "there are fifty-two vendors here, and I have fifty-two people to ask for help if I forget or need something."

Collegial masculinity was clearly on display in this space, and as time wore on, we learned why men became involved in this culture and identified with its rituals. In essence, the Throw Down and circuit competitions in general provide a social, identificatory experience for certain types of men, but often at the expense of excluding others who may want to participate.

It became clear we were observing a very regimented, particular ritual in which the competitors revered having membership. One team of retirees began participating as a hobby to get out of the house because their "wives told them to." One guy said he got into it because he and his buddies used to sit around and drink beer and cook, and it turned into something bigger. Another retired group said they go to five festivals a year, at a cost of about seven hundred dollars a festival. Deutsch (2011) asked his participants why they take part and received similar answers,

> I like the competition part of it. And I also like the *friendly* competition part of it. There's not a team here that if you needed something and they had it, they'd be happy to loan it to you whatever it is. And there's a certain type of competitive camaraderie that exists among all the teams whether you know 'em or not. It's not a cutthroat kind of thing at all. And it's an opportunity to socialize too with people who share your interests in the activity (138)

We did witness this camaraderie, but it remained a very masculine-dominated one.

Perhaps beneath this observable shroud of masculinity and exclusivity remained the ritualistic nature of barbecue that evokes primal beginnings and ongoing spiritual connections. Garner (1996) explains how eating at a classic North Carolina barbecue restaurant is like worshipping in church. For Pollan (2013), the ritualistic cooking of meat over fire acts as a communion between humans and gods, commemorating male power and the transformative nature of cooking. Egerton, (1990) too, argues that the meaning of life is passed from elders to the young at a barbecue due to its lengthy cooking time, offering a communion of spirits that transcends race, class, religion, and politics. Maybe this hyper-male universe we saw *was* an attempt by the cooks to become part of something larger than themselves, because as Deustch (2011) points out, these participants come to know barbecue in ways much different from those who grew up with this practice: "Largely white, suburban, middle-class or upper- middle-class professionals, many transplanted from other parts of the United States—are fairly unlikely to come from a barbecue tradition" (p. 132). Participants we met did give a variety of reasons for their devotion, but ultimately, it became clear that this subculture was oblivious to the spiritual needs of the one down the street. We'd argue that the spirit of community was on display in North Carolina barbecue restaurants but not at the competition.

I doubt this

Figure 4.3 Line forming for the "People's Choice" competition category

[handwritten: It's called exclusivity, and it's okay]

Whether or not the masculine competition teams intentionally closed off the rest of the community is irrelevant because the outcome was the same. A block away from the competition, little old ladies danced the shag to beach music, kids played on bouncehouses, and people shopped at little booths selling all kinds of things. A block over, machismo emanated from the tough-looking tents and elaborate RV set-ups. What was odd was that the two worlds did not really interact. We were not treated with hostility, and the competition did not seem to be cut-throat, but we certainly did not feel the welcoming, warm vibe that characterized all the other stops of the weekend. As we were leaving, a huge line was forming so that festival goers could formally sample the barbecue and vote in the "People's Choice" category of the competition (see figure 4.3). *[handwritten: It's not a restaurant. It's a comp.!]*

Those paying for the privilege of experiencing the world of competition barbecue seemed distinctly apart from the competitors, both sides losing the easy back and forth we witnessed at the other barbecue restaurants. A month later, we witnessed two types of events centered on barbecue and became more convinced that the message of singularity we received at the Throw Down in Rocky Mount was an outlier in the trope of North Carolina barbecue.

[handwritten: → It's a COMPETITION!!!!]

Rurality 3

At 11:00 a.m. on a sunny Saturday in October, I (Ashli) walked into Lexington Barbecue in North Carolina's Piedmont and stood in a long line of hungry people waiting to be seated. Finally, a seat opened at the formica-topped lunch counter. Similar to what we had noticed in Eastern North Carolina, I watched the owner, Rick, joke with regulars as he expedited orders, refilled sweet teas, and chastised diners to order particular menu items. My turn came. Just as I had been instructed by my mother, I asked him, "If I told you I wanted 'three chopped plus tomato' would you know to whom I belonged?" A beat passed, maybe two. And then the owner laughed and said, "You mean that lady who always orders the three chopped plus tomato sandwiches to go and is always in a hurry? The short lady with the salt and pepper hair?" I couldn't believe it. My mother had told me he would know who I was by *her* order. And he did. What's even more remarkable is that both of us live hours from Lexington. For the rest of the meal, I enjoyed special little things: extra "brown" on my barbecue tray, crispy pig skin to try, my to-go order packed with extra care. Upon paying my check, Rick admonished me ("You tell your mother to get back down here!"), smiled, and turned to the next customer who had eagerly grabbed my now vacant bar stool. Rick began chatting with this new customer, offering him a similar level of friendliness, welcome, and hospitality.

I (Ashli) ate at Lexington Barbecue *after* a morning at the Lexington Barbecue Festival, named one of the top ten food festivals in America. There, I witnessed the "barbecue prayer," the reciting of the Pledge of Allegiance, the singing of the National Anthem by the North Carolina–born American Idol, and the ceremonial eating of the first bite of barbecue by the mayor. I drove back to Charlotte in wonder. Lexington sits in the middle of the North Carolina Piedmont, a bustling metropolitan region that boasts numerous research universities, one of the most dynamic economies in the country, and several international airports. That morning, though, I experienced a type of rurality that shocked me with its richness and vitality. And the rural qualities expressed in that day's experience called up many observations we had while researching North Carolina barbecue as a whole. That is, barbecue invited appreciation for the small, the simple, and the familial and drew from old traditions to create new possibilities for community. By generating iden-tification through qualities associated with rural areas of the United States, participants could congregate under the same tent, inviting those unfamiliar with the barbecue tradition to come in and have a look around. While the barbecue festivals and events I attended did invite identification on the basis of shared experiences, I found them welcoming to new participants. They did not segregate their experiences from curious "outsiders," a phenomenon I witnessed in Rocky Mount at the Throw Down. The type of rurality I witnessed could be labeled stereotypical in some ways, from the colloquialisms and the invocation of food and family to the reliance on well-worn beliefs; however, my experience at these festivals and events generated opportunities for rhetorical invention, giving us a new way to consider the rural, the barbecue, and the celebrants.

Rurality is an attribute of place that suggests agricultural landscapes, isolation, small towns, and low population density, but the concept is multifaceted enough to need specification (Hart, Larson, & Lisher, 2005). Indeed, rural cultures can exist in urban places and be in close proximity to urban cores (Hart et al., 2005), a characteristic that is important when explaining the relevance of rurality in today's barbeculture in the South. Instead of associating the rural with negative qualities like "backwardness" or close-mindedness, the study of rurality seeks to generate understanding of rural lives and cultures as having "value, meaning, and complexity" (Donehower, Hogg, & Schell, 2011, p. 3). Instead of trivializing the rural past as "something left behind by a maturing nation" (Danbom, 2010, p. ix), the rural deserves rhetorical attention because it is an identity marker. Indeed, "outmigration" from rural to urban areas is now so common that such people can be seen as "operating in a diaspora" (Donehower et al., 2011, p. 7). It is this ongoing legacy of rurality in the South that makes understanding how identification functions in this context important.

To be clear, we avoid the type of rose-colored glasses nostalgia that simply longs for storied rural days gone by or blindly praises rural values. Still, rather than seeing these areas as "the other," there is rhetorical potential when "us" does not automatically default to urban or suburban (Donehower et al., 2011). We see barbecue and Southern foodways more generally as both rhetorical devices, whereby food can mark rural distinctiveness, yet simultaneously withstand and engage modernization. By this we mean that food can evolve to modern tastes and needs but still maintain its rural roots. Some rurality scholars argue that rural identities become erased when merging with urban ones, but our experiences at Mallard Creek Presbyterian Church Barbecue (MCPCB) and the Lexington festival dispute this claim. The rural natures of the church community and Lexington residents were not erased but rather acted to serve as a dynamic way for members *and* visitors to find value in the fields in the middle of metropolitan North Carolina. As Theobald (2012)

" Are the authors contradictory? — Yes, I think so

contends, "place matters," and identity formation is influenced by place but is not exclusively determined by it (p. 242). Typically, rural isolation has been discussed as a way for people to become an "us" against a "them," as when rural residents help stock each other's larders or revel in protected cultures like quilting, spinning, or woodcarving (Beall & O'Neill, 2009). What we found in these events, however, was an invitation to participate and enjoy the cultures, rather than the desire to police them. We first show how the Lexington Barbecue Festival encouraged people to find value in, and align with, a community's traditions and then explain how the MCPCB draws from ritualistic traditions to powerfully bind new members to a community.

Despite Lexington's location in a bustling metropolitan area, its rhetorical action most definitely stood apart from the surrounding urbanity. The Lexington festival is the largest one-day event of its kind in North Carolina, attended by at least two hundred thousand people and named one of the ten great places to celebrate food in the United States. The festival, which began in 1984, is based on a 1900s public cookout held in Lexington called "Everybody's Day," and today, that spirit of inclusivity remains (Garner, 1996). Originally organized to promote Lexington barbecue while minimizing the differences between the local restaurateurs, a spirit of collaboration and cooperation is evident.

Lexington's rurality helped it become one of the most welcoming and inclusive of any of our food stops; indeed, similar to someone wanting you to share their enjoyment of something special to them, Lexingtonians' barbecue pride was magnetic. On the main stage, a large assortment of people gathered, introduced by a very colorful announcer, sounding like a cross between Senator Fred Thompson and Andy Griffith ("Come on up here son, you're one of my *he*roes" . . . "Raise your hand darlin', we want to see ya and thank you for planning the best festival in America as far as I'm concerned"). From the announcer, to the mayor, to the sponsors, to the quartet who sang "God Bless America," the characteristics of small-town, rural America were on full display. It was sweet and earnest (they even had their mascot "Barbie Q" dressed up in a pink pig costume). What could have been seen as closed-minded, stuck in time, small-town America, however, quickly became emblematic of the rhetorical potential/possibility remaining in those values. That is, when Mayor Newell Clark requested of the crowd, "Raise your hand if you've been here before," and said "Welcome back to our family," and then said, "Raise your hand if you've *never* been here before. We welcome you into our family. Thank you for coming," you felt as if you *were* part of a crazy extended family of suburbanites, old farmers in overalls, and city foodies. The warmth and energy were infectious. These themes were emphasized further through the "barbecue prayer," given by Dr. Ray Howell:

On this beautiful and glorious day, we are reminded, oh God, how often you gather your people around a table. And it's always a big table, overflowing with extravagant delicacies, a table surrounded by the blessings of community, of freedom, of peace, of equality, hope, and joy. And today your people are gathered around a *big, big* table overflowing with our iconic delicacy of delicious barbecue, and it is surrounded by the blessings of community, of freedom, of peace, of equality, hope, and joy . . . Today we celebrate community, today we are all one. Bless our barbecue festival, bless our festival, keep us safe, keep us happy, and, oh God, bless the barbecue! AMEN.

You could argue that Ashli's Lexington experiences were stereotypical, simply including her in the fold of other white, lower to middle-class people who grew up with small-town barbecue experiences. What she noticed, however, was more inclusive and more interesting than that. This was not Lexington residents relying on rurality to say "our spot is not your spot" (Beall & O'Neill, 2009, p. 222). Instead, similar to what Ashli had observed at other North Carolina barbecue venues, these very traditional settings and events saw the same nontraditional attendance/diversity, appreciation, and possibility. All kinds of people were in attendance, and all seemed to be bonding through the celebration of barbecue. We watched strangers chat, community boosters talk about the possibility of pork having civic promise, and restaurateurs serving as sources of community revival. It was impressive. And it was not singular.

If Lexingtonians asked people to appreciate the old ways, the annual Mallard Creek Presbyterian Church Barbecue (MCPCB), held outside of Charlotte, offered the possibility for rhetorical connection by putting a twist on tradition. It too has a long history: the church's first barbecue was held in 1929 and began with two hogs and a goat (Reed & Reed, 2008). Ashli had heard about this event for years as a Charlotte resident, with local media featuring its history and ongoing popularity. Now in its eighty-fifth year, more than twenty thousand people attend the event. Its massive size now requires a police presence, lighted signage on the interstate, traffic control, and swooping media helicopters surveying the scene. Held the last Thursday before election day, politicians have made it a mainstay and line up to press the flesh as hungry customers move through the ordering line. Ashli simply had no idea what she would experience. The three-lane drive-through ordering lines were starting to get busy at 9:30 in the morning. By luck, the church's new pastor saw her wandering around and began talking to her, taking the time to show the different areas of the massive operation and introduce her to various people responsible for executing such a feast. Dining tables were lined up to fill an area the size of half a football field; the cookhouse was filled with working pits and sweating church volunteers; the refrigerated trucks held large amounts of slaw and applesauce. At the Brunswick stew cooking area, the daughters and granddaughters of African American women originally hired by the church eighty-five years ago stood stirring the stew with special wooden paddles, making a rhythmic smack. The scene was evocative of classic small-town America, but the event showcased a rhetorical ability to see opportunities for modern identification and community building through old rituals.

One theme, for example, was how ritualistic participation forges connection. When Ashli asked how a church could stage an event of that scale, for example, the pastor and "man in charge" explained that because the barbecue had been held so many times, everything had a history, and everyone knew what role to play, from the cooks to the decorators. "To North Carolinians, contests and festivals are an important way of keeping old customs alive" (Garner, 1996, p. 51), and that was true here, but MCPCB showed that custom did not mean burden; it meant connection. The pastor explained, "What's interesting to me is that everyone kind of has their own job they do, and they just do it. I haven't seen any written instructions on anything. The process just happens. Gets handed down. People stick to the same job year after year." Indeed. On Barbecue Day alone (everyone called it that), 250 volunteers did everything, with 125 per day in the week leading up to it. From the woman whose only job it was to grow the fresh fall flowers that graced every dining table, to the amateur photographer who had been compiling a visual history for years, to the "slaw lady" who told me to put my slaw into the stew if I wanted to be "in the know," each volunteer we spoke to had a sense of history and the importance of their role in the success of the barbecue. After hearing so many stories of how people used the same utensils year after year to do the same job, Ashli asked what happened if you wanted to do a new job. "Seems to me if you want to give up a job," said the man in charge, "you need to find your own replacement and train them. My wife does the serving line; her mother and her grandmother did the serving line. Her grandmother's cups are still used—we still use Maw-Maw's cups." And that was that. As he put it, the value of the barbecue and its rituals was its timelessness: "Our skin might get a little wrinkly, and our hair might get a little bit shorter, but the barbecue stays the same." Embedded in these old rituals, however, is new possibility.

Even as it is enveloped by the surrounding areas, we use the MCPCB as an example of rurality because it keeps its culture but deploys it in new ways, creating possibilities for connection. The church sits three miles off the interstate in the Charlotte city boundaries, the sixteenth largest city in the United States, but what was compelling rhetorically about the barbecue was the way it seemed to foster connection between the "old ways" and those new to the event and its rituals. As the pastor put it, "What I've noticed in our church, is that we have a significant number of new people in the church, and they all find their way out here. And they mingle, and the next thing you know they've got a job they are doing. It creates a sense of community more than any other event we could possibly have. We could try to force people into supper clubs and whatever. But once a year out here for a week . . ." The new pastor himself seemed shocked by the overall connective "presence" of the barbecue. "I mean they told us about it, and even brought us out here on our interview, but it was July, and it was overgrown with hay and weeds, and I couldn't envision . . . but then the barbecue rolled around, and we were shocked." He was shocked because it was not only the volunteers who seemed engaged in the community created that day. The attendees we saw, from every race and income bracket, sat at the communal tables and struck up conversation. At ten dollars a plate, the barbecue was not cheap, but a plate could easily feed two or three people. Ultimately, the MCPCB provided one of the most compelling examples of the rhetorical potential of Southern food. We met a Californian new to the church who said she "might be in culture shock" but was amazed and excited by what she saw: "It's definitely different than anything I grew up with. I grew up at a church in L.A., and we did events, but there's never been anything that brought this amount of people together. I couldn't understand it until I experienced it. I'm trying to go into [it] without any assumptions. I'm trying to go into it with a clean slate." To us, her statement showcases the rhetorical possibility surrounding barbecue and other Southern food. Barbecue does not solve problems, but it might be a way for people to meet and start talking about them. As in much of the "new South," then, busy cities sit adjacent to small towns and rural areas, providing a mix of the old and new and therefore providing opportunities for rhetorical invention.

Authenticity
Masculinity
Rurality

CONCLUSION

What is this observation?

We have provided three examples of how traditional barbecue culture still draws people together. Throughout North Carolina people from a variety of walks of life are able to participate in this community, whether or not the tradition is "theirs," because of the messages barbecue sends about authenticity and rurality. From kids to old timers, black and white, foodies or traditionalists, men and women, barbecue in North Carolina is a meal that typically invites us all in. Although the invitation is not always shared broadly, as we saw in the masculinity-ridden Throw Down example, barbecue's rhetorical strength is in its ability to make its traditions approachable and appreciable to many.

Projecting inclusivity as a Rhet. Stre.

As the South continues to change, the rhetorical strength of barbecue is in its ability to welcome more fans into its unique culture while recognizing that it must subtly, carefully, evolve to reflect their influence. Like many of the older cultural traditions found in the South, barbecue is at a crossroads because of changes in population, exposure to new and "foreign" tastes, and the push and pull between modernity and tradition (Shahin, 2012; Veteto & Maclin, 2011). The region is also experiencing the loss of local restaurants in favor of more homogenous chains. Barbecue may be an old tradition, but it is not static, watching the region change; instead, it is a "culturally constructed phenomenon that is both traditional in many regards and at the same time undergoing constant change and reformulation" (Veteto & Maclin, 2011, p. 3). To ensure that the spirit of the craft remains able to form community in light of these changes, barbecue is changing in at least three ways.

One way that barbecue is stretching carefully is in its proprietors. Specifically, as the old pitmasters retire, who carries on the legacy is important. Some worry that the barbecue competition circuit threatens the craft, with traditional pitmasters getting lost in the sea of festivals and fancy new cooking equipment. As John T. Edge worries about the proprietors of barbecue: "It was once the province of lower middle class and working class people and now it's the equivalent of the bass boat for the middle classes . . . There's no great harm in that, but once it was a job that required years of practice, and relegated to those who would endure smoke and sweat and toil. Perhaps you can excel with your basting syringe and sponsorship and 10,000 pounds, 6,000 rig. We have to question where we are going with that" (in Guarente, 2003, para. 21). The circuit does not necessarily sound a death knell for the ways of traditional proprietors, however. Not all competition groups choose the industrial product or convenience of gas and other technologies

They really can't stand competition, can they?

to compete. The Fatback Collective, for example, is an informal association of a dozen Southern chefs and pitmasters who rely on traditional cooking methods and use heritage breeds to encourage proper pork raising and the humane treatment of animals. It is not only the male-dominated circuit that presents challenges to the legacy of male proprietors. Traditional barbecue is not gender equitable, but this division is starting to be challenged. Although the women we saw at the Throw Down, for example, were largely in support roles, all-women teams do compete, and all-women barbecue food trucks and joints are popping up. The SFA crowned Brownsville, Tennessee's, Helen Turner "The Queen of Barbecue" and did a documentary about her role as one of the few female pitmasters in the South. In some ways, these "feminist versions of barbecue" allow the proprietors ways to gig the traditional system so that new possibilities become clear—sustainable meat usage, locally grown vegetables used for sides, a refusal to use industrial food service products. Whether these will "count" as having the spirit of barbecue, however, depends on how these new proprietors find new ways to express traditional practices identified in our discussion of North Carolina barbecue's authenticity.

Another way that barbecue must adapt to the changing nature of the South is in its product. As people become more cognizant of health and more attuned to agricultural industry practices, barbecue may need to better account for the product it offers its customers, while still remaining "true" to its traditions. Restaurateurs struggle with sourcing products (hogs produced by Big Agriculture can have questionable quality), health codes (smoke houses are notorious fire hazards), and rising costs. Pollan (2013) points out that the big hole in the authenticity of barbecue is the "sauce" that covers the terribly inhumane practices that produce the hogs the places cook. Jim and Nick's is a small chain of barbecue restaurants that is choosing to use more sustainable and ethically produced meat on their menu to attain the traditional taste. Additionally, meat-heavy diets are becoming less popular. That certainly doesn't mean that Southerners are cutting barbecue out of their diets altogether, but there has been a shift in diets. Scott and Rushing (2014) wonder what happens to Southern regional identity as these dietary and cooking habits change, worrying that the evolution of culinary traditions may cause individual and regional anomie. The boundaries of barbecue—of Southern food in general—must stretch in order to keep the greatest number of people in the fold as the culinary landscape changes.

The "places" of barbecue, finally, are also changing. Is it possible for the old joints to remain and also be joined by new versions? Some worry that chain restaurants now dominate interstate exits and allow travelers to bypass the rural highways with their small barbecue joints. Competition from these megachains, "unfamiliar and trendy" fusion barbecue entrees like a "redneck Reuben," and "faux-country," barbecue behemoths do not evoke the same spirit as the old places. Jim and Nick's, however, shows that "traditional" barbecue can be executed in new places, as long as the spirit of the traditional equation is followed.

Barbecue is subtly evolving in these ways, which is crucial, because the inability to stretch invites a casuistic tipping point, risking the loss of the faithful barbecue community, while stretching too far from the three elements identified here may render traditional dishes unrecognizable and unable to tie communities together. As Carlson (1992) observed in her study, "casuistry can only 'stretch' so far before the guilt created by the violation of hierarchy becomes nearly intolerable" (p. 29). It is possible that the barbecue tradition can only change so much before it loses its essence and ceases to denote "Southern" as it is interpreted through new and different lenses. Miller (1996) cautions, "Casuistry demands that we examine the data and interpretations that surround a given case, that we work through appearances in order to find those that are most reliable" (p. 222). In this way, does pork marinated in honey, garlic, and onion, deep fried, and served on a baguette with Vietnamese hot sauce and cilantro "count" as barbecue (Schaarsmith, 2006)? What about the big barbecue chains such as Sonny's, which do not use traditional smokers and offer factory-cooked meats? Do they still "count" as barbecue? What about the Weekend Warrior Barbecue Circuit teams? Do they "count"? Purists would say no, and Burke (1984) might have agreed, observing that "there comes a point when casuistry no longer serves . . . itself a way of stretching the frame, it in turn is stretched, until in the end it is felt, not as reclamation but as demoralization" (p. 134). When megachain Chili's offers fried, tossed in sweet sauce "cross cut barbecue ribs" for ten dollars, grocery stores display at least ten kinds of sweet barbecue sauce, and "North Carolina barbecue" flavored potato chips are for sale in that great state, we can see how the barbecue community might become demoralized. The barbecue frame stretched until it broke. Or did it? We believe that barbecue—Southern food in general—can evolve in new directions without crossing the tipping point as long at it is able to incorporate the rhetorical markers such as authenticity and rurality we have identified throughout this chapter.

If barbecue can stretch appropriately through the sharing of these messages, it should continue to thrive. Garner (1996) believes that barbecue has become even more important in today's South, providing a way to hold onto things that are unique in a landscape of sameness. While it is now more difficult to maintain the boundaries of regional styles, the pleasure of arguing about barbecue remains available (Franzia, 2005). As we take up in the next chapter, from a rhetorical standpoint, it matters less if the definition of what constitutes authentic barbecue evolves as people debate. What matters is that people are drawn in to talk about it, their quests for a version of its authenticity inviting connection. As North Carolina's storied tradition is shared more broadly, it should be able to retain its unifying power, because "barbecue is the glue that holds America together" (Nabhan, 2011, p. 2). As long as those who worship at the Church of Barbecue remember that permitting arguments about its essence strengthens and diversifies its community of believers, its place as one of the most rhetorically significant Southern foodways will remain.

They're starting to concern me.

Chains
vs
Authentic

CHAPTER FIVE

AUTHENTICATING SOUTHERNISM
Creating a Sense of Place through Food

On the hunt for authentic Cajun food while traveling through Louisiana, I (Wendy) came across a sign on the interstate claiming that that store's proprietor was the "King of Boudin." I was fully aware that I was falling for a tourist trap, but I thought that I might as well investigate the place. So I exited the highway and headed into Jennings, Louisiana. Sadly, the king had apparently been dethroned because the store was closed and looking for a new buyer. Hungry, though, I was determined not to prolong my drive back home, so I decided to give the well-known Southern chain Popeyes a try. Thinking it would be interesting to compare chain/fast food to our more "authentic" Southern food experiences, I walked in prepared to question the menu items, order some mass-produced food, and sit down in a corporate-manufactured environment. Instead, I walked in and was greeted with lively music—Cajun tunes and jazz—bright decorations, posters explaining the origins of different Cajun foods, and a homey-looking shelf filled with jars of spices. This was all part of the new Popeyes look, but somehow it succeeded in conveying a more authentic environment. Several elderly women were in the restaurant and shouted greetings between tables, catching up after seeing each other for the first time in a few years. This was lunchtime in small-town Louisiana, and in some ways, it didn't matter that we were sitting in a chain restaurant. The food might not have been locally sourced or made from local recipes, but the menu items certainly reflected an authentic experience. This was a perfect moment to continue to question what makes Southern food authentic.

Just like Cracker Barrel

Debate abounds over what determines authenticity in Southern food. Can a chain restaurant—such as Popeyes—produce authentic Southern food on a large scale? Or must it come from a mom and pop shop like Dooky Chase

Figure 5.1 Meat and three in Bovina, Mississippi ~~Location~~

Reality vs Performance

or Willie Mae's Scotch House, both voted among the top five fried chicken joints in New Orleans (Walker, 2014)? Are Cracker Barrel's macaroni and cheese and cornbread suspicious, but Bovina Cafe's (in Bovina, Mississippi) purple-hull peas, squash casserole, and lima beans authentic because of its location, small-town clientele, and aging building (see figure 5.1)? Are there particular boundaries to the region or its cuisine? Must it be cooked with particular ingredients, with the right techniques, and by the right people?

As a concept, authenticity can be defined and guarded. It is possible, however, to argue that the boundaries of authentic Southern cuisine do not matter; they are fluid in many ways. Elizabeth Engelhardt (2011) writes, "Southern food exists, even if we fight over what counts" (p. 7). At times, the authenticity debate seems vital to an understanding of Southern food, as evidenced in the previous chapter. The argument about which characteristics of the North Carolina barbecue experience most convey authenticity is ongoing and functions to bring patrons together, even if they disagree about the practices. This chapter will make a different argument for the role of authenticity, however.

In this chapter, we contend that the concept of an "authentic region" is rhetorically significant because it symbolizes something that binds Southerners

"Natural vs Constructed" Southern

together in important ways. The boundaries of the region and the food that defines that region must be viewed as more fluid and permeable, however. Rhetorical messages that develop a sense of authenticity—a combination of the different forms of authenticity ("true" authentic, "fake"/authentic [fauxthentic], and "new" authentic)—do rhetorical work to form stronger ties to the region and to create a sense of identification. In this case, food adds to a sense of Southern identity, folding both "insiders" and "outsiders," authentic and fauxthentic into the regional ideals and acting as a regional marker. This chapter will explore this argument by first looking at rhetorical ideas of regionalism and authenticity before analyzing examples of Southern cuisine. Finally, we will draw conclusions about Southern food's part in developing the region.

REGIONALISM

The role that regionalism plays in rhetorically influencing individuals has been explored in recent literature. As Jenny Rice (2012) notes, rhetorical research should add to our understanding of how regionalism is strategic and not only used rhetorically, but also created through rhetorical means. Regional rhetoric, as Rice describes it

> disrupts given narratives of belonging that are framed on a national level and between individuals. Regional rhetorics provide alternative ways of framing our relationships and modes of belonging. Specifically, they give us new descriptions of relationships, a power that merges together the tectonic and the architectonic impulses of rhetoric. (p. 203)

As a rhetorical concept, regionalism can be a strong component of defining identities if, as Rice suggests, it reframes relationships. In the case of Southern culture, this is particularly important since the area already has a strong influence on the people of the South. However, as Andrew Wood (2012) points out, regions are not stable concepts. "They reside beyond the comforting borders of unambiguous definition. Regions are shaped by discourse; their ephemeral markers of 'here' and 'there,' 'us' and 'them,' demand perpetual deliberation, interrogation, adjudication, and restoration" (p. 290). It takes rhetorical work to continually define borders and create connections between individuals. As Dave Tell (2012) argues, "The craft of region making, then, is a fundamentally rhetorical one: for what besides rhetoric could tie

Rly?

→ *Quasi—Ethnic Group*

particular patches of land with the broader configurations of political culture?" (p. 215). In addition to formal rhetoric—such as speeches and written pieces—the day-to-day work is an even more important part of maintaining regional boundaries. Thus, the food of a region can have a significant influence on the perception of place. Depending on locally grown produce, preparing barbecue in a way specific to the region, and offering up drinks made with locally available ingredients all help define the space and offer a sense of belonging.

But do they?

One of the most significant purposes of regionalism is the constitutive function that this rhetoric can play. If a region only exists through rhetoric, then individuals are connected based on rhetorical work. As Tell (2012) claims, "At the heart of this construction is the building of contingent bridges, the forging of tenuous links, the *articulation* of people, places, institutions, and ideologies that would not otherwise coexist in the same formation" (p. 215). Southern identity, for example, may not exist outside of rhetorical constructions. After all, the region remains fluid. Deep South states might reject the notion of Washington D.C. being a part of the Southern region; yet rhetorical work is at play in the food world, where D.C. residents happily embrace soul food, bourbon, and barbecue (Maroukian, 2012). The popularity of Southern food in decidedly non-Southern locales provides opportunities for others to embrace a Southern identity. → *Are you sure about that?*

Given that regional rhetorics can define places and people, it follows that these rhetorics can be used to bring disparate people together. Rice (2012) refers to this as creating "folds" and argues that these folds show the very fluid nature of regions. Folds, she argues, "draw together regions that were once distant or even opposed to one another" (p. 208). This can also be applied to people—with regionalism inviting people to see themselves as similar, despite historical and current perceptions of differences. Although boundaries can be used to exclude, they can also be used to define a place or people and invite others to embrace that identity.

In the end, regionalism might have an effect on perceptions of identity of self and others—drawing people together—but can also affect the way individuals perceive space. Feeling this connection between place and people can make individuals "feel at home," and that is a particularly strong feeling for overcoming alienation and difference (Rice, 2012, p. 212).

 # what does that mean?

Based on this understanding of the rhetorical nature of regionalism, there are several points that become apparent when reflecting on Southern food. First, the concept of regionalism helps explain why something as banal as food might contribute to a Southern identity and help form perceptions of how food belongs to, reflects, and defines a region. Food—Southern in particular—is an important rhetorical symbol of the area and the people, even when that space and its people are fluid. Consequently, food acts as rhetorical action, serving as one of many symbolic markers of space and identity.

The second way that Southern food acts as a regional rhetoric is by serving as a conduit. Rice (2012) argues, "Regional rhetorics and their performance thus serve as an active interface in which to engage public discourse about those global and local flows," such as food, labor, and other similar topics (p. 204). Regions are more than just intermediaries between global and local; they also function to rhetorically place people and things. Southern fare finds a way to balance between national and specifically local food, claiming a larger space. But the cuisine also serves as a symbol of a segment of American foodways, while also reflecting the regional differences that occur in the South. Southern food is still tied to the land, but it is also possible to use modern technologies to preserve and transport ingredients in order to be able to make Southern recipes in different places and at different times. Food becomes one of the ways that the Southern identity can be carved out, serving as a daily, physical reminder of the differences and similarities between people and spaces.

Another way that Southern cuisine illustrates the idea of rhetorical regionalism is that it, like the region, is not entirely geographically restricted or limited to specific ingredients. As Matt and Ted Lee (2006) point out, "great collards are grown by the truckload in New Jersey . . . and a four-star French chef proffers pickled peaches" (p. 10). In New York City, Brooklyn Borough Hall gives away sweet potatoes and collard greens each Thanksgiving, providing "hungry or homesick locals" who have relocated to New York a way to reconnect to their home (SFA, 2014, p. 25). Although there are expectations about what makes food Southern, many of those categories are fluid. Consequently, it is possible to have Southern fare in New York that challenges its geographical reaches. It is also possible to have nouveau Southern cuisine that plays with the taste boundaries. At the same time, those new takes on Southern food can subtly work to redefine it.

Finally, Southern food can serve a rhetorical function by bringing people together and emphasizing shared backgrounds. Whether it is through the concept of "folding," as Rice (2012) suggests, or merely creating a common sense of identity, Southern fare can act to emphasize the territorial bonds that Southerners share, even if they feel that they share nothing else.

If Southern food is defined by the region and, in turn, plays a role in defining it, it is then important to consider which characteristics stand out.

In other words, how does Southern cuisine create a sense of regionalism? Although the definition of Southern food was briefly discussed in the introduction, we are more concerned with the rhetorical effects of those characteristics in this chapter. The land "speaks"—it is articulated—through its food.

One characteristic that is central to understanding Southern food is the idea that the land influences what is available and, thus, what becomes a key ingredient. As Thomas Clark (1989) argues, agriculture "has had an enormous bearing on the development of a distinctive regional culture" (p. 5). Modern farming techniques might eliminate some of this cultural influence. After all, tomatoes can be grown and picked at any point in the year and then chemically treated and stored in such a way that allows shoppers to buy them year round. And yet, most savvy tomato buyers know the tricks of the trade and will avoid those cardboard-flavored monstrosities. Southerners have historically been drawn to particular ingredients, according to John Egerton (1993); he says that Southern "heritage originated in nature, in sun and earth and water. From early in its history, the South seemed to be made to be a food-conscious culture" (p. 35). Although Southerners may or may not have chosen to become connected to the land, the argument for developing a cuisine based on availability is feasible. Egerton continues,

> From the beginning, Southerners, like most Americans, were close to the soil. Their lives revolved around the seasons, around sowing and cultivating and harvesting ... Most of them grew food, either as their principal occupation or as a supplemental activity, and at various times in their history, they experienced the terrible fear of not having enough to go around. In every generation prior to World War II, the vast majority of all Southerners spent most of their waking hours in direct or indirect association with the broad subject of food. (p. 35)

Historically, this connection to the land influenced what Southerners judged to be desirable food; availability and abundance had a large influence over the foodways of the region. Changes in agricultural demands and industrialization over the years threatened the abundance of Southern produce, with much of the land shifting to cotton crops, and many of the crop workers moving over to industrial positions (Ferris, 2014). Despite the increasing urbanization of the South, however, this past behavior continues to influence Southern foodways. One of the ways that the physical region determines the identity, then, is by limiting what food is available.

imersion amongst the ppl make it authentic]

[handwritten: etc. {Think of Mexican Food / Think of Japanese food]

Southern cuisine is defined by space and time, bound up by the land and the seasons. It is also characterized by its simplicity and humble ingredients. That is, because many Southerners historically struggled to put food on the table, staples often were "make do" foods, using ingredients that were cheap and abundant. In fact, Ferris (2013) argues that the "region's poverty, isolation, and historic small number of immigrants" have been a large part of the creation of the distinctive foodways of the region (p. 283). Although this is not the case for all Southerners today, this history has still influenced the foodways of the region. As Frederick Douglass Opie (2008) points out, many black Southerners experienced the Great Depression in a very different way than Northerners because they had been struggling for many years before. Opie writes,

> In contrast, friends and relatives who never left the South had been doing without such items [good cuts of meat, sugar, etc.] for so long that many claimed to notice little change after the Depression hit. This was especially true in those regions of the South where people fished, maintained vegetable gardens, and kept dairy cows, hogs, and chickens. For Southerners, the Depression generally meant the traditional southern African American diet. (p. 85)

What was once a cuisine defined through availability and abundance, though, changed into one that *chose* to include simple ingredients. There is an increasing desire for Southerners to participate in past rituals through growing their own fruits, vegetables, and herbs and putting up preserves. Some describe this as "coming back to homestead," reflecting on the gardens of their grandparents and parents (Demetria Simpson, lecture, April 1, 2015). Additionally, chefs such as Charleston's Sean Brock (of McCrady's and Husk) actively work to bring back traditional Southern produce, growing and supporting the cultivation of heirloom seeds. This is partially because of taste, but Brock and others also recognize that the simple foodways of the South are worth preserving in an effort to strengthen the region (Brock, 2014). As Fred Sauceman (2007) writes, "Southerners have pickled watermelon rinds, made wine out of corn cobs, stewed mudbugs, killed spring lettuce with vinegar and bacon grease, and sautéed dandelion greens, thereby creating America's most diverse indigenous cuisine, appreciated all the more because of the hardships from whence it has come" (p. 104). The simple ingredients that help create the food of the region also speak to the identity that is created through the land. That is, Southerners often claim to adhere to the simplicities of life.

Another way that the region defines the food is through its abundance. The climate and soil often yield generous amounts of fruits and vegetables. Tomatoes ripening at the same time and suddenly ready to eat not only means foods driven by that abundance, but also encourages community development through the sharing of the Southern specialty. It is a common sight to find a basket of fruit or vegetables sitting beside the road with a sign inviting neighbors to help themselves. Abundance often yields hospitality and sharing and, thus, shows another way that the land articulates a particular kind of person.

In the end, many things or events can serve to mark and define a region, but food—and Southern food in particular—is one of the most obvious examples of this kind of rhetorical work. It is the act of defining and, in some ways, setting boundaries around a region that makes the rhetorical work powerful. Even if the boundaries of the region (characteristics, physical location, etc.) are stretched, or if there is disagreement over the region, the discussion itself serves a rhetorical function. Similar to the point that we make in chapter four, the act of disagreement can even serve to unite individuals when they are joined by the belief that the disagreement is worthwhile. We might argue over how to prepare our cornbread, but we are both invested in the importance of the food. Thus, the concept of Southern food as defining the region can potentially bind Southerners together and might also draw non-Southerners into an understanding of the South through the story of the regional food. As public radio host of the *Gestalt Gardener*, Felder Rushing (March 2015) states: "We have a shared heritage. If you know what olive oil smells like or what basil looks like, we're brothers. If you know how much mayonnaise to put on a tomato sandwich, we're brothers." Foods grown in Southern land seem particularly connected to the region. After all, they are dependent upon the soil, the nutrients, the water, and the climate. This connection to the land remains, even as the South has become somewhat less dependent on agricultural traditions. As Severson (2015) points out about the continuing importance of farming in the South, in the Piedmont region of North Carolina alone, "about one-third of the state's land is given over to farms . . . There are more high-quality farmers per capita in these 50 square miles than maybe anywhere else but Northern California" (para. 21). One of the topoi that emerges when discussing Southern food as a marker of the region is the idea of authenticity; thus the next section explores the ways that "authentic Southern food," based on this agricultural legacy, becomes a starting point for region making.

AUTHENTICITY

Kenneth Burke (1966) maintained that humans are "moved by a sense of order" and driven by a need for hierarchy (p. 9). This inherent desire to categorize in order to make sense of the world explains why the concept of authenticity might be so vital to cultural studies, and food studies more specifically. That is, claiming that something is "true" or not places that object into a category and allows us to understand it and place it within a hierarchy. We understand the opposite—whether it is inauthentic or authentic—in relation to the other. As Andrew Potter (2010) writes, authenticity is "a contrastive term, perhaps best understood negatively, by pointing to what it is not" (p. 6); it is "a way of talking about things in the world, a way of making judgments, staking claims, and expressing preferences about our relationships to one another, to the world, and to things" (p. 13).

Authenticity is a theme that often emerges when discussing Southern food in general. Creators of Southern food want to make sure that they are working from legitimate recipes, have the right ingredients, and have the blessing of those who know "true" Southern food. Southern restaurants strive to receive the stamp of approval from those "in the know." Authenticity as a construct, however, is anything but clear. For example, which version is valid? Must ingredients be "of the land," or can Southern food staples such as Velveeta cheese, cream of mushroom soup, and Ritz crackers also count?

Although the definition varies, many of the terms that come to mind when considering the concept have a natural connection to Southern food. Authentic foods are honest, true, pure, and connected to the people and the land. Zukin (2008) talks about the idea of something authentic as "closer to nature" (p. 728). Theodossopoulos (2013) speaks of "genuineness" and "originality" being central characteristics (p. 340). Regardless of the definitions, however, it is clear that this is largely a rhetorical construct, developed in comparison to the other and drawing its "trueness" from the falseness of the other. As Zukin (2008) argues, it is distance that allows us to recognize something as authentic. She argues, "We can only see spaces as authentic from outside them. . . . The more connected we are to its social life, especially if we grew up there, the less likely we are to call a neighborhood *authentic*" (p. 728). Whether it is constructed through absence or opposition, it is discourse that yields our understanding of the term (King, 2006).

This rhetorical construction then allows for placement within a hierarchy. When something is deemed to be authentic, it is "true" or "pure" and, thus, is seen as higher on a hierarchy and given more weight. Authenticity can also be used to create authority. As Potter (2010) argues, "That is, when something is described as 'authentic,' what is invariably meant is that it is a Good Thing. Authenticity is one of those motherhood words—like *community, family, natural, and organic*—that are only ever used in their positive sense, as terms of approbation, and that tend to be rhetorical trump cards" (p. 6). The term is used not only to judge something—to put it in its proper place—but also to pull from a certain amount of rhetorical authority. There is power in claiming that something is "the real deal." Thus, there is power in the concept.

Knowing the strength of authenticity, it then makes it clear why claims to authenticity might be an important rhetorical move. It can either be explicitly or implicitly created. Overt claims ("Grandma's recipe," "the original") can be persuasive in convincing people of the worthiness of something. But, as Dickinson (2002) argues, it is also the day-to-day messages that can be a more powerful force in its creation. It is not only the words, but also the sights, sounds, and smells that can send a message of something being "true" or "honest." Dickinson (2002) writes, "This rhetoric is powerful not because it is important but because it is banal" (p. 22). The normalcy of the messages makes them almost hidden and potentially less suspect.

Authenticity can then be rhetorically created through authority. Another way to create this sense is through performance (Albrecht, 2008). Restaurants, attempting to pull from the authority of the "true" South, might dress their staff in jeans and gingham shirts, play bluegrass, and serve their sweet tea in Mason jars. They are performing what they perceive to be the legitimate South. Zukin (2008) argues that providing a backstory can help "fabricate an aura of authenticity" (p. 736). In rhetorical terms, this might be explained through the ability of narrative to shape our perceptions of our world.

The connection between authenticity and food can be a strong one, therefore, with food drawing from all the senses and memory (as we discuss in chapter one) to add to a feeling of being honest, true, real. Moreover, establishing authenticity is a rhetorical move that further solidifies the idea of regionalism. That is, establishing the boundaries surrounding the object in question is often made possible by pulling from regional boundaries, even if they are contentious and fluid. The next section explores the particular example of Southern food in order to better understand the ways that authenticating discourse works with/uses regionalism.

[handwritten margin note: See my notes pg. 135]

[handwritten note at bottom: If the narrative is fictitious + performed, is it authentic???]

"Authentic" Southern Food and Southern Identity

This theoretical understanding of authenticity allows for a deeper under-standing of Southern food. In particular, this section looks at the different levels of authenticity, how it is rhetorically created, and the role it plays in developing an identity and a region. In particular, we are interested in ex-ploring three different types of authenticity—true authentic, fauxthentic, and new authentic.

True Authentic Southern Food

True authentic Southern food, as we are calling it here to differentiate from other types of authenticity, has many of the characteristics discussed earlier. An understanding of Southern foods starts with the "staples of Southern cooking—the pork and cornbread, the grits and greens and yams, the cor-nucopia of sweets" (Egerton, 1993, p. 5). But the food extends far beyond that; it is a diverse reflection of the complicated region that is the South. As Egerton (1993) writes:

> From the Atlantic Seaboard and the Gulf Coast to the Appalachians and the Ozarks, from the river deltas to the rolling piedmont hills, there is a wealth of gastronomic diversity in the South. The food is not just South-ern; in a historical sense, at least, it is also Indian, British, African, Hispanic, Creole, Acadian, French, German, Greek, Italian, even Asian. The South has rich food, poor food, new food, old food, hot food, cold food, fast food, slow food" (p. 5)

Thus, the idea of "true" Southern food is already complicated by the diver-sity of the region. Despite its shifting nature, it is still possible to talk about characteristics of the regional foodways.

The idea of "honest," "true," or "pure" Southern food may be difficult to determine, but there are characteristics that are emphasized in Southern foods, restaurants, cookbooks, magazines, and conversations. In some ways, Southern food is described more by what it symbolizes than what ingredients are necessary. Severson (2014) writes, "Deeply rooted in both the land and the people who have worked it, it is the original farm-to-table cooking—America's first and truest cuisine. More than a six-dollar heirloom tomato, it is beans and rice and greens. It is pork for flavor, not bacon for effect" (p. 82). For example, Southern food is traditionally connected to the people of the region and the land. Thus, it has a history in the South, appearing in historical

[handwritten margin notes: "Sub Genres of Southern food"]

cookbooks, longtime restaurant menus, and on the tables of Southerners. It typically has a story that connects it to the region on some level. At the same time, it is often physically connected to the land, demanding ingredients that might only be found in the South (grits or collards), be more prevalent and flavorful in certain seasons (tomatoes), or be driven by events in the South (crawfish boils, church suppers). In this case, it is the regionalism that also "authenticates" the food.

Greens (collard, mustard, turnip, etc.) and okra, for example, are particularly symbolic of the region. Collard greens often dominate the meat and threes, but greens in general are almost always present on the menu. Greens and okra are easy to grow in the Southern soil and climate and can flourish on small plots of land, so it is not surprising that they would become such a staple (Butler, 2007). Historically, this was an easy way for slaves to add to their rations; they might start their own small garden, create a communal garden, or forage for greens (Miller, 2013). Later, it was a matter of finding the most nutritious food for the lowest price. Butler (2007) writes, "The inclusion of vegetables, particularly those homegrown, in the southern diet reflects the economic disadvantage under which the region labored for much of its past and into the present; as meat was an expensive food item, southerners had to rely more heavily on nutrition from vegetables" (p. 170). Consequently, greens became a frequent addition to many Southern tables, although Miller (2013) argues that class distinctions did develop, with spinach, mustard, and turnip greens becoming the fare of the upper-class table, and collards "deemed low class" (p. 150).

Fourth-generation Mississippi farmer Ben Burkett is a part of the continued story of the importance of greens and okra to the Southern table. He has worked on his family farm, located in Petal, Mississippi, for forty years, with collards and okra being among the top crops in recent years (Lucas, 2014). The family farm was in danger when, during the turmoil of the 1960s anti–civil rights violence, many black residents fled the South to Chicago. Burkett stayed behind, farmed the land, and eventually decided to take over the family business. The climate was also difficult for black-owned businesses, though, so many black farmers found that it was difficult to sell their produce. As part of the civil rights movement, the Federation of Southern Cooperatives Land Assistance Fund made it possible for struggling farmers—both black and white—to hold onto farms and find viable markets (Lucas, 2014). Burkett and his family worked with the organization. In the early years of the cooperative, that market included Chicago, where many transplanted Southerners were desperate for a taste of the South (Depp, 2001).

Think of my family eating up north (handwritten annotation)

The farmers were, in essence, bringing a symbol of the region to those who had fled the South, allowing them to maintain that connection despite their separation. As Burkett mentioned in a public talk in 2015, food is a part of Southern culture—a part of all cultures—and we use food to introduce people to a culture. In this case, Burkett's group helped reify Southern culture through its culinary travels. The greens were clearly *of* the region, typically even carrying with them some of the fertile Southern soil that had produced the vegetables. They were made a Southern staple out of necessity, but remain popular because of preference. Unlike other foods that might mask the central ingredient, greens stand alone (or maybe with a touch of pork) and clearly serve as a culinary symbol of the region. Thus, eating greens can be about more than just a good meal or a sustaining meal; it might also be about the kind of consummatory action that we discuss in chapter two. Cooking and eating an authentic symbol of the South serves to reify a Southern identity, emphasizing belongingness to a region.

Similar symbols of Southern food staples can be found at typical small-town cafes and diners. Café on Main in Columbus, Mississippi, for example, serves every type of Southern side. The restaurant occupies one of the town's old anchor buildings, formerly Ruth's Department Store (with fur coat storage still available in the upper level). Columbus, Mississippi, like many small Southern towns, has a history of both de jure and de facto segregation, with remnants of that history still apparent today primarily through class distinctions. One of the recent additions to the city, however, is a Blues Trail marker, a state-recognized site of importance to the development of the Mississippi Blues tradition. The "Catfish Alley" marker proclaims that this was a spot where famous blues musicians such as B. B. King, Duke Ellington, and Little Richard performed, but audiences were drawn to this location not only because of the music, but also because of the aroma of catfish, fresh out of the water and straight into the frying pan, being sold by local fishermen. This became an important spot for the African American community in Columbus not only because of the entertainment, but because it was a place to find good food (in a time when restaurants were hard to find for black customers) and support local business people. This is ironic, because a mere two blocks away today is Café on Main, a modern day community center. Unlike Catfish Alley, though, the restaurant brings together a diverse crowd.

These days, Café on Main is a bustling meat and three, attracting business people for lunch during the week and a huge church crowd on Sundays. When I (Wendy) visited on a Sunday there were large tables of families and

[handwritten: → Who says that?]

friends catching up over a good meal. Although Sunday morning is said to be the most segregated time in America, the restaurant seemed to cross those lines, bringing African American and White crowds together to enjoy the food. The food that brought this crowd together was the food of the region. In addition to chicken cooked a variety of ways and porkchops, the "circle your item" paper menu featured the typical Southern sides: turnip greens and purple-hull peas, green beans and steamed cabbage, candied yams and fried okra. The sides change seasonally, the server assured me, and she knew the produce was fresh because she was one of the people tasked with chopping it daily.

This was an authentic Southern food experience as evidenced by the traditional dishes, seasonal availability, and simple ingredients. In this case, however, it was clearly about more than just the food. Although the food connected the restaurant to the region, it was also the small-town community members gathering together to enjoy the food, the central building that had been repurposed, and the regular customers being greeted energetically by the wait staff that signaled authenticity. *[handwritten: the people]*

Similarly, the Waysider in Tuscaloosa, Alabama, has a comparable, albeit less diverse, vibe. The meat and three has operated out of the same small house since 1951. Arguably made famous by a certain fedora-wearing football coach (Alabama's Bear Bryant was a regular at the restaurant), the food is what continues to draw community members to Tuscaloosa. Wendy visited on a quiet morning. Regulars came through the door and were warmly welcomed by the staff. The owner, Linda Smelley, eventually came into the dining area wearing her flour-covered apron—no doubt from making the restaurant's famous drop biscuits—and sat down to talk to one of the regulars. The lunch menu, changing daily, was a testament to the regional ties of the food. Not only does the menu change based on the selection of the owner, but it is also driven by the available fresh produce. On the table was a handwritten menu that listed a dozen different sides, most chosen based on their freshness and local availability, the waitress told me (see figure 5.2). As with other experiences, though, it is clear that this restaurant is not "of the region" merely because of the food, it has also become an important community gathering place. One customer commented, "We come for the biscuits, but it's really the feel of the place that shines. We are proud of Tuscaloosa when we bring people here. It sums up everything good about this town" (Mason, 2011, para. 10). Although the customer points out that it is not just the food that accounts for the community feeling at the restaurant, it is important to point out that it is the food that brings people together

[handwritten: community defines authenticity]

[handwritten: Small-town community. What about places in the North?]

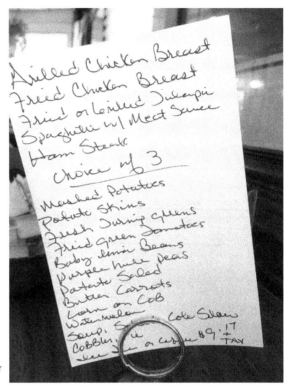

Figure 5.2 The Waysider in Tuscaloosa, Alabama

and begins the conversation. The food that is served there—grown locally, available seasonally, and historically a part of Southern culture—appeals to people in a particular way.

Biscuits, for example, are obviously an important part of the Waysider experience, but they also have significant meaning in terms of the Southern food story. As Elizabeth Engelhardt (2011) argues, biscuits and cornbread are "both quintessential southern and soul foods, hallmarks of down-home or country cooking, and sources of nostalgia for 'simpler' times" (p. 52). Interestingly, Engelhardt traces the history of the two Southern breads, noting the late nineteenth-century movement throughout the South to encourage Southern women to reject cornbread, arguing that it "symbolized ignorance, disease, and poverty" (p. 52). Biscuits, on the other hand, "demonstrated class consciousness, the ability to acquire specialized ingredients," and more, thus giving primarily white Southern women a reason to reject their cornbread recipes (p. 52). While the biscuits at the Waysider certainly do not represent a rejection of gritty Southern roots, they do speak to the customer who is looking for one of the most powerful food symbols of the region.

Taken together, these examples provide a fuller understanding of what "true" authentic Southern food is. A combination of atmosphere, ingredients, and people, it is clear why Southern food is such a strong part of the culture. The "true" authentic Southern food experience, then, can be used as a starting point to understand the differences between "true" authentic, "fauxthentic," and "new authentic."

Fauxthentic Southern Foods

It is not unusual to find examples of people, places, and things that have the underlying characteristics of the "authentic" but have somehow slowly moved away from the ideal. If authentic is seen as real, honest, true, simple, and organic, as discussed earlier, then the opposite of authentic—inauthentic—would seem to reject all of those characteristics. And yet, there seems to be a need for another category. Although inauthenticity is also a concept that brings insight into understanding rhetorical constructions of authenticity, it is the category that balances between the two—showing glimmers of the true, while also pushing the boundaries—that is most relevant when thinking of the role that food plays in developing a Southern identity.

What makes something, but Southern food specifically, fauxthentic? It starts with a connection to the original. In some fundamental ways, the food must be representative of foods of the South. The idea of the food is connected to the region, perhaps with ingredients similar to the original or a tie to the food stories of the South. Moving away from those authentic roots, however, fauxthentic Southern food loses the connection to the region in some way. It may be through the addition of an "alien" ingredient, deviating too far from the original recipe, or serving it out of season, for example. This is connected to the second characteristic—that it has been modernized, sanitized in some way, or scrubbed clean of history, deviating from popular conceptions of traditional Southern food. In some cases, this can be because modern farming or food processing techniques have made improvements over past foodways. It might also be the case that the food has been modernized and has lost some essential qualities. In some cases, that is because authenticity can be inconvenient (Zukin, 2008); authentic foods can be difficult to make, ingredients can be hard to find, and historical kitchen tools might no longer be available. Thus, Southerners move away from the more authentic foods or preparation of those foods for the sake of convenience or profit. The final reason that fauxthentic Southern food might emerge builds on the last two characteristics. Once something is only loosely tied to the original recipes and has also been sanitized in some way, it is easier to mass market the food. Thus, Southern food that is taken to a regionwide or national level can often be accused of leaving its roots behind. That might be due to mass production, an attempt to reach more consumers, or intentionally making changes in order to appeal to a wider audience.

Perhaps one of the most obvious examples of the fauxthentic Southern food is the Tennessee-based, but nationally recognized chain, Cracker Barrel. Created in 1969 by Dan Evins, the restaurant was intended to "meet the needs of folks on the road" ("Heritage & History," n.d., para. 3). Evins saw the meal as an important time to catch up with family and friends and wanted to do his part to bring people together around "simple, honest country food" (para. 4). In the words of the company web site, "What Dan had in mind was the kind of place he'd been to hundreds of times as a boy. It was a place called the country store, something every small community once had" (para. 5). In other words, Evins wanted to recreate the feeling of a small Southern town, but alongside the bustling new highways of the region. What he created was, in many ways, tied to the authentic South, but then began to deviate from that image in various ways.

This is evidenced in an observation of the restaurant itself. Stopping in a Cracker Barrel along a major Alabama highway, Wendy was struck by the comparison of that experience to the seemingly authentic Southern restaurants that both authors had visited that summer. There were four areas where it appeared that the Southern chain was trying very hard to seem authentic.

First, the visual messages that are present attempt to connect the restaurant with the region. From the highway, motorists are invited to stop into the restaurant with signs that feature an elderly man sitting in a chair (part of the logo) or the restaurant's iconic rocking chair. Driving up to the store, visitors are met with a line of rocking chairs (often filled with busily rocking customers), checkerboards spread out between the chairs, and an inviting porch. The look of the building hearkens back to the small-town country store that Evins envisioned. As Cooley (2015) argues, Evins "specifically tried to harness white southerners' sense of nostalgia for a rural past filled with vegetable-laden suppers and country stores" (p. 150). Walking through the door, a host welcomes you, visually inviting you into the restaurant. As any visitor to a Cracker Barrel will know (they are basically all set up in the same manner), you walk through the "country store," a place packed from floor to ceiling with products that might have been found in an old country store (Moon Pies, Goo Goo Clusters, and country-themed clothing, for example) and lots of others that would not (electronic yapping dogs, audio books, and gluten-free pancake mixes). Walking to the table, the photographs, signs, and

What als out white/black etc.
Creating a Sense of Place through Food   Southern
151
Food
Q.?

other memorabilia (at this location, a washboard and shotgun, for example) on the walls emphasize the connection to the location and make it appear that the chain is connected to the region and its residents (even if only particular residents) in some way.

Second, the language in the menu also attempts to link the restaurant to the past. The cover establishes the connection to the South (established in Lebanon, Tennessee), the past (established in 1969), and traditional Southern ideals ("Offering great tasting, hearty meals is a trait of Southern hospitality"). We are told that the food is "from scratch," "traditional country style," and "genuine quality." The types of food—chicken pot pie, meatloaf, "turkey 'n dressing," "Sunday Homestyle Chicken," "Momma's French Toast," and "Uncle Herschel's favorites"—also signal a connection to the past, the region, and the simple Southern foods of the past, even if we do not know the namesakes.

The sounds of the restaurant, a third aspect of the restaurant rhetorically constructing its sense of authenticity, also reflect Southern culture. The background music is generally bluegrass or country and western. Wait staff often connect with customers, interacting excitedly with regular customers. In Alabama, our waitperson hugged an older couple as they stood to leave, uttering "Love you" to them as they walked away. The sound of friends, families, and regulars interacting, in particular, adds to the sense of home that the restaurant attempts to establish. Despite the highway location and the potentially disconnected nature of the chain restaurant, certain messages add to a sense of authenticity.

The food, of course, also signals a connection to the region. The "country style cooking" menu features almost every type of Southern side dish that you might desire. Despite the claims of home cooking, though, the vegetables are mainly frozen, and they are always available (not limited by region or season). Even the memorabilia on the wall appears prepackaged (although it is actually hand selected for each location, according to the restaurant's web site; "Explore our décor," n.d.). There is a semblance of the region here, but its authenticity can be questioned. Unlike a cook in Appalachia who grows the beans, dries them, simmers them for hours, and serves them with homemade cornbread, Cracker Barrel and other fauxthentic chains benefit from that association but take shortcuts in their interpretations of these dishes.

It would be easy to dismiss a place such as Cracker Barrel and to argue that it has no place in a story about Southern food. John Currence, Oxford, Mississippi, celebrity chef and Southern food advocate, for example, says of the popular restaurant chain: "It's garbage. They're taking shit off a truck in the back door and re-warming it" (Rodbard, 2012, para. 21). Although the authenticity can be questioned, it is also worth noting that places such as Cracker Barrel and other Southern chains bring the idea of stereotypical Southern food to thousands of people each year. Although the image of the food may be skewed because of this questionable representation, it is nonetheless part of the image and contributes to a sense of regional identification.

Searching for another restaurant that might bend our understanding of authentic, we were determined to try out a Southern food restaurant outside of the region. Based on a recommendation for good soul food in Chicago, we tried Ruby's restaurant, right next to Garfield Park. We were clearly out of place; we were the only white customers except for one man who was escorted back to the kitchen area. Despite being outsiders, we were immediately welcomed, invited to try some of their finest jerk chicken, and ushered to a table where they promised to serve us, despite the fact that most customers were coming through the food line and selecting their foods. We couldn't help but wonder if we weren't experiencing privilege in the circumstance. Nevertheless, we were welcomed and well fed (see figure 5.3).

Ruby's is a new incarnation of Edna's Restaurant, a staple in the civil rights movement and an important part of the soul food scene in Chicago. Edna Stewart's family was originally from Tennessee, but she had never been to the region (SFA, Edna's Restaurant). Despite her lack of direct Southern connections, Edna's food was sought after, and it was not until her death in 2010 that the restaurant slowed down. After it was closed for a few months, a former employee was determined to bring it back to the neighborhood. Hiring back her kitchen staff and using her recipes (according to our waiter), Ruby's soon began to see its popularity rise. Interestingly, the current owner, Henry Henderson, moved to Chicago from Mississippi in 1969 and delivered produce to Edna's (Schmich, 2014). Discovering this fact after our visit and after learning more about Ben Burkett's story, we couldn't help but wonder if fate took us to this restaurant.

The stars of the show during our visit were the macaroni and cheese, black-eyed peas, yams, and collard greens. Macaroni and cheese may seem like a puzzling item on the meat-and-three menu, unlike yams, peas, and greens that are clearly remnants of the West African culinary influence over plantation food (Opie, 2008). There is, however, a connection to these foods through European influences that found their way onto plantation menus (Miller, 2013). Indeed, Miller (2013) argues that "mac 'n' cheese" "was the first major ethnic dish African Americans assimilated into their diets before the larger American public did"; thus, this dish in particular, he argues, is a black contribution to Southern food (p. 142). More than that, though, mac 'n'

Figure 5.3 Ruby's in Chicago, Illinois

cheese symbolizes a variety of things when placed on the table. "For soul food cooks," Miller says, "mac 'n' cheese had multiple identities as rich people's food, a special occasion food, a convenient comfort food, a meal-stretcher, and a poverty food" (p. 130). Alongside the greens, beans, and yams on our plate, Ruby's take on mac 'n' cheese was creamy deliciousness, but a reminder that one of the characteristics of Southern food is that it is "make do" food, with none of the menu items requiring expensive ingredients and all of the foods made in abundance.

We were both oohing and awing over the black-eyed peas and greens, savoring the fact that we had found food from back home in Chicago. At the same time, we recognized that there was something slightly different about the ingredients. After a few more bites, it struck us that what made these dishes different than what we were used to was sugar. Even the cornbread, though delicious, was sweet. Sugar in cornbread has caused ongoing debates for years, with many Southerners arguing that only a non-Southerner would dare include sugar in their cornbread (Miller, 2013). In an interview, Kathryn Tucker Windham, Alabama writer and local celebrity, decries sweet cornbread as a "terrible cooking error" and vows that she will lead "an active campaign to keep sugar out of cornbread." "Cornbread is as Southern as anything I can think of," she says, "and it *should not have* sugar in it. And I'm trying to find the source of this desecration. I'd like to do something to lop it off" (WLRH, 2012). Although neither of us shared her vehement disdain for sugar, we had to admit that the sweet flavoring did mark the food as different—not the same as "back home." Even with variations, though, the food still symbolizes the Southern home.

Despite Ruby's traditional soul food roots, the fact that the restaurant is located in the Midwest might lead some to question the authenticity of the food. Additionally, as mentioned, Ruby's potentially makes the almost fatal error of including sugar in the food for seasoning (although Miller [2013] argues that sugar is a central ingredient to soul food). Consequently, the restaurant's recipes challenge what some see as traditional ingredients. Yet it begs the question as to whether the authenticity of Southern food should be so closely guarded that Ruby's, a restaurant that clearly follows the spirit and many of the ingredients of Southern food, would be labeled "fake" or "fauxthentic." After all, the food at Ruby's drew heavily from the expected ingredients (even if some of the produce was shipped in), created a feeling of hospitality, and placed an emphasis on abundance. Almost all of the signals sent a message of authenticity, with only a few exceptions. One final example—"new" authentic—will be examined before considering the question of authenticity more fully.

New Authentic Southern Food

If authentic Southern food stays true to ingredients and recipes of the past, and fauxthentic Southern food starts with that concept, but veers away from the historical in some way, new authentic takes a similar path. In this case, new Southern food starts with the historical concept in some way and then takes artistic leeway with the ingredients or with the recipe and deviates from the historical food. However, some new Southern food is so authentic that it is almost unrecognizable because it reaches back to the true roots of the dish. That authenticity often comes at a price, and many of these restaurants are frequented by "white, educated, politically progressive southerners, even as the racial and ethnic diversity of this community expands each year" (Ferris, 2014, p. 334). Despite the demographic target of this type of restaurant, it still contributes to an understanding of Southern food authenticity.

There are several ways that this überauthenticity is created. First, many of the new South restaurants place a great emphasis on conducting historical research to determine the most authentic recipe. Occasionally, this history is shared through the menu, by the wait staff, or in chef-crafted cookbooks centrally featured in the restaurant. Charleston chef Sean Brock's *Heritage* (2014) cookbook, for example, explains how the recent revitalization of Carolina Gold rice as a crop in South Carolina allows home cooks and chefs alike to make a more "authentic" version of Hoppin' John. Second, many new South chefs are committed to serving only the most authentic ingredients. For example, they may choose to use heirloom produce, seeking out farms that have recreated historic produce (beans, tomatoes, etc.) through seeds that have been passed down through generations. Chefs may also insist on using locally sourced ingredients, some even committing to only using products (produce, breads, dairy, meat, etc.) that are sourced within one hundred or even thirty miles of the restaurant. As Brock (2014) observes, "cooking without ingredients like olive oil and vinegar was an eye-opener for me. But that challenge became a major learning experience" (p. 18). Additionally, these restaurants, because of their commitment to local ingredients, are dependent upon seasonal ingredients, sometimes frustrating restaurant-goers who have grown used to ordering what they want when they want it. These limitations serve as opportunities for innovation, with these types of restaurants relying on pickling, fermentation, and new types of farming to meet diners' expectations.

Brock's restaurant Husk, for example, seems to exemplify this kind of establishment, being committed to a recreation of the foodways of the South. Brock says, "If it doesn't come from the South, it's not coming through the door" ("About Husk," n.d., para. 3). The visitor is first struck by the historical beauty of the nineteenth-century house in which the restaurant resides. This is not an old restaurant, but it borrows from the historical stature of the building itself. Every detail of the restaurant screams Southern authenticity. The menu includes classic Southern ingredients such as catfish, tomatoes, and field peas. All of the rhetorical elements send a message of regional belonging; there is no doubt that the land and the people of the South form this restaurant. The overall message is clear, but perhaps subtler than some of the fauxthentic Southern restaurants. Although signs of the region are present in both cases, in the case of many of the signs in Husk (woodpiles, tomato garden, etc.) they are also utilized to create the food; that is, they are signs of actual ingredients, utilized tools, and histories—not just empty symbols.

Another example of this type of "new authentic" Southern food can be found at farmers' markets across the region. These markets often yield an eclectic mix of vendors, with people ranging from lifelong farmers, to newly minted farmers, to individuals who use local ingredients to create trendy items. At a Mississippi market, for example, it is possible to purchase blueberries from a family that has been farming their land for multiple generations. Just down from that stall is a man who left behind his job and started growing heirloom tomatoes for a living. Finally, a few stalls down it is possible to buy various flavors of goat cheese or handcrafted gourmet breads. In this setting, "true" authentic stands next to "new" authentic and produces a more complex understanding of what Southern food truly is. We were struck by a vendor at the Atherton Farmer's Market in Charlotte, North Carolina, who gleefully shared with us the first of her greenhouse-grown heirloom tomatoes and hydroponically grown onion sprouts in the waning winter months. She proudly used new techniques to create classic Southern flavors.

In both cases—the higher end "new South" restaurant and the modern farmers' market items—there is still a firm connection to the land, the people, and the history. There is also a new twist on some of those traditions, though. In some cases, it includes traditional ingredients, but blending those ingredients with others to make something completely different. It is a nod to tradition, but with adaptations. Given the overlap between the types of authentic Southern food, this begs the question: which is more authentic? The answer may lie in the theoretical discussion of authenticity.

Authenticating "Southernism"

In the end, this analysis helps clarify the role that authenticity can play in establishing regionalism. It is clearly the case that there are differences among Southern foods. Whether you are viewing the foodways of the region through a dive restaurant along the highway, a Southern chain that uses regional stereotypes to market the food, or a new Southern restaurant that begins with tradition and works to remake the foodways, all of these images add to an understanding of the region, the people, and the food. What this example shows is that distinctions between authentic and inauthentic might not matter, especially when it comes to understanding the creation of Southern culture. As John Besh, one of the lauded New Orleans chefs, says, "I always say the proper way to make a gumbo is the way your mama made it. It comes down to the rudimentary food, family, and table" (Fisher, 2013, para. 19). Authenticity can often be an individual experience, with many interpretations happening at once.

We often assume that something authentic is always better. And yet, in the case of Southern food, as with others, there are exceptions. As Zukin

(2008) explains, authentic spaces, although historically accurate, are often also seedy or shabby. In terms of consumption, that might not be the most desirable characteristic. That yearning for authenticity yet also comfortable and satisfying consumption often sets up a dichotomy that forces individuals to choose one or the other. In the case of Southern food, individuals might desire the kind of "new South authenticity" that is offered by places that provide historically and culturally "accurate" foods, but in a more "desirable" environment. Alternatively, some people might yearn for their grandmother's banana pudding, made not with original ingredients, but with banana-flavored Jello pudding and Nilla Wafers.

Despite the differences, each type of authenticity contributes to a sense of regionalism. This is part of Southern food's rhetorical power. While there are times to be concerned with "true" authenticity, when it comes to the influence of Southern food on Southern identity and an understanding of Southern regionalism, every type of authenticity should be considered. That is, each of the different experiences helps people in general view the region in a particular way. This is the most important finding in regard to these concepts. Although the assumption might be that there is something at stake in preserving the truth when invoking the appeals to regionalism, what this case study shows is that all types of Southerness (including those that some might consider inauthentic, such as fauxthentic and new authentic) contribute to an understanding of the region and help complicate oversimplified assumptions about the region.

In fact, the true strength of the concept lies in the *process* of authenticating rather than in establishing authenticity itself. After all, if it is relative to the perspective of the individual, then there is no way to absolutely prove something to be authentic. Instead, by signaling authenticity, we are declaring something to be true and, thus, actively involved in shaping opinions and identities. In the case of Southern food, the *signals* of authenticity might be more important to the case than the *essence* of the food itself. While Southern food purists might deny this point, their intentions are to get to that essence, while the point of this project is to determine how food is an essential part of building Southern identity.

This discussion circles back to the regionalism argument. Concern about proving authenticity is, in this case, essentially about making a claim to regionalism. To say something is authentically Southern means that it is *of the people, of the land, of the history.* Rice (2012) writes, "Regions are not so much places but ways of strategically describing relationships among places, as well as the world those doing the descriptions wish to cultivate.

Regional appeals perform critical work by cultivating space-based relations that are not grounded in territory" (p. 206). Thus, despite the trueness of the authenticity claim, if the perception is that the object is authentic, then the rhetorical point of the argument—to prove its belonging—may, in fact, be true. And, of course, by claiming something is of a region, it is also confirming the existence of a region, a concept that is also rhetorically crafted. This is one of the rhetorical possibilities of Southern food: its ability to authenticate the existence of an area and to help define that area. In turn, Southern food then reaffirms a sense of belonging, having the potential to emphasize similarities between individuals and bring them together around a common shared experience. The recent rise to fame that Southern food has enjoyed, then, does more than just put cornbread, deviled eggs, and greens on more menus. It has also helped define and refine Southernism, and that rhetorical work is noteworthy.

While the sides served next to our entrees help solidify a regional identity, desserts act in a different manner. The next chapter will explore the ways that Southern desserts sweeten the regional identity, bringing memories and rituals into play in ways that open up possibilities for connection, agency, and empowerment.

Dangerous!?

CHAPTER SIX

NOSTALGIA, RITUAL, AND THE RHETORICAL POSSIBILITY OF SOUTHERN BAKING

Eighty-eight-year-old Mava Vass might singlehandedly save tiny Hillsville, Virginia, from becoming just a gas stop at Exit 14 on Interstate 77. Hillsville is another example of a small Southern mountain town struggling to hang on. The local shops on its quaint main street have closed, and just a few factories and some agricultural activity keep residents from moving away. Amid the beauty of the Blue Ridge Mountains, people drive twenty minutes to get to the local Walmart to get what they need. I (Ashli) always feel a sense of sadness and loss driving back home. I miss the warmth of the people talking to me along Main Street, the thrill of going by myself up the street to sit at the soda fountain to order an ice cream as a child. It was the eighties, but it might as well have been Mayberry from the *Andy Griffith Show* (which does lie a mere twenty minutes south). This was a town of church fellowship dinners, Shriner Christmas parades, and high school football games that gathered the whole community together. By the mid-1990s, that spirit was gone. The recession hit; Walmart moved in. But this past summer, my dad told me to go talk to Mava, ostensibly for research about Southern desserts. What happened during our conversation not only made me feel hope for Hillsville and other small Southern towns, but it made me think quite differently about the potential of food, especially dessert, to help communities find connectedness, empowerment, and resilience in a South burdened by its history and seeking salvation.

You know you can make a good dessert when your coconut cake is featured in *Southern Living*. Mava didn't know about her achievement until

Suzanne Ray Cox told her. Someone had submitted Mava's famous recipe, time passed, and then there it was. As Mava was quick to tell me, she simply altered her friend Hope Bolen's coconut cake recipe by giving the classic Southern cake a lemon filling. Sitting in Mava's sunny den, she showed me the faded magazine clipping and the similarly aged write up in the *Carroll County News*. She was clearly proud, but she was prouder of the things she listed that can happen when a community comes together through food: welcoming new families by serving homemade ice cream at the summer concert series at the Presbyterian church, trying to revive Hillsville every summer with sweet treats at the Downtown Cruise In. She told me to go to the Dutch Oven for some country cooking, but warned me that it wasn't really a bakery because "people here still bake." Mava's generous, energetic spirit was evident in all the things she did for the community, most of them featuring dessert: the cupcake picnic for the community college band, the food she takes to shut-ins and the homemade cake trays she does for Sober House, the dessert reception she holds every year for high school graduates. Needing to get to her bridge game, Mava told me she's "not doing much." She sent me on my way by admonishing me for not having a copy of our church cookbook and gave me the phone number of her niece, the pastry chef at a Blue Ridge Parkway restaurant and winery, Chateau Morrisette. "Call Anne!" she said. "She'll tell you about dessert in the South these days." I thanked her but thought that in just thirty minutes she had told me much of what I needed to know.

Desserts have a long, valorized place in the story of the Southern food-ways. They are viewed through a particular terministic screen where some imagine their great grandmothers patting out the pastry dough and setting up the tea table, quite literally existing in the kitchen, watching the outside world spin by. When we take a bite of grandmother's hummingbird cake, we are screened to see a South that valorizes this old social order. Burke (1966) reminds us that terministic screens direct our attention to certain realities and away from others, whereby we forget that baking constituted backbreaking, sweaty repression for certain groups of Southerners. And yet, when today's cooks (and "occasional" cooks) engage in storied Southern dessert traditions, they participate in forms of nostalgia and ritual that resist repressive hegemony and carry surprising emancipatory potential. This chapter argues that familiar Southern desserts may tie us to our pasts, but through nostalgia and ritual they also provide space to help change the South's narratives about race, gender, and community. Southern desserts are suspect in limiting women's subjectivities. They seem like time-consuming relics that worry modern health sensibilities with their sweetness. They carry the weight of troubling African American history. Our meal ends, however, by investigating how these traditions might offer a taste of connection and resilience along with satisfaction.

After contextualizing some of the most famous Southern desserts to establish the roles they played previously in the culture, we then rely on the lenses of nostalgia and ritual to assess what they mean for today's Southerners and Southerners by association. We take a closer look at how pound cake connects people, the way it either reinforces gender norms or challenges them, the way Southern cakes help soothe, and the possibility of pie and cupcakes in affirming cultural health. Each section of the analysis examines how traditional dessert rituals remain relevant and may lend a hand in moving the South toward a more progressive future.

Contention between History & Progress
What is Progress?

A DELICIOUS TRADITION AMID A TROUBLED HISTORY

Like most foods in the Southern canon, desserts carry the imprint of their past. Europeans contributed many of the sweets to the Southern table, especially ones made with dairy (Smith, 2003). The African influence plays a significant role too, particularly pertaining to the use of fruit in creating dishes and for the slave labor needed to construct elaborate dessert displays. Miller (2013) points out that desserts still popular today have histories in "Elizabethan England's royal kitchens (sweet potato pie), antebellum Big Houses (peach cobbler and pound cake), and in urban American hotels and restaurants during the Southern cooking era (banana pudding)" (p. 252). A brief glimpse into these Southern dessert histories is useful in understanding how their legacies have rhetorical potential.

Following Native American recipes using indigenous fruits, the earliest Southern desserts arrived in Williamsburg, Virginia, and Charleston, South Carolina, with strong French and English influences (puddings, double-crusted pies, meringues, and cookies) (Furrh & Barksdale, 2008). Williamsburg and Charleston were important centers for entertaining and featured lavish displays of intricate desserts. Slave labor allowed for the perception that the white ladies of the house could construct fancy cakes, a difficult task that at the time required "spices to be hand-ground, flour to be dried, and butter to be washed free of salt" (Furrh & Barksdale, 2008, p. 8). New Orleans's urban lifestyle and Mississippi's rural plantations also helped develop specific dessert traditions, including pralines and desserts featuring ingredients grown on plantations, such as sweet potato pies. Whether on plantations or in the mountain South, economy and resourcefulness were important, and improvisation and invention were crucial (Furrh & Barksdale, 2008). Following the Civil War and into Reconstruction, desserts became less complex, as the slave labor system that allowed for such intricate desserts was abolished. The twentieth-century's additions of machines and packaged ingredients also changed the dessert landscape considerably (Furrh & Barksdale, 2008). Today, of course, it is less common to find scratch-made desserts because convenience products like cake mixes and store-made cookies are popular (Miller, 2013), but Southern desserts are vital and symbolic elements of Southern hospitality (Furrh & Barksdale, 2008).

Several types of desserts figure more prominently in the Southern tradition. Cakes, for example, are considered to be "the ultimate Southern dessert" (Furrh & Barksdale, 2008, p. 15) and blend Native American, African, and European traditions (Neal, 1990). Cakes are often associated with celebration, as well as with neighborly or familiar concern: "Making someone a cake is a Southerner's way of saying, 'I care'" (Furrh & Barksdale, 2008, p. 15). Popular Southern cakes include Lady Baltimore, hummingbird, Mississippi mud, Texas sheet, coconut, red velvet, all manner of pound, and caramel. Candy making, too, has been popular in the South since Colonial times. Indigenous candies like peanut brittle, pralines, and bourbon balls relied on uniquely Southern products such as peanuts, pecans, citrus, and bourbon. German and French settlers influenced the development of the still popular Southern cookie tradition (Furrh & Barksdale, 2008). Cookie making also relied on local products and resourcefulness, such as the South's bountiful supply of nuts and fruit. Puddings and pies follow a similar trajectory, with Native American, English, and French influence combining with a reliance on local ingredients and technique. Yesterday's charlottes, trifles, dumplings, and roly-polys become today's banana puddings, fruit pies, and cobblers.

To complement this historical understanding of Southern desserts, we need to interrogate their social and cultural legacy. Southern women are still characterized as excellent bakers and cooks, responsible for passing down recipes and techniques from one female family member to another. Men might mind the smoker or grill, but women bake, at least in Southern mythology (McDermott, 2007). Even as late as 2007, Southwestern Baptist Seminary offered programs for women in nutrition, meal preparation, and general homemaking because "whether a woman works outside or strictly in the home, her first priority is her family and home" (Capital Gazette, 2007, para. 10). Culturally, too, this message is shared in everything from Eudora Welty's *Delta Wedding,* to *Steel Magnolias,* to *The Help.*

Southern baking often remains gendered. Due to the South's history (a lack of a factory/labor culture and the dominance of a historically patriarchal culture dating back to Colonial times), women's traditional roles remain visible (Gantt, 2001). Mastering desserts like pound cake and coconut cake meant residing at the very top of the Southern food hierarchy, symbolizing "cultural power and with-it-ness" (Gantt, 2001, p. 66). The kitchen and the garden are areas where black and white women exercised their power and creativity traditionally. This association between women and dessert remains understudied; even in the "enlightened" post-women's movement era, the food related labor of women is still devalued and overlooked in a culture that celebrates masculinity and bravado in the kitchen (Ferris, 2014, p. 2). The expectation for women to create desserts that are sometimes elaborate, frequently economical, and always tasty has lasting rhetorical significance.

If being seen as "one who can make dessert" is still relevant in today's conception of what it means to be a Southern woman, African American women's relationship with Southern desserts is even more complex and needs rhetorical attention. As Miller (2013) points out, these women's efforts were key to the development of the Southern dessert tradition, both in the slave food period (1619–1865) and in the Southern cooking period (1865–present). Ferris (2014) argues that these women in particular deeply shaped Southern cuisine; indeed, many of today's desserts owe a debt to the creativity and skill of African American women (Twitty, 2013). Although a dessert tradition was not native to West Africa, colonization saw enslaved cooks developing a reputation for expertise in that arena (Miller, 2013). Even the harvesting of sugarcane depended on slave labor, with two-thirds of slaves being absorbed by sugar plantations (Neal, 1990). Following slavery, Neal (1990) notes that African American women supported themselves through expertise in candies, selling them on the streets of towns and cities. In New Orleans, for example, selling pralines became an entrepreneurial vehicle for free women of color (McNulty, n.d.). After reconstruction, African American cooks took knowledge gained while working in white kitchens and incorporated it into the soul food tradition (Miller, 2013). Whether baking today can work to recover the subjectivity of black women, who were defined frequently within their relationships to white women and children, needs further exploration. Classic Southern desserts are criticized by some black activists for perpetuating a stereotyped and stigmatizing cuisine of low-nutrition, obesity-causing dishes, but black women might also challenge hegemonic traditions through ownership of these traditional sweets. Finally, the possibility of opening space for new subjectivities through making dessert is complicated by another problem that affects Southerners as a group.

Southern desserts are often cast as villains in today's overweight and obese South, but whether it is Southern food in particular or mass-produced convenience food that deserves castigations is open to debate. That Paula Deen's Krispy Kreme doughnut bread pudding contains at least eight thousand calories helps indict Southern baking, but as Smith (2003) argues, "a peach cobbler made with fresh ingredients is far more nourishing than most fast food or store-bought junk" (p. 3). We will later turn to the relationship between health and Southern desserts more specifically, and as we do so we explore the idea that food is spiritual and cultural, not just nutritional, nourishment for the South's people.

Sugar may carry a heavy history in the South, but there remains the potential to see the lasting appreciation for these desserts as a source of community building. Like other foodways, dessert's celebratory qualities provide enjoyment and satisfaction that cross social divisions. Edge argues that food and music are two aspects of Southern culture that can today be celebrated jointly, because they are "byproducts of a multiracial culture, something in which we can take pride, not something we should be ashamed of" (in Jonsson, 2006, p. 1). Coming together to share a piece of delicious pie may seem somewhat anachronistic in our modern, busy lives, but Southern desserts abide, in forms that make their enjoyment more accessible as well as indisputably rhetorical.

NOSTALGIA, RITUAL, AND SWEET POTENTIAL

Nostalgia

When someone says that sweet potato pie "tastes more like memory" or takes a bite of chocolate pie and is "transported back to [his] mother's kitchen," he is living nostalgia (Miller, 2013, p. 241). A bite of a cherished dessert may invoke pleasant memories, but nostalgia has increasingly gotten a bad rap in academic circles. The term "nostalgia" comes from *nosos* (return to native land) and *algos* (suffering or grief) and evokes the bittersweet desire to return to the way one remembers things (Meyers, 2009). Whether evoked through music, movies, family members, events, or food, nostalgia can be defined as longing for the past (Holbrook, 1993). Desserts are often the Southern course most responsible for this yearning; as Miller (2013) explains, "it's the desserts that evoke the deepest sighs and the most wistful looks off into the distance, as if those reminiscing were literally eating nostalgia" (p. 24). Originally cited as a pathology in seventeenth-century medical literature, nostalgia was a "disease of an afflicted imagination," specifically tied at the time to longing for one's homeland (Boym, 2001, p. 4). From the nineteenth century forward, nostalgia became more associated with time, defined as a sentimental longing for one's past (Gabriel, 1993).

Some scholars argue that nostalgia functions conservatively and inhibits the development of progressive identities. Ritivoi (2002), for example, stresses that *restorative* nostalgia seeks to bring back the past and *reflective* nostalgic broods over an inability to return to the past, allowing no ability for evolution. Others argue that nostalgia can be used by those in power to quell resistance to change and as a tool for manipulation (McDonald, Waring, & Harrison, 2006). It can also serve to romanticize and even glamorize the past, removing struggle and divisiveness in favor of offering sanitized histories, earning the title "memory with the pain removed" (Caen, quoted in Davis, 1979, p. 37). Images of the past may tell a one-dimensional, romanticized story about race, class, and gender that perpetuates inequities (Otto, 2005). This "captured in amber" type of memory is devoid of politics where audiences are not held morally responsible for their complicity (Boym, 2001). Furthermore, scholars argue we cannot act upon nostalgia because either we cannot return to an idealized past that never existed (Smith, 2000), or we simply choose to emphasize the narratives that suit us and minimize others (Meyers, 2009).

Some forms of food nostalgia bear particular negative implications for women, presenting a selective and limited understanding of gender at both individual and collective levels. Holtzman (2010) argues that celebrating the recipes passed from grandmother to granddaughter, for example, valorizes the gender identity of the cook while simultaneously subordinating her through these activities. Indeed, whether a woman executes "grandma's pumpkin pie" and generates familial nostalgic praise or finds that her attempts fall flat, her personhood is constructed through the preparation of food (Holtzman, 2010). This legacy helps reproduce culture and collective identities in potentially problematic ways, tying women to their past roles (Mannur, 2007). Taken at face value, this legacy of complicated desserts seems to restrict women's roles and identities to the kitchen, but these traditions have the potential to move beyond mere nostalgia to perform other functions.

When writing about the potential role of nostalgia in Southern food, then, care must be taken not to be seen as advocating for the "moonlight and magnolias" South that, as we have argued earlier, is fictive. Since it is doubtful that Southern food nostalgia is going to end, however, it can be better understood as a productive rhetorical resource. Of course it is still used by those seeking to preserve the status quo and social order in the troubled historical (and present day) South, but it is also a powerful identity-supporting weapon that encourages change incrementally. If identities are created by drawing on various symbolic resources, nostalgia serves as a particularly rich discursive offering (McDonald et al., 2006). Fondly remembering Granny's rolling pin may be more useful than we thought.

The stories we may share or remember as we go through the steps of baking serve more than an instrumental purpose and shape positive identities in today's South. Some argue that nostalgia is capable of connecting people, soothing psychological distress, and increasing self-esteem (Muehling & Pascal, 2012). Others contend that nostalgic yearnings may encourage "subversive and radical readings of the present" (Meyers, 2009, p. 738) and argue for nostalgia's transformative potential, noting that it supports identity as people adjust to changed circumstances (McDonald et al., 2006). Nostalgia intensifies in times of social turmoil, helping to form community that can resist hegemonic ideology. Further, Burke's (1973) notion of "equipment for living" describes how people rely on everyday nostalgic texts, practices, and behaviors to cope with the modern world (Brummett, 1985; Burr-Miller, 2011; Ott, 2007). Eating or crafting Southern desserts serves this purpose of coping in an immediate way. We touch the dough, stir the ingredients, smell the yeast, and in doing so, find respite from the beep of emails and texts on our phones and the stress of everyday life. Indeed, connecting through pound cake invites consubstantiality over our surroundings and our histories. Unlike the "simulated substance" that serves as a materialistic mask in which "people use personal possessions such as furniture, houses, cars, clothing, or decorations to signal their substance to others," baking signals a nonmaterialistic reality that others can connect with (Gilmour, 2006, p. 58). We bake and eat and identify through the process, rather than through the purchasing of "stuff," perhaps forming community (Gilmour, 2006).

Ritual

The ritualistic nature of baking also complements the rhetorical possibilities for nostalgia, providing additional opportunities for finding expanded meaning in Southern foodways. In everyday parlance, the idea of ritual concerns handing down beliefs and customs from one generation to the next (Rogers, 2004), following a specific set of steps, and perhaps relying on memory, not specific recipes or instructions, to do so. Conceptually, ritual is constitutive, going beyond an instrumental communicative purpose, serving roles in "defining and determining the attitudes and values of the contemporary South" (Smith, 1984, p. 208). As such, the rhetorical practice of making dessert has the potential to be socially constructive, helping challenge subject positions and past meanings through small changes, nudging the South slowly forward.

Some communication scholars view ritual as largely unimportant, while others see it as delightfully complex and persuasively powerful, permeating all realms of human existence. Rather than a form of lesser communication, a momentary interruption from practical, intended activity (Putnam, Van Hoeven, & Bullis, 1991; Trice & Beyer, 1984), ritual sheds light onto how people create cultural, familial, and community meaning through shared behaviors. Called a "symbolic action system" (Smith, 1984, p. 17) and a "repetitive, patterned, sequential form of embodied performance" (Ray, 2007), ritual coherently organizes human experience.

Especially important to our study of Southern foodways, ritual provides a way to look at the nondiscursive elements of food rhetoric. The emphasis in the study of Western rhetoric has been on verbal persuasion, but words are merely one part of the many symbolic systems occurring in ritual (You, 2006). Engaging in rituals moves beyond discursive levels, with the stress on the performative nature of ritual facilitating another reading of what we really do when we make the family recipe almost the same, but in "our" way. As Robbins (2001) explains, "ritual accomplishes something simply by its performance—for example, by pronouncing man and wife you effect that union. You entreat or persuade somebody to do something through ritual" (p. 593). Thus, simply by showing someone how to make pound cake the "right" way, you persuade them to do it *your* way; as such, "rituals gain their effectiveness through being enacted or performed" (Schieffelin, 1985, p. 708). The difficulty with ritual, then, is in explaining how it is exactly that rituals do their work in making meaning (Schieffelin, 1985).

Our study of rhetorical baking rituals examines how this process of patterned behavior generates meaning and becomes a site for identity construction and management, as well as being a tool to transform culture. Rituals are tools of repressive hegemony but can become sites of invention and sources of *power*; and in our case, who can resist dessert? As with nostalgia, ritual becomes a way of dealing with social change and anxiety (Faust, 1979), provides structure and relief from "psychic noise," and also offers a way "of being together and communicating shared commitments" (Robbins, 2001, p. 599). Indeed, ritual's paradiscursiveness provides ways to transform identity, to restore or challenge social equilibrium, and to provide rebirth, making it a powerful form of persuasion.

It is no surprise, then, that ritual's persuasive power can either protect or transform the social order (Robbins, 2001). Crucially, it allows for small adaptations that allow people to remain part of a community but move it toward what they would like it to be, such that we can identify with our family's dessert traditions but also shift them over time (Hoffman, 2004). Ritual negotiates paradox, calling attention to contradiction and conflict in ways that can be transformative (Hoffman, 2004). The example of teaching your daughter to make a coconut cake shows the gradual transformation that can be made by embracing paradox. Because she can make the cake when it suits her, she discards the baggage tied to Southern baking, perhaps identifying with ritual but discarding the elements that feel unnecessary. As Hoffman (2004) explains, this process of adapting rituals in creative ways may slowly shift social structures. We may just be writing about baking chocolate cake and peach cobbler, but the selection and transformation of these storied baking rituals incrementally change how baking in today's South is viewed as a whole. Thus, today's Southern women can experience the pleasure of baking rituals without the drudgery of *having* to cook day in and day out. They can keep their fond memories while perhaps better understanding and appreciating what their forebears had to do. Women reclaim the baking ritual in ways that "resist exclusion, hierarchy, and disempowerment," embracing baking for its pleasure, not its pain (Hoffman, 2004, p. 404). And, although we address women and baking here, Southern bakers like Ben Mims (2014) describe how they, too, have adapted baking rituals for personal empowerment. Through baking, both can find new meaning by performing old rituals.

Performing old rituals or remaking them allows for tinkering, and nowhere is that concept more applicable than in baking. Most of us know a story or recipe where someone made a slight alteration to a recipe, as Mava did when making her coconut cake. Mava might have been making a recipe just taste better to her, but we can read the overall tinkering with ritual as potentially transformative. This strategic adaptation of ritual, opens rhetorical space that effects small but important changes in a system (Hoffman, 2004). Tinkering in the kitchen allows one to embrace the good parts of the South's traditional baking rituals while transcending its troubled history (but not forgetting it). The ritual and nostalgia involved in creating Southern desserts might serve an oppressive function in some cases, but we also argue that the processes connect people and foster identification, support a variety of subjectivities, and affirm the spiritual and cultural health of our communities, soothing people in times of need and supporting cultural traditions that draw people together.

Three Examples of the Creative Productivity of Ritual and Nostalgia

The South would not be the same without its well-loved pound cake. Once difficult to make, pound cake's simple ingredients and versatility make it the "original Southern cake," cutting across racial and class lines (McDermott, 2007, p. 19; Miller, 2013). Pound cake rituals connect contemporary bakers to those from another time, connecting "home cooks in twenty-first-century Atlanta, Mobile, Louisville, and New Orleans with the cooks in Southern kitchens of nearly three hundred years before" (McDermott, 2007, p. 19). Pound cake remains the "cake standard" by which good cooks are measured, the "ultimate power statement" that highlights a baker's skill (Gantt, 2001, p. 66; Miller, 2013, p. 251). People used to keep one on hand to offer visitors, and the cake remains a popular gift food in the South. Ashli, for example, received two different kinds from neighbors this past Christmas while writing this chapter. Making a pound cake is a perfect example of a baking ritual that evokes memories and forges rhetorical connections. Associations with the ritual, the simple remembrance of greasing and flouring the pans, creaming butter with sugar and eggs, and tinkering to create new flavors and variations, became tactile, immediate ways to provoke nostalgic reflection among our interviewees. These highly performative, nondiscursive, ritualistic elements of baking evoked memories and interpretive nostalgia, providing outlets for connection.

Sharing dessert illustrates the strong connective possibility of the baking ritual. The deployment of pound cake as a symbol of friendship following surgery, in one instance, led to greater connection among two friends and eventually the larger Charlotte community. Jen brought Carolee's husband, Jon, a pound cake when he was recovering from an ankle operation. Carolee recalls the pound cake sitting on the counter for a while, and after cutting into it, the family devoured it. Carolee ended up asking Jen for the recipe, which Jen gave to her in an envelope marked "confidential." Carolee made the cake and then baked another to take to her neighbor for his birthday. When the recipient reversed his car down the street to compliment her on the cake, she jokingly asked, "Would you pay money for it?" and he said yes. Now, three years later, the two women have a thriving small business.

One weekday morning in the middle of their busy holiday season, the two women sat down with Ashli in Carolee's kitchen to talk more about their story. In the corner of the kitchen, the ingredients for the next cake sat, coming to room temperature (see figure 6.1). What became apparent through the conversation is how baking bolstered a friendship and provided connective fond memories for many of the women's customers. In rhetorical terms, the women's baking ritual functioned as a site of identification, which we discuss in this section, and also a way to craft authority and develop empowerment and agency, which we discuss later.

The ritualistic process of crafting/creating food, and dessert especially, encourages connection through verbal and nondiscursive means. The performative experience of baking together and going through the steps connects cooks with each other and with larger family or community traditions, while also encouraging common ground through those who publicly pledge allegiance with a particular dessert tradition. The two ways the friends' pound cake brought people together in Charlotte, for example, are applicable to the rhetorical potential of dessert in general. Carolee and Jen explained that they generally had two groups of customers: those who liked the cake because it sparked a memory of a connection, and those who liked the cake because it represented a twist on their [own] recipe. Either way, the cake encouraged reflection, a valuable rhetorical trope. Some customers, for example, see Jen and Carolee's pound cake as a direct tie to their families' dessert rituals and traditions, and they love to talk about it. There is a "funny thing" about people's reactions to buying their pound cake: "Some of them want to buy it because they say this tastes exactly like my grandmother's pound cake that was on her counter—there's a connection—and that's why it takes people back." What is interesting rhetorically is how taste, though nondiscursive, serves the discursive function we discussed in chapter one. Instead of an old card, note, or picture that reminds someone of their loved one, it is the unique taste memory that provides the connection. Indeed, in Carolee and Jen's case, their favorite customer comment came from a ninety-six-year-old man who took a bite of the cake and said: "That tastes just like my

Figure 6.1 Pound cake ingredients coming to room temperature in Charlotte, North Carolina

grandmother's cake." Imagine that. If this gentleman was referencing his grandmother's cake, that is almost two hundred years worth of memories evoked by a single bite. It is this process of sharing, exchanging memories through taste, that creates a bond between strangers. As Jen and Carolee explain it, many of their customers are older and tell them how they used to bake and eat, and this conversation allows them to connect with people they meet casually at their sales events: "You just bond with people, and we have met more people than we have ever, ever imagined."

Even for those who make their pound cake a different way, the taste of their friends' allows them to begin a conversation through reflection. This type of rhetorical work is a bit different, because there is an element of competition as seasoned bakers square off over the "right" way to create a particular dish, similar to our argument about barbecue in chapter four. Jen and Carolee told Ashli about "little old ladies" who would say, "Oh I make a pound cake," and talk about how they have a particular recipe that has been passed down from family members. As Carolee explained, these women are not defensive exactly, but they are "very protective of that recipe because it is home to them or it's a family thing." Through this process of comparing the family cake to the friends' cake, however, a conversation starts about how everyone has her own particular way of doing a pound cake. Though the process may be slightly different, baking's ritualistic qualities provide a supportive structure that allows people to identify with each other. The women told Ashli, for example, about a man who always comes to their events joking about how he makes the best five-flavor version, but his boast, along with those of others, sparks a spirited conversation about variations in baking: "It's just fun . . . It [baking pound cake] opens people up, and they just start talking about their grandmother or their aunt."

These baking rituals seem to provide shared meaning to those who participate in them. In Carolee and Jen's case, even the specific steps taken in the ritual carved out roles for each of them in the process that simultaneously enhanced their friendship. The participation in the ritual, not just a conversation about it, provided meaning. Carolee noted how they each have their own roles in the process, such that when each baking session begins, "we don't have to talk about who is doing what . . . When we are doing it alone I'm like 'ugh, I have to grease the pans, Jen usually does that' . . . It's more fun when we do it together." Their roles make the baking process less of a chore and more a rite of friendship: "It's more of a chore, alone. It's just the friendship—it's the best part."

Such ritualistic baking roles carry performative rhetorical force in deepening connection. Ashli also talked to Tori and Mia, the Cake Makin' Sisters in Charlotte, about how the preparation of dessert was their "coming together moment." Their description of working together in their professional kitchen reads like a well-coordinated dance: "We're in here; we work on kind of this back-to-back momentum; if she turns, I turn; when she turns left, I turn right. Her arms will be messing with something, and she turns and then I am messing with it. No one ever needs to say anything in our kitchen space." Rituals connect people to others through identification with these specific, familiar processes.

Ritual is not the only trope that connects and creates consubstantiality between people or between people and a specific community. It combines with the discourse of nostalgia so strongly that recollections also connect bakers to their families and communities. All of the baking entrepreneurs we spoke with based their recipes on memories of family members and family gatherings, even if they offered a different take on the original version. Recalling the scents, sights, and sounds of foods transported interviewees back to their childhoods, connecting them to their families and histories (Rogers,

2004). The smell of Rashaa's lemon cupcake baking reminded her fondly of her grandmother and her recipe. Emma, the Southern Cake Queen, offered a variety of flavors on her bright pink food truck, all of them connected to her Southern history. Emma expressed how her memories shaped her baking:

> I love Southern treats. My cupcakes are a little bit different than anyone else's—they are a little bit heavier, have that Southern flair. My cupcakes have a pound cake base. Pound cakes to me are more like that Southern grandma baking. Of course when we were raised up whenever people had funerals or family gatherings, reunions, or holidays, we would go over to Aunt Jeannette's or Aunt Millie's house we would have a pound cake. Always a cake on the table you could slice off and offer a piece to company. That's how I was raised, so I made a few recipes based on the family and a few that are trial and error from online, following different concepts, and making them my own.

Clearly, nostalgia plays a generative role in developing recipes, as seen in Emma's recollection, but in doing so it also perpetuates a particular culture or particular cultures. When family members or friends use their memories to recreate a taste, they also recreate a culture. For many, losing that memory, those traditions, means losing community and family. Saying, "This is grandma's biscuit" means that it is more than sustenance; it connects one generation to the next (Neal, 1990, p. ix). Neal (1990) elaborates that most everyone has that special recipe handed down from someone else that means something more to them than just a way to create a dish. The recipe, the lesson, and even the equipment function as parts of the whole for signifying family and culture.

Nostalgia may have this generative potential at both the familial and community levels in helping to recreate culture, but it also must be accepting of societal change; it must be flexible. In handing down culinary knowledge, for example, the older generation must accept that rituals may change slightly. Rhetorically this may be a difficult process, as younger people may have different concerns and responsibilities and live in a different world. The passage of time seemed to be a particularly important trope in understanding how nostalgia became generative. Carolee and Jen, for example, referenced the importance of time in developing nostalgia and the willingness to engage in a baking ritual. For them, the legacy of baking provides generations of women, in particular, the opportunity to connect through the experience. Though Carolee maintained that the fond memories generated by baking were not limited to women, she did reference how the process provided women with a way to forge a lasting connection as time progressed:

> The reason the women are more intimately tied is that when you get older you begin seeking that connection . . . When you're young you are a bit ignorant of it . . . You don't really care, and you don't think about people going away, but as you get older you notice that your mom is starting to make a lot of things that her mom made regularly after she passed. My mom, for example, began churning out all kinds of Southern specialties she hadn't made in years after her own mother died. It's a way to reconnect with someone you can't connect with physically anymore. I think that pound cakes and desserts in general provide women with a connection when they can't have that face-to-face conversation with that special person anymore.

Although Carolee's story references the historical role of women in the kitchen and the legacy of that tradition, her comments are not applicable *only* to women. What seems to matter in creating a lasting connection through food is the time spent in following a process or recipe and doing it with someone else. Ben Mims, a gay man pushed away by his family in Mississippi and now cookbook author and associate food editor for *Food and Wine* magazine, talks about how, for example, baking cakes connected him to his family despite their condemnation (Reynolds, 2014).

One noted community church baker, JoAnna Goff, also noted the importance of time in developing the desire to participate in a ritual. JoAnna admitted that her mother didn't teach her everything she knew about baking "because I didn't want to learn probably." Time had to pass before bakers wanted to replicate a recipe in order to commune with a lost loved one: "You have to get to a certain age before you appreciate something. I will go back and find the things that I remember she made, and I will try to replicate that. She had an old cookbook, that was published back around 1950, and it's a Rumford Baking Powder Cookbook. She had given it to me years before, but I never paid any attention. One day I picked it up, and I just started flipping through it." For JoAnna, then, enough time had to pass before nostalgia drove her back to recalling cooking rituals important in her family. Joking about how she was going to leave her huge collection of cookbooks to her daughter: "Mom you do not need to buy one more cookbook," and I said, "But Renee, I'm leaving them to you. So you will have allllll of this."

Although JoAnna acknowledged that time needed to pass before her daughter might want to take up baking, she was resistant to losing the home-made characteristic of Southern food. She noted how her daughter had begun asking more questions about baking and cooking but took "short cuts" she did not like. As she put it,

> I can imagine that if my daughter had to bake something she would be using that Tastefully Sinful mix—I may not have said that correct. She tries to tell me, "Oh, mom it's really good; you need to try this blah de blah de blah," so I ended up buying it, and it's been sitting in my pantry for months. I'm sure I'll just say, "Hey take this, because I'm not going to use it." Because if I'm going to spend the time and the energy, I want to do it right.

For JoAnna, the new ways of baking must echo the original in some key ways, or they lose their meaning. What JoAnna seemed to intimate is that homemade tastes were most capable of creating the memories that people treasured. Another baker described a disappointing taste memory that resulted from a short cut: "The last time I ate her apple stack cake, she'd run out of energy and used a cake mix. I remember the disappointing taste. Christmas evaporated right then" (Rogers, 2004, p. 317).

Rather than arguing that people must make labor-intensive creations in order to successfully participate in nostalgic taste memories, however, there is another way. That is, the very adaptability of baking rituals shows how they can satisfy the demands of contemporary eating and entertaining and still be meaningful. The adaptability of pound cake, for example, and the ability to alter/tweak its baking ritual highlights how classic Southern desserts can be made relevant in today's world. Jen and Carolee's business allows them to provide a quality product to people who want a traditional taste but don't want to bake or don't have the time. As Jen explained, baking a pound cake takes time, effort, and planning that not everyone has, meaning that they provide a service:

> You have to have your butter room temp—it can't be four in the afternoon and you decide that you want to make a pound cake. You kind of have to know the night before to take out your eggs. And I don't know if a lot of women today just don't have time. I think we can kind of do it for them. We can make it so it tastes homemade and looks lovely. So we can do that for them, and that's what we like to do.

What the women recognize is that people want the classic, traditional taste of their memories but may not have the time or desire to do it. For busy customers with disposable incomes, then, a purchased homemade pound cake serves as a pleasing timesaver, whereby you can participate in a taste memory without the effort. You can relive the ritual without all the work.

But the power of ritual is in man a???? perfo

DESSERTS SUPPORT SUBJECTIVITY

Thus far, we've argued that dessert serves as a site of identification, but it also crafts authority, developing empowerment and agency. Baking may be viewed through some lenses as limiting subjectivity and agency because of gender expectations, but we found that engaging in dessert rituals opens up rhetorical empowerment possibilities. The baking rituals themselves produce this discursive space. The process of baking a pound cake, for example, is just similar enough that anyone who makes one has familiarity with the general steps and ingredients involved, but the ritual has enough flexibility to invite comparison and creativity. Each cook follows the basic ritual, but each also makes it "his or her thing," allowing a baker's subjectivity to emerge more strongly. As Tori and Mia put it,

> Our intent was not to grasp the whole Southern culture, but we try to keep it right where everybody is loving it, and when you get to the point where are mass producing things it kind of falls short. I think that our product has a "loving swing" rather than a "Southern swing"—a type of care. It's just got us, our swing, our flavor. It's not just the baking; it has a lot to do with the people who are preparing the product. Our baking style is funky, flavorful, and cool. We're just some cool chicks.

Another baker Ashli met was very experienced, but she also pointed out that she was still learning pound-cake variations, tweaking recipes to make them her own:

> You know, I was telling somebody recently, my daughter's boyfriend had asked me if I could make a Sun Drop (a North Carolina citrus soda) pound cake, and I had never made one. But I am baker; I bake cakes. You know, I just can't do that one. But listen, I'm not giving up on that Sun Drop pound cake.

This woman clearly identifies as a baker, yet she notes that this particular variation, although slight, requires a new approach to get it right. She will tweak the steps until it meets her expectations, and in doing so, she gains authority in "owning" that role.

The desire to tinker with flavors and tweak recipes based on family traditions to make them your own was a very prominent trope. While every baker referenced the need to follow trends and experiment, citing blogs, Pinterest, magazines, and competitors as sources of inspiration, none were stronger than family. Rashaa looked to her grandmother. Emma's Aunt Jeannette was her influence, explaining how her aunt's style of cooking inspired hers: "In the summertime she would make a blackberry dumpling. She passed away, and nobody got the recipe, so now I make the same thing, but I make the blackberry compote and make drop biscuits." Jillian Hirshaw, known for her sweet potato and pecan pies, also shared this sentiment of the importance of altering, but staying true to a family legacy:

> I had made my grandmother's sweet potato and pecan pies, and it is kind of passed down, like the recipes are passed down. Now that she has passed, some of the recipes went with her, but the one that stuck around was the sweet potato pie, and my mother put another spin on it and then I created something different. What I do is something different with my mix. Everybody's pie tastes a little different—my grandmother put lime juice, my mother did honey, different things like that, but the staple of the recipe within my family remains.

Tori and Mia also recognized that to be a true baker meant always needing to experiment:

> It's always something. Taste this, taste that. Always mixing up something. It took us a while to get these set flavors. It was a lot of add this, take that, going from place to place to taste. There are a great deal of similarities, and there's just this one thing that makes it different. It's the ones who are not afraid to venture off, to make a horrible mess in the kitchen, and try to figure it out who get it right.

In this way, baking rituals' performativity affords a sense of confidence and shared meaning to those who participate in them. The woman attempting to bake the Sun Drop cake knew enough about the pound-cake ritual to understand that adapting the recipe would allow her to solve the problem; the rest of the women's stories in this section showcase how making something their own makes them who they are. A different pinch of this, a different topping, and the recipe transforms, perhaps along with someone's subjectivity.

The argument that traditionally "female" skills can be deployed in "subjectivity-affirming" ways is particularly important in understanding some of the South's older women. Ashli went to the Poplar Tent Presbyterian Church's barbecue in Concord, North Carolina, to study that foodway but ended up learning how the nostalgia at work in making the desserts for the event bolsters the subjectivities of these women. Poplar Tent is known for its lavish dessert display, and the women of the church do their part to uphold this legacy. Ashli saw at least five different types of pound cake; red velvet, chocolate, strawberry, and caramel cakes; and pecan and sweet potato pies in the dessert tent. Sold by the slice or as a whole dessert, they were all made and donated by church members. It is true that many of these women are valorized for their ability to bake, but it is totalizing to argue that this form of nostalgia resists change, with the women (and men) of the church reflectively brooding over an inability to return to the "good old days." Rather, for these women, baking nostalgic desserts solidifies their role in a changing community and culture. The ability to bake something special gives them a way to contribute to their culture and matter; as Gantt (2001) puts it, "Through her contribution to the communal plate, she states her importance in a society that has frequently cut women out of its traditional access to power" (p. 82).

Baking was most definitely a part of these women's identities. As Neal (1990) explains, Southern cakes and other treats "show up at church suppers where cooks are often highly competitive" (p. 305). This was true at Poplar Tent, as women became known through specific desserts that are requested year after year. JoAnna explained, "A man came to the window and said, 'You used to have a lady that made the best pecan pie I ever tasted.' And I said, 'Yeah, she still bakes them and we still have some.' And he said, 'I want 4 pecan pies.'" When someone says, "I want Margaret Ann's chocolate pie," then, that woman's identity is supported. She still matters. Women become so well known for a creation at Poplar Tent that people call in advance of the barbecue to request certain desserts; as JoAnna emphasized, "So you know, word gets out." It is the case that these older women are not challenging the status quo through their baking, but they are doing something else rhetorically important—using food to emphasize their value and their subjectivities in a world that looks a lot different from the one they likely grew up in. Some may argue that these women are defined only by their roles as bakers, but being known in this way affirms their value in one particular part of their lives.

The dessert committee never knows how many desserts will be on offer until the day of the barbecue, but loaves and fishes style, there is always more than enough. The women send a rhetorical message by the sheer volume of what they make. For example, JoAnna told the story of one "matriarch" who is

> eighty years old, and she baked ten cakes, and some of them were three-layer cakes. We have another lady who is also eighty; this year, she only sent twenty-four pecan pies. She had a stroke some years ago, and it paralyzed her right side, and she was right handed. But she has taught herself to use her left hand and this year only made twenty-four because she had fallen and broken a bone. So she only got twenty-four made. The year before, when she was seventy-nine, she sent forty pies, *forty*!

Even though their baking functions as a form of edible nostalgia, harkening back to a time when this sort of cooking was the norm, this current execution serves an identity-strengthening function. In today's world, this type of baking is special, apart from the norm, and as such functions as a celebration of the people who can still bake like this.

This is not to say that baking always supports female subjectivity in empowering ways. For some, memories of baking rituals dredged up pain, calling forth remembrance of kitchen drudgery, unhappiness, and rigid female subjectivity. Though painful, these memories did, however, invite interpretive nostalgia. If reflexive nostalgia finds people moving from simply recalling the past through "rose-colored glasses" and blurring painful or uncomfortable elements, interpretive nostalgia allows even painful elements of memories to serve in encouraging change. Ashli's mother, for example, no longer bakes and proudly proclaims this decision, particularly each Christmas. She loves homemade sweets and has fond memories of some, but she is *done* baking. Ashli grew up eating home-baked goodies almost every day, from brownies after getting off the school bus, to homemade biscuits in the mornings. Each Christmas, her mother made more than twenty homemade pound-cake loaves to give as gifts. Ashli remembers going to bed during the holiday season as a child, watching as her mother kept moving about the kitchen, late into the night, sifting flour, inverting the loaf pans, tying ribbon around cellophane. Expecting her to tell stories about the glory of baking when talking about this book, Ashli was taken aback by the amount of pain that the experience called forth in her mother, now in her sixties. "Why the hell . . . I was crazy. I balanced the books for your father's hardware store (unpaid), raised you children on a very tight budget, and was still expected to serve as a shining example of small-town Southern womanhood. Crazy. What's even crazier is that I thought I *had* to do it. I bought into it." The edge of bitterness in her mom's voice eased into laughter as the conversation progressed. "You are so lucky," she said. "You have the luxury of being able to buy more than just what you need, you can select from lots of restaurants when you want to go out to eat, and you can buy great desserts when you don't want to make them. If you don't want to bake, no one will judge you in the way my generation was judged." Clearly, for Ashli's mom, baking was a ritual that was confining.

Even painful and confining, however, the ritual served a rhetorical purpose, allowing memories to be interpreted in ways that build resistance, empowerment, and subversion. These days, Ashli's mom can be found during football tailgate season and at Christmas proudly slicing a storebought (but still scratch-made) cake, telling friends and family how she can't believe anybody would bake when you can buy something so good for so little. "You couldn't pay me to bake this," she says gleefully, smiling and taking a big bite from a sour cream pound cake. It took Ashli's mom being able to break free from a small, but powerful, ritual to resist parts of a larger culture she no longer wanted. And she wasn't alone. In her interviews, Ashli heard over and over how women of a certain age, in particular, *had* to cook and *had* to bake and how that expectation sometimes led to frustration and unhappiness. However, others adapted these nostalgic rituals in ways that were meaningful to them, rather than discarding them completely. Indeed, part of the appeal of Jen and Carolee's business is its adaptability to the women's lifestyles, allowing them to work as both businesswomen and mothers, something that was very important to them: "It's a good fit for right now with our kids being young. We are definitely moms first, and really most of our baking is done before 2:00 p.m." Although these women aren't "leaning in" in the traditional sense, they are using their business to combine the paid work and maternal spheres. Carolee and Jen are white women who have the ability to engage in this type of work; nevertheless, they engage in the ritual on their terms. We cannot claim that they turn pound cake into a global high-stakes business, but we do assert that the ritual of baking provided two women with an outlet for creativity, self-determination, and profit.

As mentioned, reflection about baking rituals evokes painful memories for some and may indeed be an ongoing source of frustration and limitation, but we have seen how ritual is also affirming and liberating for others. As Ashli's mom pointed out, more people today have options that breathe new life into the pleasurable, connective, and creative potential of baking. What might be different about today's baking rituals is that they are not as mandatory as they once were. As we have seen in the previous example, ritualistic dessert expectations can reinforce gender norms, but changes in today's lifestyles allow baking to challenge them too. Some may decry the use of "convenience" products or store-bought cakes and cookies, but these choices allow the buyers to choose when and how (and whether) they want to bake. These decisions, in fact, bring more inventive rhetorical potential to the baking ritual when contemporary cooks decide to engage.

DESSERT SUPPORTS COMMUNITY RESILIENCE

When today's Southern cooks do decide to bake, they do more than com-ment upon gender norms. Certain desserts can affirm the spiritual and cultural health of our communities, soothing people in times of need and supporting cultural traditions that draw them together. Desserts feed com-munity resilience. Many Southern cookbooks and memoirs write about the comfort that can be given through food, and sweet things in particular seem to soothe anxiety or offer solace. Stories and statements like, "Her church family and neighbors knew they could depend on her for a 'cold oven pound cake' anytime they needed it," or, "From births to weddings to holidays, every-one counted on Grandma Sadie to have one or more marble cakes ready and waiting," abound in newspaper articles and cookbooks alike recounting the Southern dessert tradition (Rogers, 2004, p. 195). In a Burkean (1973) sense, then, dessert becomes a type of equipment for living or a way to cope with life, an especially sweet way to offer and receive love and care. Of course, one does not need dessert for sustenance, but the offer of a piece of pie or a warm slice of cake acts as a balm for both the giver and the recipient. People talk about the gift of Southern food blanketing them in comfort and evok-ing warm or positive memories, and not only does this nondiscursive edible nostalgia fortify the receiver, but it helps define a community's ethos. "Gift" food's edible nostalgia, then, functions as a type of resilience.

In a time of difficulty, an individual's identity is bolstered and strength-ened when he or she receives a home-baked treat because of the message of care that is delivered. These calories are loaded with meaning, and people know that they matter to someone, out of the sheer time it takes to bake and deliver something, rather than just dropping off something picked off a grocery store shelf or the restaurant takeout line (Puckett, 2006). JoAnna had baked a cream cheese pound cake for one of her church's elderly men recently home from the hospital, for example, and was excited to deliver it after our conversation. This delivery clearly meant more to her than just dropping off food to a shut in: "See if I sign up to take somebody a meal, I'm not going to the restaurant and picking it up. I want them to know that I had spent time for them because I love them, and I appreciate them, and I value them." Speaking of the time it takes to make complicated Southern drinks, bartender Terry Jordan notes, "All that complication. It's not complicated. It's just something you'll go through for somebody to make them a good drink . . . Because just like anybody that cooks in the kitchen, that's your soul going out into the glasses. The complicated part . . . not so much. The payment for a good drink is just a smile. That's the best payment. Is to know you got it right." Baking can act in the same way, with some interviewees arguing that home-baked goods share the message of love and care in ways that speak louder than their purchased, timesaving counterparts. JoAnna argued that such foods tell the recipient they are special: "I would rather receive something like that from somebody than a gift that someone purchased. Because you know they've invested themselves in it. Yeah, somebody thinks enough of you that they're going to take time out of their day or whatever to prepare this meal for you." As we've pointed out, the importance of whether something is home baked is debatable, but it did seem to send a message of care for some of our interviewees.

Providing a gift of food also works to strengthen the ethos of the givers as well. The ethos of care extended by taking loved community members food became another way that the women of the Poplar Tent defined themselves. As JoAnna explained, the "circles" of the church engage in these supportive activities "because many of them are widowers and that sort of thing, so they don't have their spouses, their wives, to bake for them anymore." There was a clear gendered division of this work, with the women serving as community carers/strengtheners through their labors of love. As JoAnna put it, the women's role in the community revolved around food and provided a special way for them to be involved in the life of the church and community:

> It's not just me that does it . . . It's any number of people in the church, and as I talk about it I realized almost everything we do, especially as the women, is, it revolves around food. We're taking care of their nourishment, maybe a little spiritual nourishment . . . I think it's part of being involved especially in the church. We look after people. I want to be involved, and so now I realize I'm involved because I'm feeding all these people. I mean in my mind I think that's typically Southern that we look after our people, you know.

Clearly, JoAnna and other women of the church derived value from their baking rituals and traditions, seemingly fortified and supported through their ability to support others. It may seem like we are thus providing yet another example of women stereotypically feeling self-worth through their ability to care for others. What we are arguing, however, is more subtle than that. JoAnna and her counterparts had careers and other responsibilities outside of the church, and their decision to participate in nostalgic baking rituals seemed to be based on how these activities made them feel about themselves.

Many of the women we spoke with used dessert in the self-supporting fashion JoAnna's experience encapsulates. Today's expression of baking rituals makes them seem less like a duty or expectation and more of a way for women to express creativity, self-determination, and love and care for others. In essence, what it came down to is whether women "used" their nostalgia and memories tied up with baking rituals or whether it let those memories and processes dominate or limit them. Baking today is about more than just fulfilling a gendered expectation and becomes equipment for living. Back in Virginia, the local Boy Scouts make "guaranteed to be good" banana pudding to raise enough money for their camping trips. Ben Mims drew upon his childhood memories of baking to come to terms with his gay identity (Reynolds, 2014). Even Carolee and Jen, who referenced historical notions of gender, illustrate how the nature of the baking ritual allowed them to develop a business in ways that suited the demands of their lives (providing authority and power and a way to "resist" the parts of culture they do not support). Indeed, all of the bakers we spoke to relied on their memories to offer ritualistic interpretations of nostalgic treats, but they did not see themselves as *just* "good cooks." All were employed formally elsewhere; thus, making dessert meant creativity, connecting with or strengthening a community, or participating in the life of a community. Dessert became equipment for life.

Indeed, some of the bakers we spoke to used their sweet equipment to help support the cultural health of their communities. Among African American women bakers in particular, opinions varied about whether traditional desserts should become healthier, but continued to be a source of cultural connection and pride. Rashaa Brown, for example, started a successful vegan cupcakery in Charlotte to meet the need for a healthier sweet. Raised in Mississippi, she ate the "old Southern way," but in Charlotte, she wanted to figure out a recipe that was both healthy and tasty. She explained, "I like food and food to taste good; it was important that it tasted good and a customer couldn't tell the difference between a conventional and healthier product."

For Rashaa, baking became a challenge to see if she could adapt recipes using less sugar, no genetically modified ingredients, and more organic ingredients. Rasha argues that education/awareness, not avoidance, is the key in preventing/reversing disturbing health trends in the African American community. Tori and Mia, the Cake Makin' Sisters, took a similar view about how to balance the desire for sweets along with the desire for health. For them, it came down to moderation: "You just need to keep in mind that this is just a treat. Just don't overdo it. Just balance. A cupcake is not going to kill you, but I would like to do some healthier options."

Jillian Hirshaw had a similar goal in improving the health of the African American community in rural South Carolina, but she also relied on her baking skills for more cultural nourishment. For Jillian, dessert became a way to get the farmers she wanted to support through her agricultural foundation to open up and trust her. In trying to record the stories of older African American farmers, some of whom had been sharecroppers, dessert became the entry point in building a relationship:

> It took years of cultivating a relationship with these farmers because they've been swindled out of land and out of money for so long so that they don't trust people whether you are black or white. And having them now trust me, they care for me like I'm a family member; it's definitely invaluable, and so when I do go down I often bring my grandmother's sweet potato pie to the farmers, and they kind of give me the validation "oh she taught you well" because it tastes good and tastes like *their* grandmother's pies.

For Jillian, the signature taste of the sweet potato pie within the African American community opens up these older farmers, but also people in general. She explained, "When I start a new job I bring in something, just to break the ice. It's a welcome gift and so that always opens up a dialogue, a warmer environment, especially if it is a baked good." Jillian talked about how in cities not considered Southern, sweet potato pie still elicited Southern taste memories, with people saying, "They don't make pies like this around here; it tastes like it is from the South; it tastes like my Grandmother's sweet potato pie."

The women differed slightly in how they saw their businesses playing into the health of their communities, but all found dessert as a source of inspiration. For Carolee and Jen, pound cake allowed them to see their roles as culinary educators, explaining, "We want to educate, and show how you can have one of these in your freezer and pull out the pound cake.... Cut it up, serve it ... and make it be what you want it to be." For Emma, the Southern Cake Queen, dessert became a mission, where she eventually wanted to leave Charlotte and go back home to Mt. Pleasant, South Carolina, to open up a bakery: "When the food truck scene is over, I want the storefront to be back home in Mt. Pleasant." Tori and Mia, too, were careful not to remain complacent, busily dreaming up the next phase of their business: "We want to expand. Being here was a blessing, and I wouldn't leave it, but you can't get stagnant, and hopefully things will happen. Go ahead and venture out." Since the sisters have been interviewed by the team that produces *Cake Boss* on the Food Network, their next venture may be bigger than even they anticipate. In their words, "We can dream a cake into reality. Tell us what you want, and we dream about it, literally. Every once in a while we may have the exact same dream." Women were not tied to the past through dessert; instead, it moved them forward in new directions.

CONCLUSION

This chapter has shown how taking the gendered expectations of Southern baking at face value leaves out an important part of their legacy in Southern culture. In the end, thinking about baking as a remaining gendered expectation is like leaving the salt out of a chocolate dessert. It loses its richness and depth. Nostalgia and ritual can be problematic, of course, but as we have illustrated, these tropes have rhetorical power along with their limitations.

The ability to "tweak" a baking recipe to make it your own while still keeping its connection to your family's past, for example, shows how nostalgia can be a generative rhetorical trope. We have shown how it is a source of connection. It can provide comfort in its traditional sense, helping us cope with the frustrations of daily life, a notion easily seen when sales of dessert rise in a downturned economy or difficult family time. Nostalgic dessert traditions may still be going strong, but they also serve as sources of inspiration and boundary pushing; as one chef explains, "There's only so much you can do with a nice piece of fish" (Shriver, 2008, para. 12).

Indeed, for the women we spoke to, dessert was far more than delimited expectation. Our interviews illustrated that women do not "re-trap" themselves when they become skilled bakers. Although it is important to acknowledge Gantt's (2001) worry that women reinscribe familiar domestic routines through these activities, we saw evidence that they were using baking rituals in new ways and for new purposes. Some women still feel pressure to fulfill domestic duties of various sorts (and perhaps the Poplar Church women did feel pressure to bake a certain number of pies, for example), but our argument is that the roles offered something else to these women, sometimes becoming sources of connection, creativity and self-expression, and cultural support. Women used dessert to pass on family stories, achieve social power, or deepen personal autonomy (Gantt, 2001). In our interviews, participating in a dessert ritual provided avenues for personal growth and understanding. In this way, examining historically female dessert rituals balances the typical cultural reliance of focusing on male chefs and male rituals such as barbecue. These rituals constitute a territory of symbolic action for women, but they are not limited to women. Food is a cultural ritual that signals power (Gantt, 2001), and dessert can be adapted by bakers in ways that show rhetorical promise.

PART THREE

AFTER-DINNER CONVERSATION

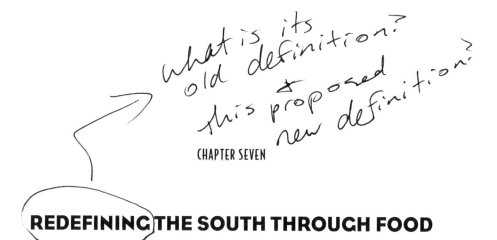

what is its definition?
old definition + this proposed new definition?

CHAPTER SEVEN

REDEFINING THE SOUTH THROUGH FOOD

As we meandered across the South in search of the definition of the region's food, the ultimate food examples, and the defining part of the area's cuisine, we found that there were not always clear-cut examples of these things. For some time, this bothered us because we began to question if there was a stable food upon which this regional identity could be defined and reified. What could we say about the Delta tamale phenomenon, the predominance of Greek-inspired restaurants in some cities, the popularity of Italian-inspired muffalettas in New Orleans, or the crawfish boils that are so fundamental to parts of the region? The more that we searched for Southern-style restaurants, the more variety we found along the way. We wondered, like other Southern foodways scholars (Forbes, 2014; Kramer, 2010), if the South was losing its culinary tradition.

Over time, we realized that this made the regional cuisine more rhetorically powerful, however. The flexibility that is bound up in today's version of Southern food invites a wider variety of individuals to the table and complements our understanding of the area's history and culture. In many ways, the authenticity of the food is less important than the role that it plays in developing a strong regional identity, creating a symbol of the South. Rather, the food itself and the discussion surrounding it are more important for the rhetorical work that they do. That is, it doesn't have to be your grandmother's type of Southern cooking _or_ the lardcore (high-end, heritage ingredients–based) version to have rhetorical possibility. Southern food helps define the area, and there is plenty of room to riff on this.

As we have argued throughout the book, Southern food provides one powerful means of contributing to a sense of individual, regional, gender, and ethnic identity. Food more broadly can influence how we see ourselves.

In other words, in addition to speaking/hearing identities, writing/reading identities, showing/seeing identities, we can also serve and consume identities. This is obviously oversimplifying the process, and we are in no way arguing that a bite of cornbread makes someone Southern. On the other hand, as symbols wash over us, we are influenced by some aspects. Some parts of those symbols remain with us, while others wash away; those that remain become a part of how we view ourselves and others. We see no reason why food—the very substance of life—would not also play a part in that process. With the study of Southern foodways, in fact, we argue that there is a strong case for food being just as powerful as other symbols in forming who we are and/or how we see ourselves. Changes in the food and foodways—how we create, serve, define, or stretch the boundaries of the food—can thus influence those identities. Consequently, attention to this type of rhetorical symbol is an important theoretical move for rhetorical studies and we hope to see Southern foodways studies contributing to that conversation.

In this final section of the book, we reflect on the different aspects of the Southern meal that we sampled through these chapters. Most importantly, this final chapter crystallizes what these stories say about the rhetorical potential of Southern food. Beyond the original story, however, this chapter will also turn to the stories that do not fit so neatly into the description of the Southern table. These are the stories that stretch the boundaries of the region, the people, and the food itself. Before turning to the final argument, though, we will first briefly revisit the Southern table.

THE SOUTHERN TABLE

Oh god... do we have to?

We have presented the argument that Southern food acts rhetorically, constitutively; that is, Southern food helps rhetorically define people and place and, consequently, has a significant impact on how individuals define themselves. The chapters in this book provided a culinary tour through the South, but also highlighted what we argue are the most powerful examples of the rhetorical potential of Southern food. What does Southern food *do*? In chapter one, "Consuming Rhetoric: How Southern Food Speaks," we explored the ways that food speaks. Food is rhetorically constructed, but also sends messages on its own through sound, smell, scent, touch, taste, and the accompanying memories that are triggered through the experience of the food. Southern food sends messages about the region, the people, and the history. While recent rhetorical research has started to account for the rhetorical potential of food, the example of Southern food provides a wealth of information about how food can speak.

Chapter two, "A Troubled Region and Its Possible Culinary Fix," looked at the ways that Southern food can affect people—partially through the movements that have emerged around the food, but also through the food itself. The fact that individuals have gathered together to show the importance of the region's foodways indicates that something significant happens through the combination of culture and food. Food can act as a uniter, but it also can define people in important ways. Southern food, through its basic characteristics, hails us to be hospitable, humble, aware of diversity, and aware of history—everything that would make the South a stronger, more united region. It also may provide opportunities for forgiveness and regional celebration. As Ben Mims argues:

? For what?

> We Southerners have a way of remembering important moments in our life through our food more than anyone else because it is our life here. Food is what we think of morning, noon, and night. So it makes sense that if there is anything that can bring Southerners to a common ground, it's our food. Not religion, not football, but food. (Reynolds, 2014)

hmmm - -

This is why we argue for the rhetorical potential of Southern food. It speaks both our past and our future; acknowledges our troubled past but points to the potential of a stronger future South.

Chapter three, "Sipping on Southern Hospitality: Drink as Rhetorical Invitation," then began the perusal of the Southern table by exploring how the offering of drinks begins the conversation that food allows. Through an initial showing of hospitality, drinks open up a conversation. Although the same could be said of the ways that food is used to show hospitality in the region, focusing on drinks allowed us to explore the complicated history that the region has with hospitality. Obviously there are complications surrounding the South and its exclusion of particular people based upon race, class, religion, and even regional biases. While acknowledging those complications, however, we argue that drink can be used rhetorically to send messages about openness to others.

Chapter four, "Turf Tussle: Uniting through North Carolina Barbecue," explored the ways that food (barbecue, in particular) creates identification among Southerners—acting to connect people by signaling authenticity through messages about barbecue's practices, place, and proprietors; performing masculine gender roles; and inviting people to connect over rural values in a contemporary context. We argue that barbecue is a big-tent food, meaning that it has the ability to welcome different people and different traditions into its long history in the South. Unlike cuisines that isolate through their formality, exclusivity, or knowledge requirements, like dining at a country club or appreciating an expensive wine, people can come to barbecue uninitiated and still connect to the experiences on offer.

Chapter five, "Authenticating Southernism: Creating a Sense of Place through Food," looked at the way that food can define us regionally and authenticate the region. Regardless of the type of food being offered—whether it is true authentic, fauxthentic, or new authentic—the rhetorical work that goes into establishing that authenticity helps establish regional boundaries. Exploring the connection to the place that is created through Southern food staples, we argue that these regional culinary creations reify our connection to place and, thus, provide a valuable argument for a regional identity.

Finally, chapter six, "Nostalgia, Ritual, and the Rhetorical Possibility of Southern Baking," showed the ways that Southern desserts provide outlets for connection, identity support, and cultural resilience through interpretations of nostalgia and ritual. Not only can food symbolize care and strength, but the act of creating and/or giving the dessert also serves identificatory purposes through the ritual of the act. Southern desserts highlight a theme that is found in the potential of Southern food generally; that is, it allows us to feel the force of our ties to the past but inspires us to stretch or break them to reach new levels of creativity or embrace new versions of subjectivity. The weight of the past grounds Southerners but does not commit them to making the same mistakes.

Our research shows that Southern food *does* significant rhetorical work. It speaks, moves people, welcomes people, identifies people, authenticates the region, and allows possibilities for nostalgia and ritual. Returning to our original argument—that Southern food has the potential to redefine the South in significant ways—this is why we believe that food offers us one way to do positive rhetorical work in the region. As Marcie Cohen Ferris (2014) argues, "In food lies the harsh dynamics of racism, sexism, class struggle, and ecological exploitation that have long defined the South; yet there, too, resides family, a strong connection to place, conviviality, creativity, and flavor" (p. 1). Southern food both defines the region (acknowledging its troubled history) and also opens up possibilities for redefining it. That is, studying and replicating Southern history through the creation of and consumption of foods while also relaxing the boundaries of the foodways to allow for diversity may provide an important route to strengthening the South. The

As what???

boundary stretching is a significant part of this possibility, though, so the next section will explore that concept in more depth.

↳ *caustic stretching?*

RHETORICAL POTENTIAL OF BOUNDARY CROSSING

hmm

Through the various chapters, then, we have argued that Southern food can act rhetorically in several ways. It can overcome a sense of alienation through courtship and hospitality. Food can be offered/read as a symbol of an identity and/or a region. It can help define and authenticate a region, allowing for a stronger sense of belongingness. It can be used as a symbol of gender performativity. It can also bring people together, emphasizing commonality when no consubstantiality seems apparent. But perhaps most importantly, while combining with the ability to welcome, identify, authenticate, signify, perform, and unify, Southern food has the potential to cross racial, class, ethnic, religious, gender, and geographical boundaries, bringing a wide variety of consumers together to celebrate one thing.

So this is the point

What we have discovered while traveling across the region, talking to and observing Southerners, and reading the plethora of books and articles that explore Southern food is that the food itself does not benefit from a single definition. Southern food does not have to be *one* thing; in fact, the food rhetorically functions more effectively when defined more broadly. This boundary stretching allows for a more diverse understanding of the region when it pushes against the borders of foods and brings more people into the conversation. For this reason, Delta tamales; Mississippi coast Vietnamese foods; Texas kolaches; and Charlotte's vibrant, crazy mishmash of Southern ethnic food combinations (Mexican-Southern, Middle Eastern–Southern, Chinese-Southern) all find a place at the Southern food table, depending on the region. There is room for ethnic boundary stretching, bringing immigrants and ethnic migration into the story of Southern foodways. That Chinese immigrant chef Chung Lam's wok-cooked okra becomes one of his most popular items in Charlotte's "new South" is rhetorically interesting. Southerners' willingness to experience a different cuisine through the lens of a familiar vegetable signals the possibility of more openness to cultural adventuring. Do a search for "boiled peanut hummus" online and find people rhapsodizing about the deliciousness of using an old Southern ingredient in a new interpretation. These more permeable boundaries mean that the region itself can be redefined. After all, there is no definitive boundary when it comes to discussions about "the South." As Elizabeth Engelhardt (2011)

explain:

But redefined as what?

puts it, "The imagined South is the South, as it were, powerful and contested" (p. 7). And, of course, food is a large part of that imagined region. The very popularity of Southern food in contemporary American culture broadly (evidenced by a nationwide explosion of Southern restaurants, popularity of Benton's bacon, sudden ubiquity of things served in Mason jars) shows that people want an anchor to the "simpler" times the South signals but also to make these traditions their own in their revisioning. There is no need to police the boundaries of Southern food so strictly when the concern is telling the story of the region—both historically and moving forward.

Why?

One conversation in particular highlighted one of the most important reasons to consider a broader definition of Southern food. As we drove away from Chicago's Ruby's Restaurant and back toward the tourist district, we chatted with our livery driver, Veronica. She asked how we had heard about Ruby's, and we began to tell her about our mission to find authentic Southern food in the city. We asked her what she thought authentic Southern food was, and in many ways, she gave us one of the best definitions of authenticity that we had come across in our travels. Authenticity, she argued, was "not just reading a recipe from a book," but creating food "like someone's grandmother makes it." Collards and tomatoes straight out of the backyard garden might have been the standard for one family. At the same time, her definition allows for that flexibility in defining Southern food that makes Velveeta, Campbell's cream of mushroom soup, and Dr. Pepper legitimate ingredients. As for "authentic" Southern restaurants, Veronica argued that they really "go into the neighborhoods" and make themselves a part of the community, rather than "just want[ing] to make money." There is an emphasis here on history, people, and a state of mind. While this boundary stretching might disturb some Southern food purists, this is more reflective of the culture and allows for more rhetorical power.

I must be more of a purist

Consequently, there is a place in the Southern food story for both historical restaurants and new South eateries. Both dives and fine dining restaurants shape our understanding of the foodways. Southern restaurant chains even have a place in the story of the foodways of the region. Rural settings and urban settings have an influence over our food. There is also room for historical recipes, even when they include processed ingredients. The Southern Methodists will carry on making casseroles out of these ingredients for funerals and other gatherings even while they start growing gardens again to make a tomato pie from scratch the way their grandmother might have. It is unnecessary to claim that the Southern recipes of a certain time period are *more* authentic. The shrimp mold served at Christmas made of ketchup,

Jello, and Ritz crackers is just as able to tell a family story as the barbecue sandwiches made from heritage breed pigs and wheat you grow yourself for the bun. What is more important than labeling certain foods as authentic or historically accurate or regionally distinct—at least when it comes to discussing the rhetorical nature of food—is how they are perceived to be a part of the region, of belonging to a certain people. For this reason, the boundary stretching that has occurred in the Southern menu represents an important part of the story of the rhetorical power of food. In Ted Ownby's (2013) words, Southern food scholars have begun to "overturn the idea of the South as a place with a biracial society with biracial foodways" and have begun to more carefully consider the ethnic diversity of the region's cuisine (p. 365). In our field research, we certainly saw signs of this complexity, which supports our argument that food can serve as a rhetorical opening between different groups of people. That we saw fried catfish, a traditional Southern food, served in an Indian-style coconut-curry–scented broth in Atlanta and Charlotteans enjoying barbecue prepared with Vietnamese influences suggests that Southern food is not static, stuck in the past. We need to continue to account for these changes and the rhetorical possibilities they invite.

For example, as a native south Texan, Wendy grew up eating tamales. Although there were stories (almost tall tales) about family attempts to create the homemade variety, it was much easier, tastier, and mentally healthier (given the amount of work that goes into tamales) to buy them from the various family-run tamale stands in the area. Moving into Mississippi and discovering that the Delta had its own tamale tradition was surprising, then. Although the exact history of the tamale in this area is contested, some associate the introduction of the food to the migrants from Mexico who came to the area to work in the cotton fields (Evans, n.d.). There is no doubt that the tradition is strong in the Delta, with plenty of tamale stands to choose from and the option to buy a dozen while filling up the gas tank at many stations. Originally a grocery store, Doe's Eat Place, in Greenville, Mississippi, is best known for its steaks, but the hot tamales are what originally allowed the restaurant to grow in its early days. The family started serving food to black customers and found that tamales were a hot seller. Word got out around town that the food was good, and in a strange turn of events, white customers started slipping in the back door to grab some grub. Charles Serna, one of the owners, explained to us that he did not really consider Doe's to be a Southern food restaurant, but the example of the tamales becoming a symbol of the Delta provides yet another example of the possibility for boundary stretching when it comes to Southern food.

The "kolache trail" offers another example of a food that has become a part of the Southern food story primarily through changes in the demographics of an area. West Texas, just south of Dallas, has become the kolache mecca, but the trail extends through the central part of Texas. Driving through this area, one is just as likely to find gas stations offering kolaches as barbecue. The pastries (filled with fruit, cheese or meat) made their way into Texas by way of the mid-1800s Czech immigration (although the Czech Republic did not yet exist, so the word "Czech" here is only loosely being used), although many claim that the Czech American version is far removed from the European versions (Walsh, 2012). Wendy's travels through this area, after leaving the State Fair of Texas in Dallas, first took her off the highway and into the newly built Slovacek's restaurant. Formerly an old gas station with a side business in kolaches and sausage, it has expanded beyond that space and is now a full-sized casual restaurant with a counter, a full deli area, and a gift shop. It has become a destination for those in the know as well as those who merely follow the signs. On this Sunday afternoon, Wendy stood in line with locals meeting up with family after church as well as tourists taking a break from the highway. Glancing around, there were many signs of cultures overlapping and even converging. There were Czech phrases written on signs ("Jak se mas?"—How are you?) next to Texas-themed T-shirts, bags, and other souvenirs. There were traditional kolaches (poppy seed) next to peach pastries (peaches are an abundant crop in central Texas), traditional Czech sausage next to jalapeno sausage. The blending of the food styles was symbolic of how permeable these boundaries are, and have always been, in Southern food. New cultures and new cuisines have always seeped into "traditional" Southern food and represent rhetorical opportunity. Of course, these stories of ethnic diversity in the region and the influence that that diversity has had on the foodways are endless. There is a long history of Italian food in the home of Creole and Cajun cuisine—New Orleans. As Justin Nystrom (2013) argues, Italian foodways had a significant influence on the food of the city, affording immigrants the opportunity to make a living in their new home, while also expressing "their homeland and its cultural heritage" (p. 130). The muffaletta sandwich has become a food that is "emblematic of both the culinary traditions of Sicily and the nature of the family business—not to mention the very identity of the French Quarter for much of the twentieth century" (Nystrom, 2013, p. 136). Greek food has become a staple in Birmingham and Jackson, Mississippi, thanks to Greek immigrants (SFA, Greeks in Birmingham; SFA, Jackson's Iconic Restaurants). The Mississippi and Louisiana coasts have been influenced by Vietnamese immigrants. North Carolina has seen a significant rise in its international community, and consequently, its food choices have changed dramatically. A visit to Charlotte's state-owned farmer's market, for example, finds mounds of Brazilian pineapple guavas and Chinese long beans next to vendors selling heritage pork and purple Cherokee tomatoes from local farms. A drive along Atlanta's Buford Highway lets visitors stop at strip malls to "eat the world," offering Vietnamese pho and banh mi, Mexican tacos, and Korean bibimbap (Knowlton, 2015).

What these brief examples show is that the food of the South is changing as the population changes. Cooley (2015) explains, "Southern foodways are often described as 'traditional'—a term loaded with racial stereotype and privilege. Far from being static, however, southern food practices are constantly evolving, a dynamic facet of a diverse regional culture" (p. 6). In many cases, those changes happen when immigrants and transplants bring food from home and integrate into the culture. In other cases, though, ethnic foods make their way into the Southern palate. The boundaries of the region's foodways are permeable and allow for these culinary traditions to inform each other, offering interesting new tastes and more important for the argument of this book, bringing more people to the table. Tom Hantchett, newly retired historian at the Levine Museum of the New South in Charlotte, North Carolina, calls this phenomenon the "Newcomer South" whereby transplants and immigrants have brought their food, ways of doing business, and perspectives about education, for example, into the character of the South (Chesser, 2011). In Charlotte, for example, it is no longer relevant to query, "You're not from around here, are you?" because "what's going on now is dramatically different than even a generation ago. No longer are people leaving the South to find opportunity in the urban North as they did for most of the 20th century. Today newcomers are arriving here from across the U.S. and around the globe" (Chesser, 2011, para. 9). Along with these changes in population comes an opportunity for Southern food because their influence enlivens the narrative of Southern foodways. Hantchett (2014) contends, "I personally would argue that 'Southern' now includes things like tres leches cake. Immigrants are a huge part of our history and culture in the past twenty-five years, and (their) impact will only grow as kids are born and grow up cooking." The interesting complexities of the "Newcomer South" are not limited to Southern cities either. Delta towns see pockets of Asian communities changing that cultural fabric, and rural Appalachia is being settled by a large Hispanic population. American culture is full of stories of how immigrant traditions changed traditional foodways, and the South is poised to become part of this larger story in more significant ways. Lest we

Lest sound like we are arguing for the wholesale mishmash of traditional South-ern foodways with immigrant ones without a glance backward, however, we should more fully consider the possibilities and limitations of Southern food in this contemporary cultural context.

POSSIBILITIES AND LIMITATIONS OF SOUTHERN FOOD

Given that Southern food can do all of this rhetorical work—creating, defin-ing, setting boundaries, crossing boundaries, performing, and so forth—there is clearly a great deal of potential for using it as one of the tools to redefine the South. That is, if food can bring people together (physically and symboli-cally); emphasize a shared history, place, and people; and open up dialogue, we should use this rhetorical tool more fully. Some entities (such as the SFA) certainly embrace this idea, but these findings indicate that foodways can be used even more widely to rhetorically emphasize shared substance. As Mar-cie Cohen Ferris (2014) argues, "In food lies the harsh dynamics of racism, sexism, class struggle, and ecological exploitation that have long defined the South; yet there, too, resides family, a strong connection to place, convivial-ity, creativity, and flavor" (p. 1). If Southern food is able to acknowledge dif-ference—defined broadly—while also exploring fundamental similarities, then there are many uses for it. Some of this rhetorical power can also be discussed more broadly when examining food in general, but as we have argued throughout the book, Southern food provides a particularly strong and unique example of this type of rhetorical work.

With these rhetorical possibilities in mind, it can be easy to veer too far into the breathless types of food writing that sing only the praises of South-ern cuisine. As we have demonstrated in each chapter of this book, each potential power that Southern food has in bringing people together must be coupled with a recognition of its limitations, an acknowledgement of the often difficult, tumultuous, and shameful history and ongoing struggles of the South. In the minds of those unfamiliar with the actual historical roots of Southern cooking, for example, one limitation of its rhetorical potential is the perception that it is unhealthy and plays too strong a role in the region's obesity crisis. As one chef summarizes, "The biggest stereotype is that our food is greasy, it's too salty, it's too sweet, and it's not healthy. It's good food, and if the chicken's greasy it means it wasn't cooked properly" (in O'Neil, 2011, para. 6). One way to combat this limitation is simply education, point-ing out that Southern diets historically were in reality vegetable based, with meat, for example, used more as a condiment and seasoning agent than as the entrée (O'Neil, 2011). Another way to overcome stereotypical understandings of Southern food is to acknowledge that the way Southerners (and by extension, Americans in general) used to live has changed, and with the move toward more sedentary lifestyles comes the need to change the way we eat. Southern cattleman Will Harris points out that the South was a particularly agrarian society that allowed for big dinners and ways to work off any extra calories: "We were an agrarian society. When you're bailing hay, you don't need to go jogging" (in O'Neil, 2011, para. 12). Dori Sanders expresses the same notion, acknowledging that even as Southern society became less agricultural, "people still ate like they were sweating in fields when they were commuting in air-conditioned cars" (in Auchmutey, 1995, para. 28). While these criticisms may hold truth, we contend that dealing with the issue of health is not unique to Southern food. Whether it is Chicagoans enjoying deep-dish pizza, Californians appreciating a variety of Mexican tacos, or Bostonians eagerly awaiting their Sunday "gravy" of tomato sauce and pasta, Americans collectively have seen major changes to their diets that, arguably, do not suit their current lifestyles.

Related to this problem of stereotyping the Southern diet is the concern that economic conditions often lead to the consumption of too much of the "wrong" calories (processed food and the like) or not having access to enough calories in general. While there is an obvious need to address hunger in the region, there is also a tendency to use the consumption of a particular *type* of food to denigrate and ostracize. As Chris Offutt (2015) warns, "Economic status dictates class and diet. We arrange food in a hierarchy based on who originally ate it until we reach the diet of the poor. The food is called trash, and then the people are" (para. 30). Offutt (2015) is convinced, however, that learning about these foods and sharing them is also the only way out of the damaging nature of these stereotypes, arguing that is a boundary "that only food can cross" (para. 30). Whether it is correcting stereotypes or providing opportunities for people to partake of particular foods so that they can better help groups understand each other, there is a great deal of work left to do. How we talk about Southern food matters.

Finally, the biggest limitation of the rhetorical potential of Southern food is that the food is not a cure all. We may be arguing for possibilities for connection in each of our preceding chapters, but it is important to acknowledge that you cannot bring food to a crisis moment. It is ridiculous to think that a casserole will stop bigoted police from making suspicious arrests or that a cake can get people to sit down, take a bite, and stop rioting. Of course we are not making this argument; the wounds are too deep. What food can do, however, is intervene before that moment occurs. If we learn about each other through what we eat, maybe we will realize that we have more in common than we think and become more willing to work together on the problems that plague us.

Just as we were wrapping up this book, Ashli took a chance and expressed these beliefs in an entry for an essay contest sponsored by the *Charleston Post and Courier*. In 1865, renowned black chef and caterer Nat Fuller held a reunification banquet in Charleston that was unheard of at the time for inviting both blacks and whites to celebrate the end of the Civil War. The feast was recreated 150 years later, in April 2015, by a group of chefs, writers, and food producers led by University of South Carolina professor David Shields. Seventy-four of the guests were preselected for their commitment to social justice through food by Shields and his team, and the other six seats were up for grabs through the contest. In her winning essay, Ashli reflected on the possibility of food serving as a contemporary example of the type of social justice that Fuller sought to create all those years ago. She wrote:

I wouldn't have been invited to Nat Fuller's reunification banquet in April of 1865. Far away from Charleston, I would likely have been working deep within the mountains of Virginia, planting crops and making do with my cornmeal, leather-britches, and cast-iron skillet until spring's ramps and asparagus provided some color and variety. A White woman, yes, and a Southern one at that, but I'm certain I wouldn't have counted; instead, I would have been a woman without means, without membership in a community beyond my hazy blue horizon, without even the ability to read the storied news about the feast. That those desperation dishes of cornbread and beans have come to symbolize authenticity, community, and regional pride showcase the renewed possibilities of using food, as Nat Fuller did, as radical hospitality. I wouldn't have known it then, but my use of cornmeal connected me to the African American cooks in Charleston at the time. Like them, I made do; and like Nat Fuller, I made it delicious.

That is why Southern food brims with such possibility. Our churches may still remain largely segregated and some of our neighborhood schools still divided by color, but remarkably, stunningly, we can sit down with someone different from us, eat something delicious, and find some common ground that acts as a balm in soothing these wounds. We can go to Chicago, that bastion of Southern Black migration, and though we may be the only white women in the place, be welcomed (warmly, truly, fully) to enjoy soul food specialties in a neighborhood that even the taxis avoid. We can go to a BBQ joint in Eastern North Carolina and marvel at how take out line and table service patrons alike crowd around for the char, the smoke, and the taste of community. We can sit at lunch counters across the South (those tiny battlefields of the Civil Rights Movement) and strike up a conversation with someone who looks nothing like us but likes at least one thing we do.

Post Ferguson, we remain hungry for solace. We still thirst for kinship. But food sends messages that help build and repair these relationships. Everything we eat and choose to serve says something, intentional or not, about our upbringing, about how we view ourselves and others, and about the cultural ties that help create who we are, as individuals, as a community, as a region, and as a nation. Food tells our stories, both past and present. And, because Southern food tells such important stories, it provides a meaningful way to open up dialogue. By sharing and celebrating the stories of Southern food, but more importantly by sharing the actual food, Southerners are able to focus on similar histories and traditions, despite the division that has plagued and continues to plague the South. The ritual of radical hospitality, of cooking and eating Southern food, is a small, but significant, way to reaffirm the strength of our region and to continue to build connections across racial and class lines. Southern food is not monolithic, and celebrating its many differences helps us come to terms with societal difference. The possibility of using Southern food to open up opportunities for celebrating a shared food culture is a noteworthy moment. Food might lead the way. When we eat together, we become full, satisfied with the hope of a better South. We take a bite in the right direction. Maybe that's what Nat Fuller was betting on, all those many years ago. (in Raskin, 2015, para. 35)

On the night of the recreation of the reunification banquet, Ashli found herself surrounded by the performance of these ideals. Charleston chef Kevin Mitchell assumed the role of Fuller at the feast, calling the group of eighty to attention with the words: "All things are ready, come to feast; come for the table is spread, ye weary, ye famishing, come and thou shall be richly fed." And indeed we were, from nine courses that would not have been characterized as "Southern" in today's estimation. We ate roasted capon, Bradford watermelon pickles, and venison with currant demiglace, dishes that would have appeared on the menus at the time and were very much "authentic," with no fried chicken or grits in sight. Speaking as Fuller, Mitchell encouraged us to "talk with your neighbor, make a new friend, and hear someone tell his or her story." As the seating for the banquet was done by place card, strategically designed to seat strangers together, the diners enacted this performance. As they did so, the potential to encourage true listening, through the sharing of a meal, emerged. The relevance of reconciliation remained clear, with Mitchell, again as Fuller, noting, "These have not been hospitable times, strife and sorrow have for too long held the upper hand." Indeed, the prospect of racial justice seemed dim: a week before, unarmed Walter Scott had been gunned down by a police officer in north Charleston; the riots in Baltimore over Freddie Gray's death would occur two weeks later. And yet, as Mitchell/ Fuller intoned, "it is an ancient custom that once people sit at a table and break bread and share salt, that they will do no harm to one another." The diners were a reflective crew, encouraged by the hosts to follow the dinner with toasts, speaking whatever sentiment of reconciliation the banquet had cultivated among them. One of Ashli's fellow essayists, Shelia Anderson, an African American and a longtime resident of Charleston, put the rhetorical potential of the evening best in her toast. She said:

> Today we've come home. Our hearts swelling with anticipation that home brings. Yes, we've taken identities not of our own. We've sinned against God and human kind. But oh how we have longed to return home, how we've longed for fellowship around home's great bountiful table, as they did so long ago, native and stranger together, in a great feast of remembrance and thanksgiving. We have returned to where liberty, freedom, and equality dwell. We have come home to the heart of America.

Foodways are rhetorical, and Southern foodways are rhetorical in particular ways. Their humble, hospitable, and diverse characteristics define a people and a region, as the essayist so eloquently toasted. When we consume food born of Southern hands and the troubled Southern story, we consume parts of our identities. What's left is to see how much eating at the Southern table redefines who we are and where we are headed.

So we really don't do much at all, seems we just go along for the ride.

REFERENCES

Abarca, M. (2004). Authentic or not, it's original. *Food and Foodways, 12,* 1–25.

Abramson, R., & Haskell, J. (2006). *Encyclopedia of Appalachia.* Knoxville: University of Tennessee Press.

Acheson, H. (2011). *A new turn in the South.* New York: Clarkson Potter.

Albala, K. (Ed.). (2013). *Routledge international handbook of food studies.* London: Routledge.

Albrecht, M. M. (2008). Acting naturally unnaturally: The performative nature of authenticity in contemporary popular music. *Text and Performance Quarterly, 28*(4), 379–395.

Allen. J. (2011, March 1). The Southern Foodways Alliance shares the stories of the South at the Potlikker Film Festival. *Charleston City Paper.* Retrieved from http://www.charlestoncitypaper.com.

Aller, J. E. (2010). *Cider beans, wild greens, and dandelion jelly: Recipes from southern Appalachia.* Kansas City, MO: Andrews McMeel.

Althusser, L. (1971). Ideology and ideological state apparatuses (notes toward an investigation). In L. Althusser, *Lenin and philosophy and other essays* (B. Brewster, Trans.) New York: Monthly Review.

Amy, E. G. (2007). Katrina and colonialism: The sins of our forefathers perpetuated? *Administrative Theory & Praxis, 29,* 512–533.

Anderson, B. (2012). *Cornbread nation 6: The best of Southern food writing.* Athens: University of Georgia Press.

Anderson, C., Johnson, V., Gregory, L., Roberts, K., Eshleman, T., Morris, K. B., Fox, B. P., Winiecki, S. (January 1, 2011). Southern food guide. *Richmond: The Magazine of Metropolitan Richmond* (pp. 78–95).

AP. (2013, August 13). Viewers flock to "Duck Dynasty" in record numbers. Retrieved from http://www.huffingtonpost.com.

Apuzzo, M., & Williams, T. (2015, April 8). Video of Walter Scott shooting reignites debate on police tactics. *New York Times.* Retrieved from http://nytimes.com.

Askegaard, S., & Kjeldgaard, D. (2007). Here, there, and everywhere: Place branding and gastronomical globalization in a macromarketing perspective. *Journal of Macromarketing, 27*(2), 138–147.

Atkins-Sayre, W. (2010). Articulating identity: People for the Ethical Treatment of Animals and the animal/human divide. *Western Journal of Communication, 74,* 309–328.

Atkins-Sayre, W., & Stokes, A. Q. (2014). Crafting the cornbread nation: The Southern Foodways Alliance and Southern identity. *Southern Communication Journal, 79*(2), 77–93.

Auchmutey, J. (1995, October 12). Soul food's new look: Cooks eye past as they stir up a lighter menu. *Atlanta Journal Constitution.* Retrieved from Lexis Nexis database.

Auchmutey, J. (2007). Barbecue. In John T. Edge (Ed.), *Foodways: The New Encyclopedia of Southern Culture,* vol. 7 (pp. 22–26). Chapel Hill: University of North Carolina Press.

Baer, H. A., & Jones, Y. (1992). *African Americans in the South: Issues of race, class, and gender*. Athens: University of Georgia Press.

Bauer, M., Ramírez, M., & Southern Poverty Law Center. (2010). *Injustice on our plates: Immigrant women in the U.S. food industry: A report by the Southern Poverty Law Center*. Montgomery, AL: Southern Poverty Law Center.

Beall, S., & O'Neill, M. (2009). *The Blackberry Farm cookbook: Four seasons of great food and the good life*. New York: Clarkson Potter.

Beall, S., Stets, M., & Blackberry Farm (Walland, Tenn.). (2012). *The foothills cuisine of Blackberry Farm: Recipes and wisdom from our artisans, chefs, and Smoky Mountain ancestors*. New York: Clarkson Potter.

Beasley, V. B. (2002). Engendering democratic change: How three U.S. presidents discussed female suffrage. *Rhetoric & Public Affairs, 5*, 79–103.

Beckham, S. B. (1989). Porches. In C. R. Wilson & W. Ferris (Eds.), *Encyclopedia of Southern culture* (p. 515). Chapel Hill: University of North Carolina Press.

Bell, L. A. (2010). *Storytelling for social justice: Connecting narrative and the arts in antiracist teaching*. New York: Routledge.

Benford, R., & Gough, B. (2006). Defining and defending unhealthy practices. *Journal of Health Psychology, 11*, 427–440.

Biesecker, B. A. (2002). Remembering World War II: The rhetoric and politics of national commemoration at the turn of the 21st century. *Quarterly Journal of Speech, 88*, 393–409.

Black, E. (1970). The second persona. *Quarterly Journal of Speech, 73*, 133–150.

Blair, C. (1999). Contemporary U.S. memorial sites as exemplars of rhetoric's materiality. In J. Selzer & S. Crowley (Eds.), *Rhetorical bodies* (pp. 16–57). Madison: University of Wisconsin Press.

Blend, B. (2001). "I am an act of kneading": Food and the making of Chicana identity. In S. A. Inness (Ed.), *Cooking lessons: The politics of gender and food* (pp. 41–62). Lanham, MD: Rowman & Littlefield.

Bloom, L. Z. (2008). Consuming prose: The delectable rhetoric of food writing. *College English, 70*, 346–362.

Blount, R. (2006). *Long time leaving: Dispatches from up South*. New York: Knopf.

Bluewater Marketing (Firm) & North Carolina Association of Festivals & Events. (1996). *A taste of North Carolina: A collection of recipes from festivals and events of North Carolina*. Wilmington, NC: Bluewater Marketing.

Boorstein, M. (2004, June 13). Barbecue event aims to raise V.A.'s interest. *The Washington Post*. Retrieved from Lexis Nexis database.

Bowen, D. (2006, October 13). Pulled pork, pulled corks. *New York Times*. Retrieved from http://lexisnexis.com.

Boym, S. (2001). *The future of nostalgia*. New York: Basic Books.

Brock, S. (2014). *Heritage*. New York: Artisan.

Brock, W. (2005, August 11). Turning over a new leaf raised on sweet tea, southerner looks beyond his roots and embraces world of exotic variations. *The Atlanta Journal-Constitution*, K1.

Brown, A. (2010). Foreword. *The Southern Foodways Alliance community cookbook*. Athens: University of Georgia Press.

Brown, J. (2012, December 13). The surprising history of the cocktail. *Telegraph*. Retrieved from http://www.telegraph.co.uk.

Brown, W. (2009). "Eat it to save it": April McGreger in conversation with tradition. *Southern Cultures, 15*, 93–102.

Browne, S. H. (1995). Reading, rhetoric, and the texture of public memory. *Quarterly Journal of Speech, 81*, 237–265.

Browning, L. (2014, August 20). Are women better grillers than men? *Newsweek*. Retrieved from http://www.newsweek.com.

Bruce, T. (2010, December). A tale of two tamales. *Southern Living*. Retrieved from www.southern living.com.

Brummett, B. (1985). Electronic literature as equipment for living: Haunted house films. *Critical Studies in Mass Communication, 2*, 247–261.

Buncombe, A. (2005, May 29). Southern barbecue pork lovers split over short and sweet and sweet or slow and sharp sauce. *Independent on Sunday*. Retrieved from http://www.lexisnexis.com.

Burke, K. (1966). *Language as symbolic action*. Berkley: University of California Press.

Burke, K. (1950/1969). *A rhetoric of motives*. Berkeley: University of California Press. (Original work published 1950).

Burke, K. (1973). *The philosophy of literary form: Studies in symbolic action*, 3rd ed. Berkeley: University of California Press.

Burke, K. (1984). *Attitudes toward history*. Berkeley: University of California Press.

Burns, R. (2012, November 1). How southern are we? *Atlanta Magazine*. Retrieved from www .atlantamagazine.

Burr-Miller, A. C. (2011). What's your fantasy? Fantasy baseball as equipment for living. *Southern Communication Journal, 76*, 443–464.

Butler, J. (1988). Performative acts and gender constitution: An essay in phenomenology and feminist theory. *Theatre Journal, 40*, 519–531.

Butler, J. (1990). *Gender trouble: Feminism and the subversion of identity*. New York: Routledge.

Butler, B. (2007). Greens. In J. T. Edge (Ed.), *Foodways: The new encyclopedia of Southern culture*, vol. 7 (pp. 170–172). Chapel Hill, NC: University of North Carolina Press.

Carlson, A. (1992). Creative casuistry and feminist consciousness: The rhetoric of moral reform. *Quarterly Journal of Speech, 78*, 16–32.

Carr, D. (1986). *Time, narrative, and history*. Bloomington: Indiana University Press.

Carr, S. (2012, December). In Southern towns, "segregation academies" are still going strong. *The Atlantic*. Retrieved from http://www.theatlantic.com.

Carroll, B. E. (2012). Rhetoric of "Buy Irish Food" campaigns: Speaking to consumer values to valorise the "local" and exclude "others?" *Irish Geography, 45*, 87–109.

Carter, H. (1963). *First person rural*. Garden City, NY: Doubleday.

Cash, W. (1941). *The mind of the South*. New York: Vintage Books.

Center for a Better South (2011). Special Louisiana edition of Gravy. Retrieved from www.better south.org.

Charland, M. (1987). Constitutive rhetoric: The case of the Peuple Quebecois. *Quarterly Journal of Speech, 73*, 133–150.

Chavez, K. R. (2011). Counter-public enclaves and understanding the function of rhetoric in social movement coalition-building. *Communication Quarterly, 59*, 1–18.

Cherry, E., Ellis, C., & DeSoucey, M. (2011). Food for thought, thought for food: Consumption, identity, and ethnography. *Journal of Contemporary Ethnography, 40*, 231–258.

Chesser, J. (2011, November 18). You're not from around here, are you? UNC Charlotte Urban Institute. Retrieved from http://www.ui.uncc.edu.

Clark, T. (1989). Agriculture. In C. R. Wilson & W. Ferris (Eds.), *Encyclopedia of Southern culture*. Chapel Hill, NC: University of North Carolina Press.

Cobb, C. (2008). Despite unhealthy reputation, influence of Southern cuisine expands. *Nation's Restaurant News*. Retrieved from LexisNexis Database.

Cobb, J. C. (2011). *The South and America since World War II*. Oxford, UK: Oxford University Press.

Cohen, D., Vandello, J., Puente, S., & Ratilla, A. (1999). "When you call me that, smile!" How norms for politeness, interaction styles, and aggression work together in Southern culture. *Social Psychology Quarterly, 62,* 257–275.

Cole, J. & Lewis, H. (2013, February). The South's most storied recipes. *Southern Living,* 78–87.

Conser, W. H., & Payne, R. M. (2008). *Southern crossroads: Perspectives on religion and culture.* Lexington: University Press of Kentucky.

Cooley, A. J. (2015). *To live and dine in Dixie: The evolution of urban food culture in the Jim Crow South.* Athens: University of Georgia Press.

Cooren, F. (2012). Communication theory at the center: Ventriloquism and the communicative constitution of reality. *Journal of Communication, 62,* 1–20.

Cooren, F., Kuhn, T., Cornelissen, J. P., & Clark, T. (2011). Communication, organizing and organization: An overview and introduction to the special issue. *Organization Studies, 32,* 1149–1170.

Cordova, N. (2004). The constitutive force of the Catecismo del Pueblo in Puerto Rico's popular democratic party campaign of 1938–1940. *Quarterly Journal of Speech, 90,* 212–233.

Counihan, C. M. (1999). *The anthropology of food and body: Gender, meaning and power.* New York: Routledge.

Counihan, C. M. (2009). *A tortilla is like life: Food and culture in the San Luis Valley of Colorado.* Austin: University of Texas Press.

Craig, R. (2000). Dewey and Gadamer on practical reflection: Toward a methodology for the practical disciplines. In D. K. Perry (Ed.), *Pragmatism and communication research* (pp. 131–148). Mahwah, NJ: Lawrence Erlbaum.

Cramer, J. M., Greene, C. P., & Walters, L. M. (2011). *Food as communication/communication as food.* New York: Peter Lang.

Crescent City Farmers Market. (n.d.). Who we are. Retrieved from http://www.crescentcityfarmers market.org.

Croke, D. (2009). Cavemen and firebuilders: Barbecue and masculinity. In E. Engelhardt, (Ed.), *Republic of barbecue: Stories behind the brisket* (pp. 122–127). Austin: University of Texas Press.

Cross, K., & Street, E. (2011, August). What stands in a storm, part II: Food. *Southern Living.* Retrieved from http://www.southernliving.com.

Dabney, J. E. (2010). *The Food, folklore, and art of lowcountry cooking: A celebration of the foods, history, and romance handed down from England, Africa, the Caribbean, France, Germany, and Scotland.* Naperville, IL: Cumberland House.

Danbom, D. (2010). *Born in the country: A history of rural America.* Baltimore: Johns Hopkins University Press.

Davis, F. (1973). *Yearning for yesterday: A sociology of nostalgia.* New York: Free Press.

Dean, S. (2013, April 4). The Southern Foodways Alliance John Edge on the New South family supper. *Bon Appetit.* Retrieved from http://www.bonappetit.com

Deen, P. H., & Clark, M. (2011). *Paula Deen's Southern cooking bible: The classic guide to delicious dishes.* New York: Simon & Schuster.

Degler, C. (2000). *The other South: Southern dissenters in the nineteenth century.* Gainesville: University of Florida Press.

DeLind, L. B. (2011). Are local food and the local food movement taking us where we want to go? Or are we hitching our wagons to the wrong stars? *Agriculture and Human Values, 28,* 273–283.

DeLuca, K. (1999). *Image politics: The new rhetoric of environmental justice.* New York: Guilford.

Depp, M. (2001, September 9). The legacy of a family farm. Retrieved from http://americanprofile. com.

Deutsch, J. (2011). Swine by design: Inside a competition barbecue team. In J. R. Veteto & E. M. Maclin (Eds.), *The slaw and the slow cooked: Culture and barbecue in the mid South.* Nashville: Vanderbilt University Press.

Devine, J. B. (2009). "Hop to the top with the Iowa Chop": The Iowa Porkettes and cultivating agrarian feminisms in the Midwest, 1964–1992. *Agricultural History, 83,* 477–502.

Dickinson, G. (2002). Joe's rhetoric: Finding authenticity at Starbucks. *Rhetoric Society Quarterly, 32*(4), 5–27.

Donehower, K., Hogg, C., & Schell, E. E. (2011). *Reclaiming the rural: Essays on literacy, rhetoric, and pedagogy.* Carbondale: Southern Illinois University Press.

Dooky Chase Restaurant. About the chef. Retrieved from http://dookychaserestaurant.com.

Draper, C. (2013, February 1). Talking food, folks, and lore with Amy C. Evans. *Magic City Post.* Retrieved from http://www.magiccitypost.com.

Drzewiecka, J. (2002). The structural-cultural dialectic of diasporic politics. *Communication Theory, 12,* 340–366.

Dubriwny, T. (2005). Consciousness-raising as collective rhetoric: The Redstockings' abortion speak-out of 1969. *Quarterly Journal of Speech, 91,* 395–422.

Dubriwny, T. (2009). Constructing breast cancer in the news: Betty Ford and the evolution of the breast cancer patient. *Journal of Communication Inquiry, 33*(2), 104–125.

Dunaway, W. (1995). The "disremembered" of the antebellum South: A new look at the invisible labor of poor women. *Critical Sociology, 21,* 89–106.

DuPuis, E. M., & Goodman, D. (2005). Should we go "home" to eat?: Toward a reflexive politics of localism. *Journal of Rural Studies, 21,* 359–371.

Dupree, N. (2004). *New Southern cooking.* Athens: University of Georgia Press.

Dupree, N., & Graubart, C. S. (2012). *Mastering the art of Southern cooking.* Salt Lake City, UT: Gibbs Smith.

Dutch, J. (2011). Buffalo wings and brussels sprouts. Food, football and the rhetoric of healthy super bowl snacks. *Appetite, 56,* 527–527.

Eatocracy. (2010, November 10). Southern food: More voices from the field. CNN. Retrieved from http://eatocracy.cnn.com.

Economist. (1997, September 6). William Faulkner, past and future. *The Economist, 344,* 30. Retrieved from ProQuest database.

Eckstein, J., & Conley, D. (2012). Spatial affects and rhetorical relations: At the Cherry Creek farmers' market. In J. J. Frye & M. S. Bruner (Eds.), *The rhetoric of food: Discourse, materiality, and power* (pp. 171–189). New York: Routledge.

Eddy, J. (2013, December). The Senegalese roots of Southern cooking. *Food and Wine.* Retrieved from http://www.foodandwine.com.

Edge, J. T. (2010). Preface. *The Southern Foodways Alliance community cookbook.* Athens: University of Georgia Press.

Edge, J. T. (2011a). BBQ nation: The preservation of a culinary art form. *Saveur Magazine,* 48–55.

Edge, J. T. (2011b, March/April). Q & A with John T. Edge. *Imbibe Magazine,* 20–21.

Edge, J. T. (2012, October/November). Good eats. *Garden and Gun.* Retrieved from http://garden andgun.com.

Edge, J. T. (2013a). Personal communication.

Edge, J. T. (2013b). Why Southern food matters (so much). In D. DiBenedetto (Ed.), *The Southerner's handbook: A guide to living the good life* (pp. 3–7). New York: HarperCollins.

Edge, J. T., Engelhardt, E., & Ownby, T. (2013). *The larder: Food studies methods from the American South.* Athens: University of Georgia Press.

Edge, J. T., & University of Mississippi. (1999). *A gracious plenty: Recipes and recollections from the American South.* New York: Putnam.

Edge, J. T., & University of Mississippi. (2007). *Foodways.* Chapel Hill: University of North Carolina Press.

Edible Nation. (2011). Oral history is waiting for its close-up. Retrieved from www.ediblecom munities.com.

Edwards, J. L., & Winkler, C. K. (1997). Representative form and the visual ideograph: The Iwo Jima image in editorial cartoons. *Quarterly Journal of Speech, 83,* 289–310.

Egerton, J. (1990). *Side orders: Small helpings of Southern cookery and culture.* Atlanta: Peachtree.

Egerton, J. (1993). *Southern food: At home, on the road, in history.* Chapel Hill, NC: University of North Carolina Press.

Elie, L. (1996). *Smokestack lightning: Adventures in the heart of barbecue country.* New York: Farrar Straus & Giroux.

Elie, L. E., & Southern Foodways Alliance. (2004). *Cornbread nation 2: The United States of barbecue.* Chapel Hill: University of North Carolina Press.

Enck-Wanzer, D. (2006). Trashing the system: Social movement, intersectional rhetoric, and collective agency in the Young Lords Organization's garbage offensive. *Quarterly Journal of Speech, 92,* 174–201.

Endolyn, O. (2013, April). A taste of the South's culinary evolution. *Atlanta Magazine.* Retrieved from http://www.atlantamagazine.com.

Engelhardt, E. (2013). Redrawing the grocery: Practices and methods for studying Southern food. In J. T. Edge, E. Engelhardt, & T. Ownby (Eds.), *The larder: Food studies methods from the American South* (pp. 1–6). Athens: University of Georgia Press.

Engelhardt, E. S. D. (2011). *A mess of greens: Southern gender and Southern food.* Athens: University of Georgia Press.

Evans, A. C. (n.d.). An introduction: Hot tamales & the Mississippi Delta. Retrieved from http://www .southernfoodways.org/interview/hot-tamales-the-mississippi-delta/.

Evens, T. M. (1990). Introduction. In T. M. Evens & J. I. Peacock (Eds.), *Comparative social research, suppl. 1: Transcendence in society: Case studies.* Greenwich, CT: JAI.

Faust, D. G. (1979). The rhetoric and ritual of agriculture in antebellum South Carolina. *The Journal of Southern History, 45,* 541–68.

Ferris, M. C. (2009). The edible South. *Southern Cultures, 15*(4), 3–27.

Ferris, M. C. (2010). Why study Southern food? In F. Sauceman and J. T. Edge (Eds.), *Cornbread nation 5* (pp. 5–6). Athens: University of Georgia Press.

Ferris, M. C. (2013). The "stuff" of Southern food: Food and material culture in the American South. In J. T. Edge, E. Engelhardt, & T. Ownby (Eds.), *The larder: Food studies methods from the American South* (pp. 276–311). Athens: University of Georgia Press.

Ferris, M. C. (2014). *The edible South: The power of food and the making of an American region.* Chapel Hill: University of North Carolina Press.

Fertel, R. (2011). Identity, authenticity, persistence, and loss in the west Tennessee whole-hog barbecue tradition. In J. R. Veteto & E. M. Maclin (Eds.), *The slaw and the slow cooked: Culture and barbecue in the Mid-South* (pp. 83–104). Nashville: Vanderbilt University Press.

Fertel, R. (2013, June). Sweetest smoke. *Southern Living.* Retrieved from http://www.southernliving. com.

Finnegan, C. A. (2003). *Picturing poverty: Print culture and the FSA photographs.* Washington: Smithsonian Books.

Fisher, C. (2013, February 1). Sweat, sorghum and Southern grit. Retrieved from https://carlyafisher .wordpress.com.

Forbes, P. (2014, November 13). Cookbook review: Sean Brock's *Heritage.* Eater.com. Retrieved from http://www.eater.com.

Foust, C. R. (2011). Considering the prospects of immediate resistance in food politics: Reflections on the garden. *Environmental Communication: A Journal of Nature and Culture, 5,* 350–355.

Franzia, M. (2005, May 23). On N.C. barbecue, east and west don't meet—except to argue. *The Washington Post*. Retrieved from Lexis Nexis database.

Frye, J., & Bruner, M. S. (2012). *The rhetoric of food: Discourse, materiality, and power*. New York: Routledge.

Furrh, M., & Barksdale, J. (2008). *100 greatest desserts of the South, the 100 greatest recipes series*. Gretna, LA: Pelican.

Gabriel, Y. (1993). Organizational nostalgia: Reflections on the golden age. In S. Finemen (Ed.), *Emotion in organizations* (pp. 118-141). London: Sage.

Ganguly, K. (2001). *States of exception: Everyday life and postcolonial identity*. Minneapolis: University of Minnesota Press.

Gantt, J. E. (2002). *The ultimate Gullah cookbook: A taste of food, history and culture from the Gullah people*. Beaufort, SC: Sands.

Gantt, P. (2001). Taking the cake: Power politics in Southern life and fiction. In S. Inness (Ed.), *Cooking lessons: The politics of gender and food* (pp. 63-85). New York: Rowman and Littlefield.

Garner, B. (1996). *North Carolina barbecue: Flavored by time*. Winston-Salem, NC: Blair.

Gentilcore, D. (2010). *Pomodoro!: A history of the tomato in Italy*. New York: Columbia University Press.

Gibson, C. (2010). Geographies of tourism: (Un)ethical encounters. *Progress in Human Geography, 34*, 521-527.

Giddens, A. (1984). *The constitution of society: Outline of the theory of structuration*. Berkeley: University of California Press.

Gilbert, J., & Wallmenich, L. V. (2014). When words fail us: Mother time, relational attention, and the rhetorics of focus and balance. *Women's Studies in Communication, 37*(1), 66-89.

Gilmour, D. (2006). Nostalgia for sale: Extending Burke's theory of substance to idealized images of home. *Kaleidoscope: A Graduate Journal of Qualitative Communication Research, 5*, 57-72.

Glatz, J. (2011, April 14). The fascinating anthropology of Midwestern food. *Illinois Times*. Retrieved from http://www.illnoistimes.com.

Glazer, S. (2007). *Slow food movement*. Washington, DC: CQ.

Glock, A. (2013). Sweet tea: A love story. In D. DiBenedetto (Ed.), *The Southerner's handbook: A guide to living the good life* (pp. 105-110). New York: Harper Wave.

Gold, D. (2010). Beyond grits. *Women in Business, 62*(2), 14-16. Retrieved from EBSCO*host*.

Goodale, G. (2010). The presidential sound: From orotund to instructional speech, 1892-1912. *Quarterly Journal of Speech, 96*, 164-184.

Goodman, D., & Head, T. (2011). *The happy table of Eugene Walter: Southern spirits in food and drink: An ardent survey of Southern beverages and a grand selection of Southern dishes employing spiritous flavorings*. Chapel Hill: University of North Carolina Press.

Gray, R. (2002). Inventing communities, imagining places: Some thoughts on Southern self-fashioning. In S. M. Jones and S. Monteith (Eds.), *Foreword to South to a new place: Region, literature, culture* (pp. xiii-xxiii). Baton Rouge: Louisiana State Press.

Green, S. D., & Abney, L. (2001). *Songs of the new South: Writing contemporary Louisiana*. Westport, CT: Greenwood.

Greene, C. P. (2015). *Gourmands & gluttons: The rhetoric of food excess*. New York: Peter Lang.

Greene, R. W. (1998). Another materialist rhetoric. *Critical Studies in Mass Communication, 15*, 21-41.

Griffin, L. J. (2000). Southern distinctiveness, yet again, or, why America still needs the South. *Southern Cultures, 6*. Retrieved from Gale Cengage Literature Resource Center.

Gros, J. G. (2010). Indigestible recipe: Rice, chicken wings, and international financial institutions. *Journal of Black Studies, 40*, 974-986.

Guarente, M. (2003, June 15). Griller warfare: In the city where Elvis ate himself to death, meat will always come first. *Independent on Sunday*. Retrieved from Lexis Nexis database.

Guerin-Gonzales, C. (1994). Conversing across boundaries of race, ethnicity, class, gender, and region: Latino and Latina labor history. *Labor History, 35,* 547–563.

Gunn, J. (2010). On speech and public release. *Rhetoric & Public Affairs, 13,* 175–215.

Haan, A., & Maxwell, S. (1998). Poverty and social exclusion in North and South: [Special topic]. *IDS Bulletin, 29,* 1.

Hahne, E. (2008). *You are where you eat: Stories and recipes from the neighborhoods of New Orleans.* Jackson: University Press of Mississippi.

Hall, B., & Wood, C. (1995). *Big muddy.* New York: Random House.

Hanchett, T. (2014, March 7). The newest new South. PRX. Retrieved from https://beta.prx.org

Hariman, R., & Lucaites, J. L. (2003). Public identity and collective memory in U.S. iconic photography: The image of "Accidental Napalm." *Critical Studies in Media Communication, 20,* 35–66.

Hariman, R., & Lucaites, J. L. (2007). *No caption needed: Iconic photographs, public culture, and liberal democracy.* Chicago: University of Chicago Press.

Harris, E., & Nowverl, A. (2000). What's happening to soul food? Regional and income differences in the African American diet. *Ecology of Food and Nutrition, 38*(6), 587–603.

Harris, J. (2011). *High on the hog: A culinary journey from Africa to America.* New York: Bloomsbury USA.

Harris, J. (2012). Big houses. In Brett Anderson & J. T. Edge (Eds.), *Cornbread nation 6* (pp. 22–23). Athens: University of Georgia Press.

Hart, L. G., Larson, E. H., & Lisher, D. M. (2005). Rural definitions for health policy and research. *American Journal of Public Health, 95,* 1149–1155.

Harwell, R. B. (2007). Mint julep. In John T. Edge (Ed.), *Foodways: The New Encyclopedia of Southern Culture,* vol. 7 (94–96). Chapel Hill: University of North Carolina Press.

Hayden, S. (2011). Constituting savvy aunties: From childless women to child-focused consumers. *Women's Studies in Communication, 34,* 1–19.

Heinz, B., & Lee, R. (1998). Getting down to the meat: The symbolic construction of meat consumption. *Communication Studies, 49,* 86–99.

Hemenway-Forbes, M. (2007, January 3). Family friendly spa offers dose of Southern hospitality. *WCF Courier.* Retrieved from: http://wcfcourier.com.

Henderson, A., Weaver, C., & Cheney, G. (2007). Talking facts: Identity and rationality in industry perspectives on genetic modification. *Discourse Studies, 9,* 9–41.

Henderson, L. (2007). Ebony Jr. and soul food: The construction of middle-class African American identity through the use of traditional Southern foodways. *Melus Amherst, 32,* 81–98.

Henderson, M. B. (2008). *The great Southern food festival cookbook: Celebrating everything from peaches to peanuts, onions to okra.* Nashville, TN: Nelson.

Hess, A. (2011). Critical-rhetorical ethnography: Rethinking the place and process of rhetoric. *Communication Studies, 62,* 127–152.

Hoffman, M. F., & Medlock-Klyukovski, A. (2004). "Our creator who art in heaven": Paradox, ritual, and cultural transformation." *Western Journal of Communication, 68,* 389–410.

Holbrook, M. B. (1993). Nostalgia and consumption preference: Some emerging patterns of consumer tastes. *Journal of Consumer Research, 20,* 245–256.

Holtzman, J. (2010). Remembering bad cooks: Sensuality, memory, personhood. *The Senses and Society 5,* 235–243.

Holtzman, J. D. (2006). Food and memory. *Annual Review of Anthropology, 35,* 361–378.

Huey, T. A. (2005). Thinking globally, eating locally: Website linking and the performance of solidarity in global and local food movements. *Social Movement Studies, 4,* 123–137.

Innes, S. (2007). Slow food growing fast: International movement even has Tucson branch. *Arizona Daily Star.* Retrieved from: http://www.slowfood.com.

Inness, S. A. (2001a). *Cooking lessons: The politics of gender and food*. Lanham, MD: Rowman & Littlefield.

Inness, S. A. (2001b). *Kitchen culture in America: Popular representations of food, gender, and race*. Philadelphia: University of Pennsylvania Press.

Jackall, R., & Hirota, J. M. (2000). *Image makers: Advertising public relations and the ethos of advocacy*. Chicago: University of Chicago Press.

Jakes, K. (2013). France en chantant: The rhetorical construction of French identity in French protest songs. *Quarterly Journal of Speech, 99*, 317–340.

Jasinski, J. (1998). A constitutive framework for rhetorical historiography: Toward an understanding of the discursive (re)constitution of "Constitution" in *The Federalist Papers*. In K. J. Turner (Ed.), *Doing rhetorical history: Concepts and cases* (pp. 72–92). Tuscaloosa: University of Alabama Press.

Jasinski, J. (2001). *Sourcebook on rhetoric: Key concepts in contemporary rhetorical studies*. Thousand Oaks, CA: Sage.

Jenkins, M. (2006). Gullah island dispute resolution. *Journal of Black Studies, 37*, 299–319.

Johnson, D. (2007). Martin Luther King Jr.'s 1963 Birmingham campaign as image event. *Rhetoric & Public Affairs, 10*, 1–25.

Johnston, J., & Baumann, S. (2011). *Foodies: Democracy and distinction in the gourmet foodscape*. New York: Routledge.

Johnston, J., Szabo, M., & Rodney, A. (2011). Good food, good people: Understanding the cultural repertoire of ethical eating. *Journal of Consumer Culture, 11*, 293–318.

Jones, A. G., & Donaldson, S. V. D. E. (1997). *Haunted bodies: Gender and Southern texts*. Charlottesville: University Press of Virginia.

Jones, P., Comfort, D., & Hillier, D. (2013). Local food and the UK's leading food retailers: Rhetoric and reality. *World Review of Entrepreneurship, Management and Sustainable Development, 9*, 26–36.

Jones, W. (2007). Culinary creations: Classic Southern cuisine. *Prepared Foods, 176*, 1, 67.

Jonsson, P. (2006, February 6). Backstory: Southern discomfort food. *Christian Science Monitor*. Retrieved from http://www.csmonitor.com.

Jordan, C. (2010). *Southern plate: Classic comfort food that makes everyone feel like family*. New York: Morrow.

Katz, S. H., & Weaver, W. W. (2003). *Encyclopedia of food and culture*. New York: Scribner.

Kein, S. (2000). *Creole: The history and legacy of Louisiana's free people of color*. Baton Rouge: Louisiana State University Press.

Kierner, C. A. (1996). Hospitality, sociability, and gender in the Southern colonies. *The Journal of Southern History, 62*, 449–480.

King, S. A. (2006). Memory, mythmaking, and museums: Constructive authenticity and the primitive blues subject. *Southern Communication Journal, 71*(3), 235–250.

Kinsman, K. (2010, November 10). Reclaiming the soul of Southern food. *Eatocracy*. Retrieved from eatocracy.cnn.com.

Kittler, P. G., & Sucher, K. (2004). *Food and culture*. Belmont, CA: Thomson/Wadsworth.

Kniazeva, M., & Belk, R. W. (2010). Supermarkets as libraries of postmodern mythology. *Journal of Business Research, 63*, 748–753.

Knipple, P., & Knipple, A. (2012). *The world in a skillet: A food lover's tour of the new American South*. Chapel Hill: University of North Carolina Press.

Knoblauch, M. (2002). Cornbread nation 1 (Book). *Booklist, 99*(6), 562. Retrieved from EBSCO*host*.

Knowlton, A. (2015, April 28). Eat the world (yes, the entire world) along Atlanta's Buford Highway. *Bon Appetit*. Retrieved from http://www.bonappetit.com.

Kramer, J. (2010, December 8). Culinary heritage: What does it mean to you? *Durham Foodie*. Retrieved from http://www.durhamfoodie.com.

Krølner, R., Rasmussen, M., Brug, J., Klepp, K. I., Wind, M., & Due, P. (2011). Determinants of fruit and vegetable consumption among children and adolescents: A review of the literature. Part II: Qualitative studies. *The International Journal of Behavioral Nutrition and Physical Activity, 8, 1–38*.

Kummer, C. (2005, October). Sweet home Louisiana. *Atlantic Monthly*. Retrieved from http://www.theatlantic.com.

Kurlansky, M., Hoye, S., United States, & Tantor Media. (2009). *The food of a younger land: [a portrait of American food—before the national highway system, before chain restaurants, and before frozen food, when the nation's food was seasonal, regional, and traditional—from the lost WPA files]*. Old Saybrook, CT: Tantor Audio.

Latshaw, B. A. (2009). Food for thought: Race, region, identity, and foodways in the American South. *Southern Cultures, 15*(4), 106–128.

Launay, R. (2003). Tasting the world: Food in early European travel narratives. *Food and Foodways, 11*(1), 27–47.

Lee, M., & Lee, T. (2013, April 14). Southern exposure. *The New York Times*. Retrieved from http://tmagazine.blog.nytimes.com.

Leeman, R. (2014). Personal communication.

Lien, M. E., Nerlich, B., & European Association of Social Anthropologists. (2004). *The politics of food*. Oxford, NY: Berg.

Link, D., & Disbrowe, P. (2014). *Down south: Bourbon, pork, gulf shrimp & second helpings of everything*. New York: Clarkson Potter.

Littlejohn, S. J., & NC Digital Online Collection of Knowledge and Scholarship (NCDOCKS). (2008). *The rhetoric of food narratives: Ideology and influence in American culture*. Greensboro: University of North Carolina at Greensboro.

Liu, H., & Lin, L. (2009). Food, culinary identity, and transnational culture: Chinese restaurant business in Southern California. *Journal of Asian American Studies, 12, 135–162*.

Long, L. (2001). Nourishing the academic imagination: The use of food in teaching concepts of culture. *Food and Foodways, 9, 3–4*.

Lucas, S. (2014, July 17). Petal farmer to get James Beard Leadership Award. *Clarion-Ledger*. Retrieved from http://clarionledger.com.

Macartney, S., Bishaw, A., & Fontenot, K. (2013, February). Poverty rates for selected detailed race and Hispanic groups by state and place: 2007–2011. U.S. Census Bureau. Retrieved from http://www.census.gov.

Madden, H., & Chamberlain, K. (2010). Nutritional health, subjectivity and resistance: Women's accounts of dietary practices. *Health, 14, 292–309*.

Magkos, F., Arvaniti, F., & Zampelas, A. (2006). Organic food: Buying more safety or just peace of mind? A critical review of the literature. *Critical Reviews in Food Science and Nutrition, 46, 23–56*.

Mannur, A. (2007). Culinary nostalgia: Authenticity, nationalism, and diaspora. *MELUS: Multi-Ethnic Literature of the United States, 32*(4), 11–31.

Maroukian, F. (2012, December 29). The new food capital: 15 D.C. restaurants serving up Southern fare. Retrieved from http://thedailysouth.southernliving.com.

Marsden, T., Murdoch, J., & Morgan, K. (2006). *Worlds of food: Place, power, and provenance in the food chain*. NY: Oxford University Press.

Martin, A. (2009). Is a food revolution now in season? *New York Times*. Retrieved from http://www.nytimes.com.

Mason, C. (2011, October 31). The Waysider: Best breakfast. Retrieved from http://www.tuscaloosanews.com.

Massa, D. (2013, June 17). "Miss Dot" Domilise, matriarch of uptown poor boy restaurant, dies at 90. Retrieved from http://www.wwltv.com/.

Massey, D. S. (2008). *New faces in new places: The changing geography of American immigration.* New York: Russell Sage Foundation.

Maynard, W. (2012, February/March). Southern food revival: Living in the golden age of Southern cuisine. *The Local Palate*, 86–93.

McDaniel, R. (2011). *An irresistible history of Southern food: Four centuries of black-eyed peas, collard greens & whole hog barbecue.* Charleston, SC: History.

McDermott, N. (2007). *Southern cakes: Sweet and irresistible recipes for everyday celebrations.* New York: Chronicle Books.

McDonald, R., Waring, J., & Harrison, S. (2006). At the cutting edge? Modernization and nostalgia in a hospital operating theatre department. *Sociology 40*(6), 1097–1115.

McEntee, J. (2010). Contemporary and traditional localism: A conceptualisation of rural local food. *Local Environment, 15,* 9–10.

McHendry, G. F., Middleton, M. K., Endres, D., Senda-Cook, S., & O'Byrn, M. (2014). Rhetorical critic(ism)'s body: Affect and fieldwork on a plane of immanence. *Southern Communication Journal, 79,* 293–310.

McIntyre, L., Thille, P., & Rondeau, K. (2009). Farmwomen's discourses on family food provisioning: Gender, healthism, and risk avoidance. *Food and Foodways, 17,* 80–103.

McKeithan, S. S. (2012). Every ounce a man's whiskey?: Bourbon in the white masculine South. *Southern Cultures, 18*(1), 5–20.

McLaughlin, L. (2011, January 4). Amy Evans Streeter. *Jackson Free Press.* Retrieved from http://www.jacksonfreepress.com.

McLeod, G. E. (2010, October 1). Day trips: Historic dance halls in Texas still offer a cold beer and a welcoming dance floor. *Austin Chronicle.* Retrieved from http://www.austinchronicle.com.

McMurry, A. (2012). Framing Emerson's "Farming": Climate change, peak oil, and the rhetoric of food security in the twenty-first century. *Interdisciplinary Studies in Literature and Environment, 19,* 548–566.

McPherson, T. (2003). *Reconstructing Dixie: Race, gender, and nostalgia in the imagined South.* Durham, NC: Duke University Press.

McNulty, I. (n. d.) The creole confection–New Orleans pralines. Retrieved from http://www.frenchquarter.com/new-orleans-pralines/

Meister, M. (2001). Cultural feeding, good life science, and the TV Food Network. *Mass Communication & Society, 4,* 165–182.

Meyers, O. (2009). The engine's in the front, but its heart's in the same place: Advertising, nostalgia, and the construction of commodities as realms of memory. *The Journal of Popular Culture, 42*(4), 733–755.

Middleton, M. K., Senda-Cook, S., Endres, D. (2011). Articulating rhetorical field methods: Challenges and tensions. *Western Journal of Communication, 75,* 386–406.

Miller, A. (2012, June 21). Barbecue digest: Don't whitewash BBQ. *CNN.* Retrieved from http://www.cnn.com.

Miller, A. (2013). *Soul food: The surprising story of an American cuisine, one plate at a time.* Chapel Hill: University of North Carolina Press.

Miles, J. (2013, February/March). Drink with style. *Garden & Gun.* 72.

Mintz, S. W., & Du Bois, C. M. (2002). The anthropology of food and eating. *Annual Review of Anthropology, 31,* 99–119.

Mkono, M. (2011). The othering of food in touristic eatertainment: A netnography. *Tourist Studies, 11,* 253–270.

Morago, G. (2012, October 13). Po'boys are the flavor of New Orleans. *Austin American Statesman.* Retrieved from http://www.statesman.com.

Morgan, K., Marsden, T., & Murdoch, J. (2006). *Worlds of food: Place, power, and provenance in the food chain.* Oxford, UK: Oxford University Press.

Moskin, J. (2011, December 27). Southern farmers vanquish the clichés. *New York Times.* Retrieved from http://www.nytimes.com.

Moskin, J. (2013). A culinary birthright in dispute. *New York Times.* Retrieved from http://www.nytimes.com.

Moss, K. (2013). *Seeking the historical cook: Exploring eighteenth-century Southern foodways.* Columbia: University of South Carolina Press.

Moss, R. (2010). *Barbecue: The history of an American institution.* Tuscaloosa: University of Alabama Press.

Mudry, J. (2006). Dissecting dinner: The USDA Food Guide Pyramid and the decline of taste at the table. *Appetite, 47,* 395.

Muehling, D. D., & Pascal, V. J. (2012). An involvement explanation for nostalgia advertising effects. *Journal of Promotion Management, 18*(1), 100–118.

Mumby, D. (1989). Ideology & the social construction of meaning: A communication perspective. *Communication Quarterly, 37,* 291–304.

Mumby, D. (1993). *Narrative and social control: Critical perspectives.* Newbury Park, CA: Sage.

Murphy, M. (2011). *Off the eaten path: Favorite Southern dives and 150 recipes that made them famous.* Birmingham, AL: Oxmoor House.

Nabhan, G. P. (2011). From coa to barbacoa to barbecue. In J. R. and E. M. Maclin (Eds.), *The slaw and the slow cooked: Culture and barbecue in the mid-South* (pp. 83–104). Nashville: Vanderbilt University Press.

National Public Radio. (2008, June 26). New Orleans declares Sazerac its cocktail of choice. Retrieved from http://www.npr.org.

Neal, B. (1990). *Biscuits, spoonbread, and sweet potato pie.* Chapel Hill: University of North Carolina Press.

Neuhaus, J. (1999). The way to a man's heart: Gender roles, domestic ideology, and cookbooks in the 1950s. *Journal of Social History, 32,* 529–555.

Newman, H. (2000). Hospitality and violence: Contradictions in a Southern city. *Urban Affairs Review, 35,* 541–558.

Nolan, J. (2011). Piney woods tradition at the crossroads: Barbecue and regional identity. In J. R. Veteto & E. M. Maclin (Eds.), *The slaw and the slow cooked: Culture and barbecue in the mid-South* (pp. 51–65). Nashville: Vanderbilt University Press.

Nysrom, J. A. (2013). Italian New Orleans and the business of food in the immigrant city. In J. T. Edge, E. Engelhardt, & T. Ownby (Eds.), *The larder: Food studies methods from the American South* (pp. 128–154). Athens: University of Georgia Press.

Offutt, C. (2015, April 10). Trash food. *Oxford American.* Retrieved from http://www.oxfordamerican.org

O'Gorman, N. (2008). Eisenhower and the American sublime. *Quarterly Journal of Speech, 94,* 44–72.

O'Neil, C. (2011, November 9). Southern cooking: "It's good food". *Atlanta Journal Constitution,* 4D.

Olson, L. C., Finnegan, C. A., & Hope, D. S. (2008). Visual rhetoric in communication: Continuing questions and contemporary issues. In L. C. Olson, C. A. Finnegan, & D. S. Hope (Eds.), *Visual rhetoric: A reader in communication and American culture* (pp. 1–14). Thousand Oaks: Sage.

Onorato, P. H. (2008, August 27). Southern hospitality is alive and well. *The Dispatch.* Retrieved from ProQuest.

Opel, A., Johnson, J., & Wilk, R. (2010). Food, culture and the environment: Communicating about what we eat. *Environmental Communication, 4,* 251–254.

Opie, F. D. (2008). *Hog & hominy: Soul food from Africa to America.* New York: Columbia University Press.

Ott, B. (2007). *The small screen: How television equips us to live in the information age.* Malden, MA: Blackwell.

Ott, B. L, & Keeling, D. M. (2011). Cinema and choric connection: *Lost in Translation* as sensual experience. *Quarterly Journal of Speech, 97,* 363–386.

Otto, S. (2005). Nostalgic for what? The epidemic of images of the mid 20th century classroom in American media culture and what it means. *Discourse: Studies in the Cultural Politics of Education, 26*(4), 459–575.

Ownby, T. (2013). Conclusion: Go forth with method. In J. T. Edge, E. Engelhardt, & T. Ownby (Eds.), *The larder: Food studies methods from the American South* (pp. 363–370). Athens: University of Georgia Press.

Ozersky, J. (2010, October 27). Lardcore: Southern food with hardcore attitude. *Time.* Retrieved from http://www.time.com.

Packel, D. (2011). Snacking with the sons of the soil. *Gastronomica: The Journal of Food and Culture, 11,* 67–70.

Page, L. G., & Wigginton, E. (1992). *The Foxfire book of Appalachian cookery.* New York: Gramercy Books.

Parrott, N. (2003). Spatializing quality: Regional protection and the alternative geography of food. *Sage Urban Studies Abstracts, 31,* 3–133.

Peace, A. (2006). Barossa slow: The representation and rhetoric of slow food's regional cooking. *Gastronomica: The Journal of Food and Culture, 6,* 51–59.

Peace, A. (2008). Terra Madre 2006: Political theater and ritual rhetoric in the slow food movement. *Gastronomica: The Journal of Food and Culture, 8,* 31–39.

Penrice, R. (2012, November 1). My piece of Africa came by way of Mississippi. *Atlanta Magazine.* Retrieved from http://www.atlantamagazine.

Percy, W. (1991). *Signposts in a strange land.* New York: Farrar, Straus, and Giroux.

Petrini, C. (2007). *Slow food nation: Why our food should be good, clean, and fair.* NY: Rizzoli Ex Libris.

Pezzullo, P. (2007). *Toxic tourism: Rhetorics of travel, pollution, and environmental justice.* Tuscaloosa: University of Alabama Press

Phillips, K. R. (2004). Introduction. In K. R. Phillips (Ed.), *Framing public memory* (pp. 1–14). Tuscaloosa: University of Alabama Press.

Poe, T. N. (February 1, 1999). The origins of soul food in black urban identity: Chicago, 1915–1947. *American Studies International, 37,* 4–33.

Pollan, M. (2009). Introduction. In W. Berry (Ed.), *Bringing it to the table.* (pp. ix–xv). Berkeley, CA: Counterpoint.

Pollan, M. (2013). *Cooked: A natural history of transformation.* New York: Penguin Books.

Poniewozik, J. (2013, June 20). Less than accidental racist: Why Paula Deen's comments insult her fans too. *Time.* Retrieved from http://entertainment.time.com.

Potter, A. (2010). *The authenticity hoax: How we got lost finding ourselves.* Toronto: McLelland & Stewart.

Pramuk, J. (2015, March 27). The South gets in on the craft beer boom. CNBC.com. Retrieved from http://www.cnbc.com.

Preston-Werner, T. (2009). "Gallo Pinto": Tradition, memory, and identity in Costa Rican foodways. *The Journal of American Folklore, 122,* 483, 11–27.

Puckett, S. (2006, October 5). The taste of innocence: Breathe in—something's baking, a wonderful treat that stirs the memories of childhood. *The Atlanta Journal Constitution.* Retrieved from http://www.ajc.com.

Pullen, M. C., & Crocker, S. (2012). *Martha Pullen's Southern family cookbook: Reflect on the past, rejoice in the present, and celebrate future gatherings with more than 250 heirloom recipes & meals.* Avon, MA: Adams Media.

Purvis, K. (2009). "Peace and a smile to the lips:" Favorite Southern food dishes. *Southern Cultures, 15,* 29–35.

Putnam, L. L., Van Hoeven, S. A., & Bullis, C. A. (1991). The role of ritual and fantasy themes in teachers' bargaining. *Western Journal of Speech Communication, 55,* 85–103.

Ramage, J., Callaway, M., Clary-Lemon, J., & Waggoner, Z. (2009). *Argument in composition.* West Lafayette, IN: Parlor.

Randall, M. (1997). *Hunger's table: Women, food & politics.* Watsonville, CA: Papier Mache.

Raskin, H. (2011, June 23). Reviewing the review: Just like grandma used to make. Retrieved from http://blogs.seattleweekly.com.

Raskin, H. (2015, March 25). Winners chosen for Nat Fuller dinner essay contest. *Charleston Post and Courier.* Retrieved from http://www.postandcourier.com.

Ray, A. G. (2007). The rhetorical ritual of citizenship: Women's voting as public performance, 1868–1875. *Quarterly Journal of Speech, 93,* 1–26.

Ray, K. (2006). "Invisible trumpet in the unseen marketplace." Food in three media: Print, radio and TV. *Appetite, 47,* 398.

Ray, K. (2008). Nation and cuisine: The evidence from American newspapers Ca. 1830–2003. *Food and Foodways, 16,* 259–297.

Reed, J. (2004). Barbecue sociology: The meat of the matter. In L. E. Elie (Ed.), *Cornbread nation 2* (pp. 78–87). Chapel Hill: University of North Carolina Press.

Reed, J., & Reed, D. V. (2008). *Holy smoke: The big book of North Carolina barbecue.* Chapel Hill: University of North Carolina Press.

Rehder, J. B. (2004). *Appalachian folkways.* Baltimore, MD: Johns Hopkins University Press.

Reynolds, L. K. (2014, November 12). Ben Mims on sweet tea in the shade for #SFA14. Retrieved from https://www.southernfoodways.org/watch-ben-mims-at-sfa14/.

Rice, J. (2012). From architectonic to tectonics: Introducing regional rhetorics. *Rhetoric Society Quarterly, 42*(3), 201–213.

Rienstra, J. (2013, October 25). Shiner, Texas seduces travelers with more than just good beer. *Culture Map—Dallas.* Retrieved from http://dallas.culturemap.com.

Ritivoi, A. D. (2002). *Yesterday's self: Nostalgia and the immigrant identity.* Lanham, MD: Rowman & Littlefield.

Roahen, S., Edge, J. T., & Southern Foodways Alliance. (2010). *The Southern Foodways Alliance community cookbook.* Athens: University of Georgia Press.

Roberson, L. (2012). What does it mean to be Southern? *Exchange, 6*(1), 12–15.

Robbins, J. (2001). Ritual communication and linguistic ideology: A reading and partial reformulation of Rappaport's theory of ritual. *Current Anthropology, 42,* 591–614.

Rodbard, M. (2012, May 16). John Currence, the chef who happily banned pork specials. *Food Republic.* Retrieved from http://www.foodrepublic.com.

Rogers, A. (2004). *Hungry for home: Stories of food from across the Carolinas with more than 200 favorite recipes.* Winston-Salem, NC: Blair.

Rosello, M. (2001). *Postcolonial hospitality: The immigrant as guest.* Stanford: Stanford University Press.

Rothblum, E. D., & Solovay, S. (2009). *The fat studies reader.* New York: New York University Press.

Rubin, L. C. (2008). *Food for thought: Essays on eating and culture.* Jefferson, NC: McFarland.

Rufca, S. (2010). Southern food gets new respect (and a terrible name) with lardcore. *Culture Map: Houston.* Retrieved from http://houston.culturemap.com.

Sampson, S. (2007). A word with the ambassador of barbecue. *The Toronto Star*. Retrieved from Lexis Nexis database.

Sarup, M. (1993). *An introductory guide to post-structuralism and postmodernism*. Reprint. Athens: University of Georgia Press.

Sassatelli, R., & Davolio, F. (2010). Consumption, pleasure and politics. *Journal of Consumer Culture, 10*, 202–232.

Sauceman, F. (2007). Social class and food. In C. R. Wilson & W. Ferris (Eds.), *Encyclopedia of Southern culture* (pp. 102–104). Chapel Hill: University of North Carolina Press.

Saulsbury, C. V. (2005). *Consuming home cooking: An investigation of the contemporary meaning of cooking and identity in the domestic sphere*. Dissertation. Indiana University.

Schaarsmith, A. M. (2006, October 15). Southern food rises again and again, as culture stirs the mix. *Pittsburgh Post-Gazette*. Retrieved from Lexis Nexis database.

Schely-Newman, E. (2001). Remember Shushan?: Counter-nostalgia in gendered discourse. *Text-Interdisciplinary Journal for the Study of Discourse, 21*(3), 411–436.

Schieffelin, E. L (1985). Performance and the cultural construction of reality. *American Ethnologist, 12*(4), 707–24.

Schmich, M. (2014, February 26). Kale's out? Take a look at the next edible miracle. *Chicago Tribune*. Retrieved from http://www.tribunecontentagency.com.

Schmidt, M. S., & Apuzzo, M. (2015, April 7). South Carolina officer is charged with murder of Walter Scott. Retrieved from http://www.nytimes.com.

Scollon, R. (2006). Food and behavior: A Burkean motive analysis of a quasi-medical text. *Text & Talk, 26*, 107–125.

Scott, M., & Rushing, W. (2014). Barbecue tofu and the most Southern place on earth. *Arkansas Review: A Journal of Delta Studies, 45*(3), 146–155.

Selzer, J. (1999). Habeas corpus: An introduction. In J. Selzer & S. Crowley (Eds.), *Rhetorical bodies* (pp. 3–15). Madison: University of Wisconsin Press.

Senda-Cook, S. (2012). Rugged practices: Embodying authenticity in outdoor recreation. *Quarterly Journal of Speech, 98*, 129–152.

Severson, K. (2012, February). A Southern fried education. *Bon Appetit*. Retrieved from http://www.bonappetit.com.

Severson, K. (2014, August/September). The comfort of Southern food. *Garden & Gun*, 82.

Severson, K. (2015, January 27). The North Carolina way: A food sisterhood flourishes in North Carolina. *New York Times*. Retrieved from http://www.nytimes.com.

Shahin, J. (2012, November 7). Barbecue's having an identity crisis. *The Washington Post*. Retrieved from http://www.highbeam.com.

Shaw, T. (1993). *The archaeology of Africa: Food, metals, and towns*. London: Routledge.

Shriver, J. (2008, August 22). Americans always make room for dessert. USAToday. Retrieved from http://www.usatoday.com

Shugart, H. A. (2008). Sumptuous texts: Consuming "otherness" in the food film genre. *Critical Studies in Media Communication, 25*, 68–90.

Simon, M. (2006). *Appetite for profit: How the food industry undermines our health and how to fight back*. New York: Nation Books.

Singer, R. (2011). Anti-corporate argument and the spectacle of the grotesque rhetorical body in *Super Size Me*. *Critical Studies in Media Communication, 28*, 135–152.

Slawter-Volkening, L. (2008, November). Roads to American identity: The material and constitutive rhetoric of the interstate highway system. Paper presented at the National Communication Association Conference, San Diego, CA.

Smalls, A., & Jones, H. (1997). *Grace the table: Stories and recipes from my Southern revival*. New York: HarperCollins.

Smith, B. (2003). *B. Smith cooks Southern-style*. New York: Scribner.

Smith, K. (2000). Mere nostalgia: Notes on a progressive paratheory. *Rhetoric & Public Affairs, 3,* 505–527.

Smith, K. L., & Zepp, I. G. (n. d.). Martin Luther King's vision of the beloved community. Retrieved from http://www.religion-online.org.

Smith, R., & Eisenberg, E. (1987). Conflict at Disneyland: A root metaphor analysis. *Communication Monographs, 54,* 367–380.

Smith, S. (1984). Food for thought: Comestible communication and contemporary Southern culture. In E. Mayo (Ed.), *American material culture: The shape of things around us* (pp. 208–217). Bowling Green: Bowling Green State University Press.

Smith, S. L., Quandt, S. A., Arcury, T. A., Wetmore, L. K., Bell, R. A., & Vitolins, M. Z. (2006). Aging and eating in the rural, Southern United States: Beliefs about salt and its effect on health. *Social Science & Medicine, 62,* 189–198.

Smyth, L. (2008). Gendered spaces and intimate citizenship. *European Journal of Women's Studies, 15,* 83–99.

Snyder, J. (2011, August 10). Chef Ashley Christensen bets it all on downtown Raleigh. *Indyweek.* Retrieved from http://www.indyweek.com.

Sohn, M. (1996). *Appalachian home cooking: History, culture, and recipes.* Lexington: University Press of Kentucky.

Soper, K. (2007). Re-thinking the "good life." *Journal of Consumer Culture, 7,* 205–229.

Southern Foodways Alliance. (n. d.). Bowen's Island. Oxford, MS: Southern Foodways Alliance. Retrieved from http://southernfoodways.org/documentary/film/bowens-island.html.

Southern Foodways Alliance. (n. d.). Cured. Oxford, MS: Southern Foodways Alliance. Retrieved from http://southernfoodways.org/documentary/film/cured.html.

Southern Foodways Alliance. (n. d.). Dori. Oxford, MS: Southern Foodways Alliance. Retrieved from http://southernfoodways.org/documentary/film/dori.html.

Southern Foodways Alliance. (n. d.). Greeks in Birmingham. Oxford, MS: Southern Foodways Alliance. Retrieved from http://www.southernfoodways.org/oral-history/greeks-in-birmingham/.

Southern Foodways Alliance. (n. d.). Hot, wet goobers. Oxford, MS: Southern Foodways Alliance. Retrieved from http://southernfoodways.org/documentary/film/hot-wet-goobers.html.

Southern Foodways Alliance. (n. d.). Jackson's iconic restaurants. Oxford, MS: Southern Foodways Alliance. Retrieved from http://www.southernfoodways.org/oral-history/jacksons-iconic-restaurants/.

Southern Foodways Alliance. (n. d.). Saving seeds. Oxford, MS: Southern Foodways Alliance. Retrieved from http://southernfoodways.org/documentary/film/saving_seeds.htm.

Southern Foodways Alliance. (n. d.). SFA history. Retrieved from http://southernfoodways.org/about/history.html.

Southern Foodways Alliance. (n. d.). SFA mission. Retrieved from http://southernfoodways.org/about/mission.htmlSouthern Foodways Alliance (2004). Interview: Leah Chase. Retrieved from http://southernfoodwaysalliance.org/leah-chase.

Southern Foodways Alliance. (n. d.). An SFA film primer. Oxford, MS: Southern Foodways Alliance. Retrieved from http://southernfoodways.org/documentary/film/sfa_primer.html.

Southern Foodways Alliance. (2004). Interview: Welcome Table. Retrieved from http://southern foodways.org/film/welcome-table/.

Southern Foodways Alliance. (2006). Interview: Chuck's BBQ. Retrieved from http://southernfood waysalliance.org/chuck's-bbq.

Southern Foodways Alliance. (2006). Interview: Prince's Hot Chicken. Retrieved from http://southern foodwaysalliance.org/interview/princes-hot-chicken-shack.

Southern Foodways Alliance. (2007). Interview: Mama Dips. Retrieved from http://southernfood waysalliance.org/interview/mama-dips-traditional-country-cooking.

Southern Foodways Alliance. (2010). Interview: Buford Highway farmers market. Retrieved from http://southernfoodways.org/interview/buford-highway-farmers-market.

Southern Foodways Alliance. (2011). Interview: Spooney's Barbecue. Retrieved from http://southern foodwaysalliance.org/interview/spooneys-bar-b-que.

Southern Foodways Alliance. (2006). Interview: Swett's. Retrieved from https://www.southern foodways.org/interview/swetts/

Southern Foodways Alliance. (2012). Interview: The Pie Wagon. Retrieved from http://southernfood waysalliance.org/interview/the-pie-wagon.

Southern Foodways Alliance. (2014). A democratic way of looking. *Gravy, 54,* 12–25.

Spurlock, C. M. (2009). Performing and sustaining (Agri)Culture and place: The cultivation of environmental subjectivity on the Piedmont Farm Tour. *Text and Performance Quarterly, 29,* 5–21.

Stein, S. (2002). The "1984" Macintosh ad: Cinematic icons and constitutive rhetoric in the launch of a new machine. *Quarterly Journal of Speech, 88,* 169–192.

St. John, R. (2006). *Deep South staples, or, how to survive in a southern kitchen without a can of cream of mushroom soup.* New York: Hyperion.

St. John, W. (2004, October 6). Greens in black and white. *New York Times.* Retrieved from http://www.nytimes.com.

St. Paul's Church (Lynchburg, Va.). (1946). *Favorite foods of Virginians: A compilation of selected and tested recipes of Virginians and other famous folk.* Lynchburg, VA: Circles Two, Seven and Nine of the Church Service League of St. Paul's Church.

Stokes, A. Q. (2013). You are what you eat: Slow Food USA's constitutive public relations. *Journal of Public Relations Research, 25,* 68–90.

Stormer, N. (1997). Embodying normal miracles. *Quarterly Journal of Speech, 83,* 172–191.

Street, E. (2012). Heroes of the new South awards. *Southern Living.* Retrieved from http://southern living.com.

Stuckey, M. (2006). Establishing the rhetorical presidency through presidential rhetoric: Theodore Roosevelt and the Brownsville Raid. *Quarterly Journal of Speech, 92,* 287–309.

Sweet, D., & McCue-Enser, M. (2010). Constituting 'the people' as rhetorical interruption: Barack Obama and the unfinished hopes of an imperfect people. *Communication Studies, 61,* 602–622.

Symposium on American Cuisine & FSA Group. (1987). *The sixth Symposium on American Cuisine: September 13–26, 1987, the Omni Hotel at Charleston Place, Charleston, S.C.* Louisville, KY: FSA Group.

Szczesiul, A. (2007). Re-mapping Southern hospitality: Discourse, ethics, politics. *European Journal of American Culture, 26,* 127–141.

Tate, H. (2005). The ideological effects of a failed constitutive rhetoric: The co-optation of the rhetoric of white lesbian feminism. *Women's Studies in Communication, 28,* 1–31.

Taylor, J. G. (1982). *Eating, drinking, and visiting in the South: An informal history.* Baton Rouge: Louisiana State University Press.

Taylor, J. R., & Cooren, F. (1997). What makes communication "organizational"? How the many voices of a collectivity become the one voice of an organization. *Journal of Pragmatics, 27,* 409–438.

Tell, D. (2012). The meanings of Kansas: Rhetoric, regions, and counter regions. *Rhetoric Society Quarterly, 42*(3), 214–232.

Theobald, P. (2012). Afterword. In K. Donehower, C. Hogg, and E. Schell (Eds.), *Reclaiming the rural: Essays in literacy, rhetoric, and pedagogy* (pp. 239–246). Carbondale: Southern Illinois University Press.

Theodossopoulos, D. (2013). Laying claim to authenticity: Five anthropological dilemmas. *Anthropological Quarterly, 86*(2), 337–360.

Thompson, A. (2005, December). New Orleans cocktail: A sip of Southern comfort. *Southern Living.* Retrieved from http://www.southernliving.com.

Thompson, T. (2013a). *The new mind of the South.* New York: Simon and Schuster.

Thompson, T. (2013b, June 25). No, we are not all like Paula Deen. *Slate.* Retrieved from http://www.slate.com.

Thomson, D., & Hassenkamp, A. M. (2008). The social meaning and function of food rituals in healthcare practice: An ethnography. *Human Relations, 61,* 1775–1802.

Thomson, D. M. (2009). Big food and the body politics of personal responsibility. *Southern Communication Journal, 74,* 2–17.

Trice, D. (2011, February 4). Army & Lou's, one of the last soul food icons, closes. *Chicago Tribune.* Retrieved from http://www.chicagotribune.com.

Trice, H. M., & Beyer, J. M. (1984). Studying organizational cultures through rites and ceremonials. *Academy of Management Review, 9,* 653–669.

Tucker, S. (2009). *New Orleans cuisine: Fourteen signature dishes and their histories.* Jackson: University Press of Mississippi.

Twiss, K. C. (2007). *The archaeology of food and identity.* Carbondale: Center for Archaeological Investigations, Southern Illinois University Carbondale.

Twitty, M. W. (2013, June 25). An open letter to Paula Deen. Retrieved from http://afroculinaria.com.

Ulla, G. (2012, February 22). Eater Interview—Linton Hopkins. *Eater.* Retrieved from http://www.eater.com.

Vaughn, G. C. (2011). *Southern soul food cooking with a multicultural flavor: The Rouse family cookbook.* Bloomington, IN: AuthorHouse.

Veteto, J. R., & Maclin, E. M. (2011). *The slaw and the slow cooked: Culture and barbecue in the mid-south.* Nashville, TN: Vanderbilt University Press.

Vignali, C., Kenyon, A. J., & Vignali, C. (2007). Food we eat: A range of perspectives. *British Food Journal, 109,* 8.

Vines-Rushing, A., & Rushing, S. (2012). *Southern comfort: A new take on the recipes we grew up with.* Berkeley, CA: Ten Speed.

Visser, M. (1986). *Much depends on dinner: The extraordinary history and mythology, allure and obsessions, perils and taboos of an ordinary meal.* New York: Grove.

Vivian, B. (2010). *Public forgetting: The rhetoric and politics of beginning again.* University Park: Pennsylvania State University Press.

Vlahos, J. (2007, September 9). Scent and sensibility. *New York* Times. Retrieved from http://www.nytimes.com.

Von Burg, R., & Johnson, P. E. (2009). Yearning for a past that never was: Baseball, steroids, and the anxiety of the American dream. *Critical Studies in Media Communication, 26,* 351–371.

Vranica, S. (2012, January 18). Paula Deen pitch hard to swallow. *Wall Street Journal,* B8.

Walker, J. (2014, September 19). The best fried chicken in New Orleans award goes to Dooky Chase's restaurant. Retrieved from http://www.nola.com/food.

Walonen, M. K., & Hackler, M. B. (2012). Class, identity, and anxiety at the plantation table: British travellers and antebellum Southern foodways. *Studies in Travel Writing, 16,* 17–30.

Walsh, R. (2012). *Texas eats: The new lone star heritage cookbook.* Berkeley: Ten Speed Press.

Warnes, A. (2008). *Savage barbecue: Race, culture, and the invention of America's first food.* Athens: University of Georgia Press.

Watson, H. L. (2009). Front porch. *Southern Cultures, 15*(4), 1–2.

Watts, E. K. (2001). Cultivating a black public voice: W. E. B. Du Bois and the "Criteria of Negro Art." *Rhetoric & Public Affairs, 4*(2), 181–201.

Watts, R. (2008). *Contemporary Southern identity: Community through controversy.* Jackson: University Press of Mississippi.

Wessell, A. (2004). There's no taste like home: The food of empire. In K. Darian-Smith, P. Grimshaw, K. Lindsey, & S. Mcintyre (Eds.), *Exploring the British world: Identity, cultural production, institutions* (pp. 811–821). Melbourne: RMIT.

What Is Bourbon Anyway? In D. DiBenedetto (Ed.), *The Southerner's handbook: A guide to living the good life* (pp. 119–120). New York: Harper Wave.

Wheeler, B. (2012, March 21). The slow death of prohibition. *BBC News Magazine.* Retrieved from http://www.bbc.com/news/magazine.

White, J. (1985). *Heracles' bow: Essays on the rhetoric and poetics of law.* Madison: University of Wisconsin Press.

Whitelegg, D. (2005). From smiles to miles: Delta Airlines attendants and Southern hospitality. *Southern Cultures, 11*(4), 7–27.

Wiggins, S., Potter, J., & Wildsmith, A. (2001). Eating your words: Discursive psychology and the reconstruction of eating practices. *Journal of Health Psychology, 6,* 5–15.

Wile, K. (2015, February 17). Bob Peters behind the bar at Punch Room. *Charlotte Magazine.* Retrieved from http://www.charlottemagazine.com.

Wilk, R. (2010). Power at the table: Food fights and happy meals. *Cultural Studies/Critical Methodologies, 10,* 428–436.

Wilkins, R., & Wolf, K. (2011). The role of ethnography in rhetorical analysis: The new rhetorical turn. *Empedocles: European Journal for the Philosophy of Communication, 3*(1), 7–23.

Willard, B. E. (2003). The American story of meat: Discursive influences on cultural eating practice. *Communication Abstracts, 26,* 155–298.

Willis, V., Dujardin, H., & Willan, A. (2011). *Basic to brilliant, y'all: 150 refined Southern recipes and ways to dress them up for company.* Berkeley, CA: Ten Speed.

WLRH. (2012, December 3). Kathryn Tucker Windham "No sugar in the cornbread". Writer's Corner. Retrieved from http://www.wlrh.org/WritersCorner/kathryn-tucker-windham-no-sugar-cornbread

Wohl, K. (2012). *New Orleans classic cocktails.* Gretna: Pelican.

Wondrich, D. (2007). *Imbibe: From absinthe cocktail to whiskey mash, a salute in stories and drinks to "Professor" Jerry Thomas, pioneer of the American bar.* New York: Perigree.

Wood, A. (2012). Regionalization and the construction of ephemeral co-location. *Rhetoric Society Quarterly, 42*(3), 289–296.

Woodward, C. V. (1974). *The strange career of Jim Crow.* NY: Oxford University Press.

You, X. (2006). The way, multimodality of ritual symbols, and social change: Reading Confucius's Analects as a rhetoric. *Rhetoric Society Quarterly, 36,* 425–448.

Zagacki, K. (2007). Constitutive rhetoric reconsidered: Constitutive paradoxes in G. W. Bush's Iraq war speeches. *Western Journal of Communication, 71,* 272–293.

Zelizer, B. (2004). The voice of the visual in memory. In K. R. Phillips (Ed.), *Framing public memory* (pp. 157–186). Tuscaloosa: University of Alabama Press.

Zukin, S. (2008). Consuming authenticity. *Cultural Studies, 22*(5), 724–748.

INDEX

abundance, 141
Acheson, H., 7
action, 25, 45–46, 47
African Americans, 55; contributions to Southern cuisine, 28–29, 58–59, 152; and desserts, 161, 162, 163–64, 183–84; experience of Great Depression, 140; pitmasters, 61, 67, 107; travel by, 9. *See also* race; segregation; slavery
agriculture, 46–47, 139, 141
Albrecht, M. M., 143
alcohol, 14, 84–86, 94–95. *See also* drink
Allen, J., 52
Althusser, L., 26
Anderson, Sheila, 202
Appalachia, 151, 197, 207
Apuzzo, M., 52
Athens, Ga., 21–22, 48
Atkins-Sayre, W., 42
Atlanta, Ga.: Evans Fine Foods, 64; JCT, 43; Miller Union, 43; presentation of to outsiders, 90
Atlantic Monthly, 23
Auchmutey, J., 104, 107, 199
authenticity, 16, 64; and barbecue, 111, 112–18, 131, 191–92; and boundary stretching, 194–95; concern about proving, 157; as connection through remembrance, 112; and connection to land, 156; connection with food, 143; creating through performance, 143; defining, 142, 194–95; determining, 134–35; drawbacks to, 157; and empowerment, 168, 176, 180; and establishing regional boundaries, 192; fauxthentic Southern foods, 149–54; and ingredients, 153–54, 155; and need for hierarchy, 142–43; new authentic

Southern food, 154–56; and place, 114–17; and practices, 112–14; and proprietors, 117–18; and region making, 142–58; signals of, 157; significance of, 135–36; and smell, 37; strength of, 143; true authentic Southern food, 144–49; and visuals, 42

baking, 192; and community building, 166; and connections, 173–74; and cultural nourishment, 184; and female subjectivity, 176–81; and gender roles, 162–64, 183, 185–86; and identity, 178. *See also* dessert; ritual
Baltimore, Md., 202
barbecue, 15, 36, 69, 191–92; in airports, 35; and authenticity, 111, 112–18, 131, 191–92; and casuistic stretching, 111, 132; changes in, 130; and community, 105, 122, 126–29; competitions, 119–23, 130; and congregation, 111–12; and culture, 104; experience of, 117; and health, 131; importance in South, 132–33; and inclusion through exclusion, 110; interpretations of, 106; Mallard Creek Presbyterian Church Barbecue, 125, 126; and masculinity, 119–23, 130; National Barbecue Month, 67; in North Carolina regions, 107–8; pitmasters, 61, 67, 107, 117, 130; and place, 109, 131; practices, 112–14; proprietors, 130; and race, 106–7; rhetorical potential of, 117, 130; rhetorical themes of, 111 (*see also* authenticity; masculinity; rurality); and ritual, 122, 127; and rurality, 124–29; and side dishes, 113; and slavery, 106–7; and Southern identity, 104–5, 108, 109–10; and sustainability, 131; tradition of, 104; women in, 120–21, 131
Barbecue Pitmasters (television show), 120

Barber, Robert, 46, 47
Barksdale, J., 161, 162
bartenders, 79–80
Beall, S., 127
Beasley, V. B., 26
Beckham, S. B., 101
beer, 40, 41, 85, 93–95, 97, 101
beer halls, 92–93
Bell, L. A., 29
beloved community, 62–63
Besh, J., 156
Bessinger, Maurice, 110
Best, Bill, 37, 46
beverages. *See* drink
Beyer, J. M., 167
biscuits, 7, 9, 41, 148, 157, 158, 177, 189
Bishaw, A., 52
Bitter Southerner, 7
Black, E., 26
Blair, C., 26, 38, 39, 47
Boorstein, M., 105
boundary stretching, 192, 193–97
bourbon, 84–85, 96
Bowens Island, 40–41
Bowens Island (film), 40, 46–47
Boym, S., 165
Brock, Sean, 7, 31–32, 140, 155
Brown, J., 82
Brown, Rashaa, 183–84
Brown, W., 56
Browning, L., 106, 107, 120
Brummett, B., 166
Bruner, M. S., 3, 4
Bullis, C. A., 167
Buncombe, A., 106
Burke, K., 3, 5, 15, 16, 60, 62, 81, 111, 181; on
    casuistic stretching, 15, 108, 110–11, 132; on
    courtship, 15, 81, 86–87, 89, 91; definition
    of man, 55; on desire for order, 16, 86, 142;
    on division, 90; on equipment for living,
    166; on identification, 25, 90, 108, 109; on
    identity, 13; on terministic screens, 160
Burkett, Ben, 145, 146, 152
Burns, R., 13
Burr-Miller, A. C., 166
Butler, B., 145
Butler, J., 3, 25

Café on Main, 146–47
Cajun cuisine, 6
Cake Makin' Sisters, 172, 184
Callaway, John W., 61
Callaway, M., 87
Carlson, A., 108, 111, 132
Carr, S., 52
Cash, W., 53
casuistic stretching, 15, 108, 110–11, 132
Center for a Better South, 67
Center for the Study of Southern Culture, 23,
    59. *See also* Southern Foodways Alliance
Charland, M., 3, 5, 25, 26, 32, 45, 74
Charleston, S.C.: Husk Restaurant, 31–32, 155;
    Macintosh, 43; reunification banquet,
    200–202
Charleston Post and Courier, 200
Charlotte, N.C., 38, 79, 197
Chase, Leah, 13, 62, 63, 66, 67
Chavez, K. R., 10
chef culture, 120
Chesser, J., 197
Chicago, Ill., 152–54, 194
chicken, fried, 6, 22, 31, 38, 43, 58, 66, 68, 104, 201
church: Mallard Creek Presbyterian Church
    Barbecue, 125, 126; Poplar Tent Presbyterian
    Church barbecue, 178, 182; and Southern
    food customs, 62. *See also* religion
civil rights movement, 55, 63, 68
Clark, M., 7
Clark, Newell, 126
Clark, T., 23, 139
Clary-Lemon, J., 87
class: and breads, 148; confronting issues of, 73;
    and courtship, 87; and diet, 199; and greens,
    145; and history of Southern food, 65–66;
    and hospitality, 88, 90; and Southern food,
    54
Cobb, C., 7, 52
Cobb, J. C., 7
cocktail, 92; design of, 84; origins of, 80, 82–83;
    in Southern culture, 91. *See also* drink
coffee, 36, 44
Cohen, D., 90
Cole, J., 13, 66
Columbus, Miss., 146–47
commonalities, 27, 39–40, 66, 72, 74
community, 63–64; and baking/desserts,
    159–60, 164, 166, 181–84; and barbecue, 105,

122, 126–29; and coming together through food, 105; and ritual, 127, 128
community building, 164
community resilience, 181
competitions, barbecue, 119–23
congregation, 108, 111–12, 124–25, 126–27
Conley, D., 37, 44
connections: and baking/desserts, 170–71, 173–74; building, 22, 70, 81; and drink, 91–94; and nostalgia, 172–74; and ritual, 128–29, 170
constitutive rhetoric, 24–31, 32–33, 46, 47–48
consumption, 43–44
control, 119
conversations: about food, 57; and desserts, 171–72; at Domilise's, 34, 35
Cooley, A. J., 8, 9, 55, 150, 197
Cooren, F., 23, 24, 45, 46, 47–48
Cordova, N., 23, 25, 26, 45
cornbread, 153–54
cornbread nation, 60, 148
Cornbread Nation (SFA), 67
Cornelissen, J. P., 23
courtship, 81, 86–87, 91
Cox, Suzanne Ray, 160
Cracker Barrel, 150–52
Craig, R., 24
Cramer, J. M., 3
Creole cuisine, 6
Croke, D., 119, 120
Cross, K., 69
Crow, James, 84
cuisine, Southern. *See* food, Southern
culture: articulating identity through, 13; experiencing, 70
culture, Southern, 50–51
Currence, J., 112, 151
Czech influences, in Texas, 196

Dan B, 62
Danbom, D., 125
dance halls, 92–93
Davis, F., 165
Dean, S., 55
Deen, Paula, 7, 8, 28–29, 52, 164
Degler, C., 53
Delta, 71, 195, 197
DeLuca, K., 41
Depp, M., 145

desserts, 16, 192; and African Americans, 161, 162, 163–64, 183–84; and changing narratives, 160–61; and community, 159–60, 164, 181–84; and connections, 170–71; and conversations, 171–72; as equipment for life, 183; and health, 164, 183–84; and history, 161–62; and hospitality, 162; and nostalgia, 164–66; pound cake, 169–72, 175–76; and reinforcement of gender norms, 179–80, 181; and ritual, 167–76; sharing, 169; as source of inspiration, 184–85; and subjectivity, 176–81; viewed through terministic screen, 160. *See also* baking
Deutsch, J., 119, 120, 122
dialogue, 48, 56, 65, 72
Dickinson, G., 33, 36, 57, 143
differences, 68, 81, 87, 90, 109, 137, 138, 201
discursive practice, Southern food rhetoric's influence on, 46–48
discursive space, opening, 73
diversity, 61–65; in South, 53; of Southern food, 189, 193, 195–97; at Weaver D's, 22
division, 5, 15, 22, 86, 201
Doe's Eat Place, 41, 42, 70–71, 195
Domilise's Po-Boys, 33–34, 35, 48
Donehower, K., 125
Dooky Chase, 67–68
Draper, C., 74
drink, 14, 79, 191; alcohol, 14, 84–86, 94–95; and building relationships, 79–80; choice of, 95–96, 97–98; and connections, 91–94; connection to place, 96–97; and hospitality, 80, 86, 88, 91; and performance, 79, 98–100, 101; and religion, 94–95; rhetorical aspects of, 91–100; role of in Southern culture, 81–86; Southern relationship with, 100; sweet tea, 85; symbolism of, 100–101. *See also* cocktail
Drzewiecka, J., 27
Dubois, C. M., 108
Dubriwny, T., 27, 29
Dujardin, H., 7
Dupree, N., 6, 7, 58

Eastern Carolina Barbecue Throw Down, 119–21, 130
eating, as communal experience, 40, 47, 114, 118
Eckstein, J., 37, 44
Economist, The, 8
Eddy, J., 26

Edge, J. T., 6, 7, 11, 23, 50, 56, 59, 62, 66, 69, 107, 164; on barbecue, 130; on race, 55, 58; on SFA's films, 23–24

Edible Nation, 71

Edna's Restaurant, 152

Edwards, J. L., 41

Egerton, J., 6, 7, 8, 60, 62, 66, 80, 84, 94, 98, 104, 113, 139, 144; on barbecue, 122; on drinks, 84, 85, 94, 98; on heritage, 139; on hospitality, 80, 88

Elie, L., 120

Enck-Wanzer, D., 13, 32

Endolyn, O., 61

Endres, D., 10

Engelhardt, E., 7, 10, 54, 135; on authenticity, 135; on breads, 148; on foodways, 3; on imagined South, 193–94; on Southern foods, 55

equipment for living, 166, 183

Evans, A. C., 195

Evans Fine Foods, 64

Evens, T. M., 62

Evins, Dan, 150

exclusion: at barbecue competitions, 121–22, 123; and hospitality, 88–90, 101; inclusion through, 110; and narratives, 28

experience, and understanding Southern foodways, 10–12

farmers, 145–46

farmers' markets, 65, 70, 73, 155–56, 197

farm-to-table movement, 58. *See also* sustainable food movement

Faust, D. G., 168

fauxthentic Southern foods, 149–54

Federation of Southern Cooperatives Land Assistance Fund, 145

Ferris, M. C., 7, 9, 30, 55, 58, 90, 139, 154, 163, 192, 198

Fertel, R., 69, 104, 105, 113, 117

Finnegan, C. A., 41

Fisher, C., 156

folds, 137, 138

Fontenot, K., 52

food: ability to build relationships, 4; ability to send messages, 4; centrality to Southern experience, 6; as communication, 3; connection to race, 8; as constitutive rhetoric, 23–24, 33; and identity, 5, 17; and nuanced

understanding of past, 65; in regional culture, 50–51; rhetoric about, 46; rhetorical function of, 72; as rhetorically powerful narrative, 29; role in cultural understanding, 72; symbolic message of, 45

food, Southern: ability to authenticate existence of South, 158; broadening narratives about, 111; categories, 6; changes in, 197; connection to land, 139; constitutive function of, 51, 74, 190; and cultural identity, 7–8; difficulty in defining, 6–7; diversity of, 6–7, 189, 193, 195–97; effects on people, 191; founding moments, 26–27; and identity, 189–90; messages sent by, 190–91; and opportunity for dialogue, 56; popularity of, 7, 50, 194; potential to redefine South, 192–93, 198 (*see also* boundary stretching); and poverty, 140, 145; and regionalism, 137–38, 139; rhetoric about, 45; as rhetorical, 12; rhetorical actions of, 193–97; rhetorical potential of, 190–91, 198–201; rhetorical power of, 64, 189–90; rhetorical work of, 9, 12; as source of identification and reconciliation, 55–56; stereotypes of, 198–99

food culture, 12, 22–23, 28, 38, 46, 58

food deserts, 16

foodie culture, 71

food movements: local food movement, 57–58; Slow Food movement, 42–43, 46, 47; Southern food movement, 14, 26–27, 51, 57–58, 72, 74–75; Southern Foodways Alliance (*see* Southern Foodways Alliance); sustainable food movement, 8, 57–58, 131

food organizations, 57

food rhetoric, constitutive function of, 5, 13, 14, 60, 137

foodways, 3–4

Forbes, P., 189

founding moments, 26–27, 49

Franzia, M., 107, 133

frugality, 16

Frye, J., 3, 4

Fuller, Nat, 200, 201, 202

Furrh, M., 161, 162

Gabriel, Y., 165

Gantt, P., 163, 169, 178, 185, 186

Garner, B., 107, 108, 109, 110, 122, 126, 128, 132

gender: and baking/desserts, 162–64, 183; and hospitality, 89; and nostalgia, 165–66; as performance, 25; and ritual, 179–80, 181

Gestalt Gardener (radio program), 141

Giddens, A., 46

gift food, 181–82

Gilbert, J., 10

Gilmore, Ga., 63

Gilmour, D., 166

Glatz, J., 59

Glock, A., 85

Goff, Joanna, 174–75, 178, 179, 181–83

Gold, D., 6

Goodale, G., 32, 34, 35

Graubart, C. S., 7

Gray, Freddie, 202

Gray, R., 88

Great Depression, 140

Greene, C. P., 3, 4

Greene, R. W., 26

greens, 22, 65, 145, 146

Greenville, Miss.: Doe's Eat Place, 41, 42, 70–71, 195

Greenwood, Miss., 63

Griffin, L. J., 51

Gruene Hall, 92–93

Guarente, M., 121, 130

Gunn, J., 32

Gus's World Famous Fried Chicken, 38, 48

Hahne, E., 7

Hall, B., 53, 54

Hantchett, T., 197

Hariman, R., 41

Harris, J., 67, 107

Harris, Will, 199

Harrison, S., 165

Hart, L. G., 125

Harwell, R. B., 84

Hattiesburg, Miss., 97

Hawkins, Martha, 63

Hayden, S., 26, 27

health: and barbecue, 131; and desserts, 164, 183–84; and Southern food, 9, 198–99

Henderson, Henry, 152

Heritage (Brock), 155

Hess, A., 10

hierarchy, 132, 142

Hillsville, Va., 159

Hirshaw, J., 177, 184

history, 64; and desserts, 161–62; and new authentic Southern food, 154–55; and Southern Foodways Alliance, 65–66, 73. *See also* past

Hoffman, M. F., 168

Hogg, C., 125

Holbrook, M. B., 165

Holtzman, J., 30, 165

Hope, D. S., 41

hospitality, 6, 14–15, 69–71, 73, 80–81, 87–88; and abundance, 141; and class, 88, 90; and desserts, 162; as discourse, 88; and drink, 80, 86, 88, 91; and exclusion, 88–90, 101; food's role in communicating, 101–2; and gender, 89; and identification with others, 86; as performance, 89; politics of, 87; and race, 90; and rejection, 101; and religion, 89

hospitality, radical, 200, 201

Howell, Ray, 126

Husk Restaurant, 31–32, 155

identification: as key to persuasion, 86; and ritual, 128; through division, 108–10

identity: and action, 25; articulated through culture, 13; and baking, 178; and drink, 95–98; and food, 5, 17; and food choices, 57; and nostalgia, 165, 166; perception of, and regionalism, 137; as rhetorically shaped, 24–31; and shared experience, 25; and Southern food, 23, 189–90

identity, collective, 26, 27

identity, cultural, 7–8

identity, Southern: and barbecue, 104–5, 108, 109–10; complexity of, 13–14; and food, 7–8, 13, 22, 189–90; influenced by past, 54; negotiating, 72; problems with, 51–56; shift in, 5; and smell, 36

identity building. *See* constitutive rhetoric

identity scholarship, 3

immigrant(s), 53, 196–97

inauthenticity, 149

inclusion, 61; and barbecue, 126–27; through exclusion, 110

ingredients, 31, 140, 153–54, 155

Innes, S., 8

interaction: and barbecue restaurants, 114–17; and Southern food experiences, 48

Jakes, K., 28, 29, 32
Jasinski, J., 23, 24, 25, 26, 28, 29, 45, 46
JCT, 43
Jim and Nick's, 131, 132
Johnson, D., 42
Johnson, J., 56
Johnson, P. E., 69
Jones, W., 54
Jonsson, P., 164
Jordan, Christy, 7
Jordan, Terry, 79–80, 81, 84, 97, 182

Katrina (hurricane), 73
Keeling, D. M., 33
Kentucky, 96–97
Kierner, C., 87, 89
King, Martin Luther, Jr., 62–63
King, S. A., 142
Kinsman, K., 6, 57
Knoblauch, M., 6
Knowlton, A., 197
kolaches, 196
Kramer, J., 189
Kuhn, T., 23
Kummer, C., 23

lardcore movement, 7, 50, 58
Larson, E. H., 125
Latshaw, B. A., 13, 54, 56
Lee, Matt, 138
Lee, Ted, 138
Leeman, R., 109
Lewis, H., 13, 66
Lexington, N.C., 124
Lexington Barbecue, 124–25
Lexington Barbecue Festival, 125, 126
lifestyle, 104, 180, 181, 199
Link, D., 91
Lisher, D. M., 125
listeners, 26
local food movement, 57–58
Lowcountry cuisine, 6
Lucaites, J. L., 41
Lucas, S., 145

macaroni and cheese, 152–53
Macartney, S., 52
Macintosh, 43
Maclin, E. M., 15, 104, 107, 108, 109, 130

Mallard Creek Presbyterian Church Barbecue
    (MCPCB), 125, 126
Mannur, A., 165
Maroukian, F., 137
Martin, A., 8
masculinity, and barbecue, 119–23, 130
Mason, C., 147
Massa, D., 34
mass marketing, 149–50
materialism, constitutive, 26
Maynard, W., 7, 59
McCue-Enser, M., 26, 49
McDermott, N., 169
McDonald, R., 165, 166
McHendry, G. F., 10
McKeithan, S. S., 96
McLaughlin, L., 72
McLeod, G. E., 92
McNulty, I., 163
McPherson, T., 89
meaning: multiple layers of, 32; and ritual,
    167–68, 172
memorials, 39
memories, 30–31, 32, 37
memory, taste, 170–71, 175
Memphis, Tenn., 35; Gus's World Famous Fried
    Chicken, 38, 48
message. See rhetoric
methodology, 9–12
Meyers, O., 164, 165
Middleton, M. K., 10, 11
Miles, J., 95, 100
Miller, A., 9, 67, 132, 145, 152, 153, 154, 161, 163,
    164, 165, 169
Miller Union, 43
Mims, Ben, 168, 174, 183, 191
mint julep, 83–84
Mintz, S. W., 108
Mississippi, University of, 23, 59. See also
    Southern Foodways Alliance
Mississippi Delta, 71, 195, 197
Mitchell, Kevin, 201–2
Morago, G., 34
Moskin, J., 8, 50, 58, 59
Moss, R., 104, 106, 107
Muehling, D. D., 166
Mumby, D., 29, 46, 47
Museum of the American Cocktail, 82
mystery, 15, 86, 87

Nabhan, G. P., 133
narratives: examining underlying assumptions
    of, 29; rhetorical function of, 28–29. *See
    also* stories
Nashville, Tenn., 62, 66, 69
National Barbecue Month, 67
Neal, B., 162, 163, 173, 178
Negro American Labor Council, 70
new authentic Southern food, 154–56
Newcomer South, 197
Newman, H., 90
New Orleans, La.: Crescent City farmers'
    market, 65, 73; and dessert traditions, 161;
    Domilise's Po-Boys, 33–34, 35, 48; Dooky
    Chase, 67–68; and history of cocktail, 82;
    history of Italian food in, 196; Purloo, 83;
    Sazerac Bar, 98; Southern Food and Bever-
    age Museum, 73, 82, 83
Nolan, J., 104
North Carolina, 11, 38, 79, 156, 171, 176, 178, 196.
    See also barbecue
nostalgia, 17, 68–69, 164–66, 178, 185–86; and
    connection, 172–74; and Cracker Barrel,
    150; defined, 164–65; flexibility of, 173–75;
    and recreating culture, 173; rhetorical pos-
    sibilities of, 167; and rurality, 125
nourishment, 164
Nystrom, J., 196

O'Bryne, M., 10
Offutt, C., 199
okra, 145, 147, 193
Olson, L. C., 41
O'Neil, C., 198, 199
O'Neill, M., 127
Onorato, P. H., 80
Opel, A., 56
Opie, F. D., 9, 106, 140, 152
order, desire for, 16, 86, 142
Ott, B. L., 33, 166
Ownby, T., 195
oysters, 40–41, 46–47
Ozersky, J., 7, 50, 58

Pascal, V. J., 166
past, 192; and nostalgia, 165; nuanced under-
    standing of, 65; struggle with, 51–52. *See
    also* history
Penrice, R., 14

Percy, Walker, 84–85
performance: and drink, 79, 98–100, 101; gen-
    der as, 25; hospitality as, 89
persuasion: and ritual, 167. *See also* rhetoric
Peters, Bob, 79
Petrini, C., 46
Pettus, Henry, 61
Peychaud, Antoine, 82
Pezzullo, P., 10
Phillips, K. R., 30
Pie Wagon, 62
pitmasters, 61, 67, 107, 117, 130
place, 71; and authenticity, 114–17; and barbe-
    cue, 109, 131; celebration of, 68; connection
    to, 192; and drink, 96–97; perception of,
    and food, 137
po-boy, 33–34
Pollan, M., 57, 104, 106, 107, 112, 113, 119, 122, 131
Poniewozik, J., 52
Poplar Tent Presbyterian Church barbecue,
    178, 182
porches, 101
pork, 106. *See also* barbecue
Potter, A., 142, 143
pound cake, 169–72, 175–76
poverty, 48, 52, 140, 145, 153
power, food as source of, 55
Pramuk, J., 85, 94
Price's Chicken, 38
Prohibition, 84
Puckett, S., 181
Puente, S., 90
punches, 92
Purloo, 83
Purvis, K., 30
Putnam, L. L., 167

race: and barbecue, 106–7; confronting issues
    of, 73; food's connection to, 8; and history
    of Southern food, 65–66; and hospitality,
    90; and Southern food, 58–59; and South-
    ern food movement, 74–75
racism, 13, 51, 52, 106
Ramage, J., 87
Ramos, Henry, 98
Ramos Gin Fizz, 98–99
Raskin, H., 69, 201
Ratilla, A., 90
Ray, A. G., 167

Reed, D. V., 104, 109, 114, 127
Reed, J., 104, 107, 109, 114, 127
regionalism, 136–41
regions, defining, 136–37
relationships, 4, 79–80
religion, 15, 54; and alcohol, 94–95; and hospitality, 89; and Southern food customs, 62. *See also* church
religious symbolism, 43
restaurants: barbecue, 114; Café on Main, 146–47; and community building, 63–64; Cracker Barrel, 150–52; decor, 114, 150–51; Doe's Eat Place, 41, 42, 70–71, 195; Domilise's Po-Boys, 33–34, 35, 48; Dooky Chase, 67–68; Evans Fine Foods, 64; Gus's World Famous Fried Chicken, 38, 48; Husk Restaurant, 31–32, 155; JCT, 43; Jim and Nick's, 131, 132; Lexington Barbecue, 124–25; Macintosh, 43; Miller Union, 43; in Nashville, 66, 69; Pie Wagon, 62; Price's Chicken, 38; Purloo, 83; Ruby's restaurant, 152–54, 194; soul food, 70, 152–54, 194; Waysider, 147–48; Weaver D's, 21–22, 48
reunification banquet, 200–202
Reynolds, L. K., 174, 183, 191
rhetoric, 10; emphasis on verbal persuasion, 167. *See also* constitutive rhetoric
rhetoric, regional, 136–41
rhetoric, Southern food, 45, 46–48, 49
rhetoric, visual, 41–43
rhetorical criticism, 9
rhetorical fieldwork, 10, 23
rhetorical studies, 12
Rice, J., 136, 137, 138, 157
Richmond Times Dispatch, 112
Rienstra, J., 85
Ritivoi, A. D., 165
ritual, 17; and barbecue, 122, 127; and community building, 127, 128; and connections, 128–29, 169, 170; and desserts, 167–76; flexibility of, 176–77; and identification, 128; importance of, 167; and meaning, 167–68, 172; persuasive power of, 168; and possibility, 129; and reinforcement of gender norms, 179–80, 181; remaking, 168–69; rhetorical purpose of, 180
Roahen, S., 7, 59, 66, 69
Robbins, J., 167, 168
Roberson, L., 54

Rodbard, M., 151
Rogers, A., 175, 181
Ruby's restaurant, 152–54, 194
Rufca, S., 57
rurality, 124–29
Rushing, Felder, 141
Rushing, W., 109, 131

salads, 43, 44
Sampson, S., 104
Sanders, Dori, 199
Sauceman, F., 140
savage ideal, 53
Saving Seeds (film), 37, 46
Sazerac, 84
scent: as rhetorical marker, 35. *See also* smell
Schaarsmith, A. M., 132
Schell, E. E., 125
Schieffelin, E. L., 167
Schmich, M., 152
Schmidt, M. S., 52
Scott, M., 109, 131
Scott, Walter, 202
segregation, 8–9, 15, 22, 55, 66, 68, 146–47
Senda-Cook, S., 10
sensory experiences: as constitutive discursive practices, 45–48; at Husk, 31–32; as rhetorically constitutive, 31–33; sight, 41–43; smell, 35–37; sound, 33–35; taste, 43–44, 170–71, 175; touch, 38–41
Serna, Charles, 195
Severson, K., 6, 7, 56, 62, 67, 141, 144
Shahin, J., 130
shared food culture, 12
Shields, David, 200
Shiner, Texas, 85
Shinn, Howard, 70, 72
Shirley, Wilbur, 117–18
Shriver, J., 185
side dishes, 15–16, 113, 147, 151
sight, and food experience, 41–43
Signa, Charles, 70–71
Simpson, D., 140
slavery: and barbecue, 106–7; and desserts, 161, 162, 163–64
Slow Food movement, 42–43, 46, 47
smell, 35–37
Smelley, Linda, 147
Smith, B., 161, 164

Smith, K., 165
Smith, S., 105, 114, 167
smoke, 113–14
social justice, 200
soul food, 6, 58, 66, 70, 152–54, 194
sound, 33–35
South (region): defining, 53, 88; diversity in, 53; negative image of, 52; opening dialogue in, 5; rhetorical problem of, 13; stereotypes about, 110; struggle with past, 51–52
Southerner's Handbook, The, (DiBenedetto), 85
Southern Food (Egerton), 6
Southern Food and Beverage Museum, 73, 82, 83
Southern food movement: constitutive function of, 14, 51; founding moment, 26–27; and local food movement, 57–58; participation in, 72; and race, 74–75; and sustainable food movement, 57–58
Southern food rhetoric, 46–48, 49
Southern foodways, 17–18
Southern Foodways Alliance (SFA), 7, 23, 26, 56, 59–72; Bowens Island, 40, 46–47; celebration of people of South, 61; celebration of place, 68; Cornbread Nation, 67; and diversity, 61–65; films, 23–24, 48; mission and values, 60, 62, 63, 65, 69, 71, 72, 73, 75; oral histories, 66, 69, 70; rhetorical work of, 59–61; Saving Seeds, 37, 46; and Southern history, 65–66, 73; and Southern pride, 68–72; "The Spoken Dish," 44; themes of rhetoric, 60
Southern revival, 50
Spoetzel Brewery, 85
"Spoken Dish, The," 44
Starbucks, 36
Stein, S., 27, 46
St. John, W., 58, 59
Stokes, A. Q., 43
stories, 4; and food's rhetorical strength, 27–28; and memory, 30–31. See also narratives
stories, alternative, 29
Stormer, N., 42
Street, E., 65, 69
Stuckey, M., 26
subjectivity, female, 176–81
sugar, 153–54, 164
Sundrop soft drink, 176
sustainable food movement, 8, 57–58, 131

Sweet, D., 26, 49
sweet tea, 85
Swett, David, 69
symbolism, religious, 43
symbols, 3, 5, 10, 86, 146, 148, 190
Szczesiul, A., 87, 88, 89

table, as communal space, 39, 129
tamales, 66, 195
taste, 43–44
taste memory, 170–71, 175
Tate, H., 27
Taylor, J. G., 90, 95
tea, sweet, 85
Tell, D., 136, 137
terministic screens, 16–17, 160
Texas, 85, 92–93, 195–96
texts, 10, 23, 29–30, 32, 33, 105
Theobald, P., 125
Theodossopoulos, D., 142
Thomas, Jerry, 82
Thompson, A., 82
Thompson, T., 7, 51, 52, 89
time, experience of, 28
tomatoes, 37, 46, 139
touch, 38–41
traditions, 48
Trice, D., 70
Trice, H. M., 167
true authentic Southern food, 144–49
Turner, Helen, 131
Tuscaloosa, Ala.: Waysider, 147–48
Twitty, M. W., 28, 163

Ulla, G., 50

Vandello, J., 90
Van Hoeven, S. A., 167
Vass, Mava, 159–60
vegetables, 8, 131, 140–41, 145, 198–99
Veteto, J. R., 15, 104, 107, 108, 109, 130
virtue, public display of, 89
Visser, M., 50
visual rhetoric, 41–43
Vlahos, J., 36
Von Burg, R., 69

Waggoner, Z., 87
Walker, J., 135

Wallmenich, L. V., 10
Walsh, R., 116, 196
Walters, L. M., 3
Waring, J., 165
Warnes, A., 106, 107
Watson, H. L., 74
Watts, E. K., 54, 55
Watts, R., 5
Waysider, 147–48
Weaver D's, 21–22, 48
Wheeler, B., 94
Whitelegg, D., 89
Wile, K., 79
Wilk, R., 56
Wilkins, R., 10
Willan, A., 7
Williams, T., 52
Willis, V., 7
Windham, Kathryn Tucker, 153–54

wine, 84
Winkler, C. K., 41
Wohl, K., 82
Wolf, K., 10
women, 55; and African American women's contributions, 163; and baking, 162–64, 176–81; in barbecue, 119, 131; in barbecue competitions, 120–21; and food nostalgia, 165–66; left out of conversation of food, 61; as Southern, 162–63; and subjectivity, 176–81
Wondrich, D., 82, 84, 91, 92, 98
Wood, A., 136
Wood, C., 53, 54
Woodward, C. Vann, 53

Zagacki, K., 27, 32
Zelizer, B., 30, 42
Zukin, S., 142, 143, 149, 156

CPSIA information can be obtained
at www.ICGtesting.com
Printed in the USA
BVHW03s0749250818
525137BV00001B/3/P